# NATIONAL PETROLEUM COUNCIL

*An Oil and Natural Gas Advisory Committee to the Secretary of Energy*

1625 K Street, N.W.
Washington, D.C. 20006-1656

Phone: (202) 393-6100
Fax: (202) 331-8539

April 23, 2024

The Honorable Jennifer M. Granholm
Secretary of Energy
Washington, D.C. 20585

Dear Madam Secretary,

In response to your request dated November 8, 2021, the National Petroleum Council (Council) conducted a comprehensive study on the deployment of low carbon intensity (LCI) hydrogen at scale in the United States across the entire value chain, including production, storage, transportation, and end uses, to support decarbonization of various energy and key market sectors. If deployed at scale, LCI hydrogen technology applications in the hard-to-abate sectors can support achieving U.S. carbon emissions reduction ambitions at a lower cost to society.

This report, *Harnessing Hydrogen: A Key Element of the U.S. Energy Future*, evaluated the key economic, policy, regulatory, technical, and public acceptance challenges and critical enablers along the hydrogen value chain that must be addressed to achieve at-scale LCI hydrogen deployment. The study effort involved a diverse team of approximately 300 experts from more than 100 organizations, 70 percent of which come from outside of the oil and gas industry. This study leveraged scenario-based modeling, partnering with the Massachusetts Institute of Technology (MIT) Energy Initiative.

The report generates unique insights due to the diverse perspectives of the study participants, many of whom have practical experience executing large-scale projects, informing the technoeconomic and life cycle assessment models. The Council would like to highlight three key findings from the report:

**First, LCI hydrogen can play a key role in reducing emissions in hard-to-abate sectors at a lower cost to society.** The study determined that, while existing policies and legislation are expected to double the current U.S. demand for hydrogen by 2050, these levers, along with anticipated cost reductions, are insufficient to stimulate the growth of LCI hydrogen deployment needed to support the country's net zero ambitions by 2050 at a lower cost to society. LCI hydrogen, when applied in hard-to-abate applications within the Industrial, Transportation, and Power sectors, could abate approximately 8 percent of total U.S. emissions by 2050, but achieving net zero ambitions by deploying multiple technology solutions could cost up to 3 percent of the Gross Domestic Product (GDP) annually. Achieving that same outcome without leveraging LCI hydrogen would likely increase this annual cost by an incremental 0.5 to 1 percent of GDP.

**Second, the LCI hydrogen production mix will be driven by multiple aspects of the various hydrogen production pathways, including their relative speed to scale, delivery cost reductions, and carbon intensities.** LCI hydrogen production is expected to be initially driven by hydrogen produced via natural gas reforming with carbon capture and storage, due to its lower production cost and the ability to rapidly scale production and infrastructure. The production mix under a net zero emissions scenario is expected to include an increasingly larger share of renewable electrolytic hydrogen due to its lower carbon emissions and the projected higher future cost of carbon. Deployment of LCI hydrogen from the two key production pathways will be needed to support net zero objectives and will require addressing specific constraints for each pathway.

**Third, LCI hydrogen deployment will be marked by regional variation in production development and demand activation by sector.** LCI hydrogen production can activate now in regions with abundant renewable or natural gas resources, existing anchoring demand, access to infrastructure, or supportive policies. Expanding LCI hydrogen more broadly across the United States will require additional federal policy and investment in technologies and infrastructure.

Significant and rapid progress across many areas must occur to move through three phases of LCI hydrogen market development: Activation, Expansion, and At-Scale. This report identifies three categories of critical enablers that could aid in rapid LCI hydrogen deployment and progression across all regions: policy and regulation; societal considerations, impacts (SCI) and safety; and targeted investments in technology and research, development, and deployment (RD&D). The Council provides key recommendations for the critical enablers:

- **Policy and Regulation:** Develop additional legislation to overcome cost gaps between incumbent fuels and feedstocks and LCI hydrogen, increase investor confidence, and streamline regulatory frameworks.

- **SCI and Safety:** Ensure reliable value chains while providing societal benefits, improving community engagement, and enabling workforce development.

- **Technology and RD&D Investments:** Prioritize investments to close technology gaps across the LCI hydrogen value chain, address technical bottlenecks, and support public/private research programs.

The recommendations provided by the Council in this *Harnessing Hydrogen* report aim to accelerate the deployment of LCI hydrogen in the United States, contributing to the country's net zero target by 2050. The Council identifies clear areas of opportunity and challenge, while maintaining a focus on how the United States can leverage its existing infrastructure, abundant resources, and capabilities to reach at-scale deployment of LCI hydrogen. The Council looks forward to sharing additional details with you, your colleagues, and broader government and public audiences about the critical enablers.

Respectfully submitted,

Alan S. Armstrong
Chair
National Petroleum Council

Enclosure

# HARNESSING HYDROGEN

## A Key Element of the U.S. Energy Future

### VOLUME III • REPORT APPENDICES

**A Report of
the National Petroleum Council
April 2024**

**Committee on Deployment
of Low Carbon Intensity Hydrogen At-Scale
Mike Wirth, Chair**

**NATIONAL PETROLEUM COUNCIL**

Alan S. Armstrong, Chair
Ryan M. Lance, Vice Chair
Marshall W. Nichols, Executive Director

**U.S. DEPARTMENT OF ENERGY**

Jennifer M. Granholm, Secretary

---

The National Petroleum Council is a federal
advisory committee to the Secretary of Energy.

The sole purpose of the National Petroleum Council
is to advise, inform, and make recommendations
to the Secretary of Energy on any matter
requested by the Secretary
relating to oil and natural gas
or to the oil and gas industries.

---

Cover photos: Adobe Stock
Hydrogen molecule model: Anusorn
Solar panel: Jess Rodriguez
Hydrogen pipeline: Yingyaipumi
Electric powerlines: TebNad
Hydrogen transport fleet: Visual Voyager
Refinery plant: Vectorizer88
Wind turbines farm: Rafa Irusta

# TABLE OF CONTENTS

## VOLUME III – REPORT APPENDICES

The Report Summary, Chapters, Appendices, and other study materials
can be downloaded at no charge from the NPC report website,
harnessinghydrogen.npc.org.

# Appendix D

# MODELING METHODOLOGY

## I. OVERVIEW

This appendix describes the modeling approach used in the development of the NPC report *Harnessing Hydrogen: A Key Element of the U.S. Energy Future* (NPC H$_2$ study).

The modeling objectives were twofold:

1. Evaluate the cost and carbon intensity (CI) of different options for the production, handling, and use of low carbon intensity hydrogen (LCI H$_2$).

2. Evaluate the role of LCI H$_2$ in the energy system in the United States under two scenarios for how energy sector CO$_2$ emissions might evolve over 2025–2050. The emissions trajectories assumed for these scenarios are depicted in Figure D-1.

   - The **Stated Policies** scenario assumes current state and federal policies continue, but no additional policies are enacted. This emissions trajectory follows the projection for the United States under the *Stated Policies* scenario of the International Energy

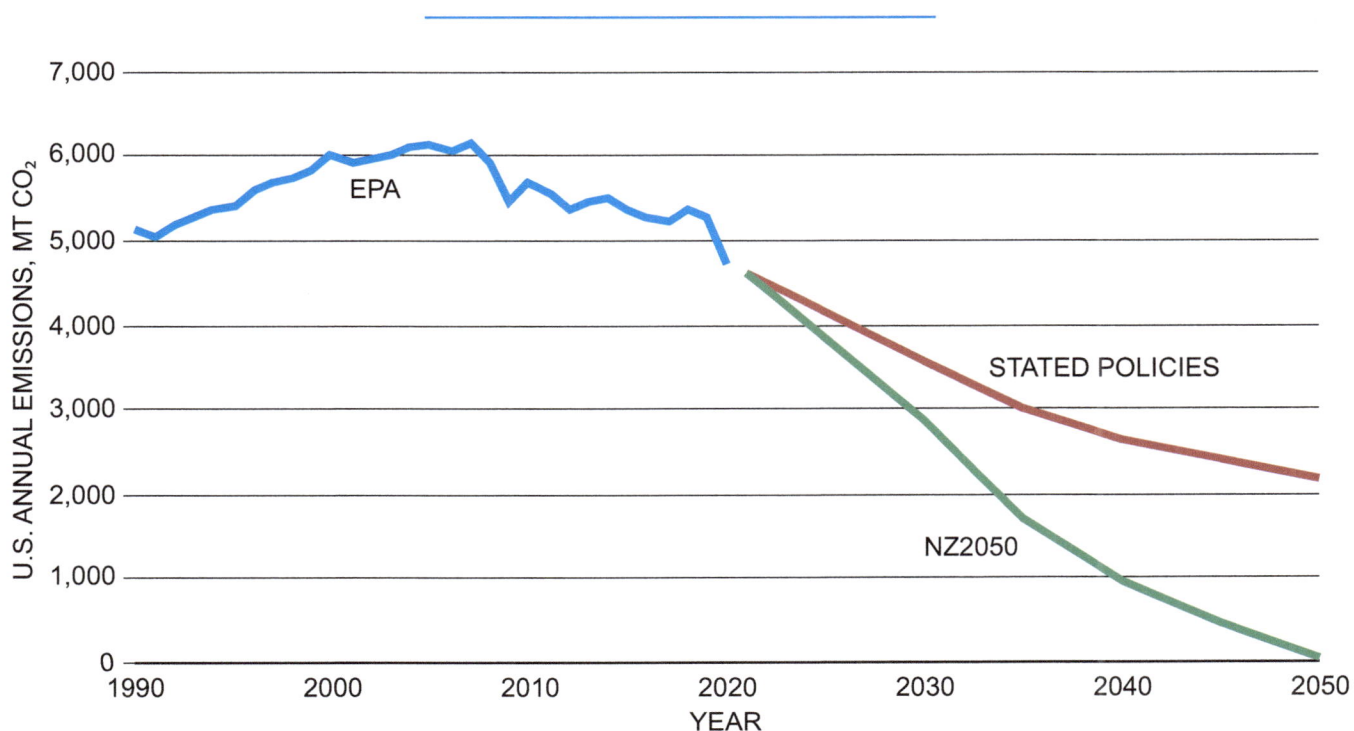

Notes: "EPA" denotes historical data from the U.S. Environmental Protection Agency, while projections reflect the emissions trajectory under the two scenarios assumed for the study. This plot only reflects CO$_2$ emissions, not total GHG emissions.

***Figure D-1.** U.S. Emissions for Study Scenarios*

Agency (IEA) 2022 World Energy Outlook, which estimates U.S. energy sector emissions in 2050 will have fallen 64% below their peak in 2005.

- The **Net Zero in 2050** (NZ2050) scenario assumes a more aggressive reduction resulting in the U.S. energy sector becoming carbon neutral by the end of the study period. This emissions trajectory follows the projection for the United States under the *Advanced Policies* scenario of the IEA 2022 World Energy Outlook.

The study worked with the Massachusetts Institute of Technology (MIT) to accomplish these objectives by leveraging two modeling platforms developed there, SESAME and USREP.

## A.  SESAME

The *Sustainable Energy System Analysis Modeling Environment* (SESAME), developed at the MIT Energy Initiative, is a modular platform for exploring the impacts of technology choices on the evolving energy system.[1, 2] The focus is assessment of the cost and life cycle greenhouse gas (GHG) emissions of established and emerging technologies. The modules are grouped by the key steps in an energy vector: upstream, midstream, production, delivery, and end use. A pathway to produce a specific product is formulated by selecting appropriate modules under each step. As a result, SESAME can be used to interrogate more than 1,000 energy pathways, covering fossil resources (coal, natural gas, and crude oil), renewable energy sources (solar, wind, hydropower, and biomass), major energy transformation processes (e.g., power generation and refining), and major end-use sectors (Industrial, Transportation, and Power). Cost and life cycle assessments for chosen pathways are conducted on an internally consistent basis, which supports robust comparisons. SESAME also includes modules for the optimization of intra- and inter-pathway trade-offs with high temporal and geospatial resolution, to identify critical parameters and best practices.

SESAME's Hydrogen-Power System module is a $H_2$ supply chain capacity expansion model. All necessary data, including cost and life cycle assessments, are collected and preprocessed to allow the user to explore the impact of different $H_2$ generation mixes and carbon policies on system costs and emissions over multiple connected regions.

## B.  USREP

The *U.S. Regional Energy Policy* (USREP) model is based on the *Economic Projection and Policy Analysis* framework developed under the MIT Joint Program on the Science and Policy of Global Change.[3] USREP is a multisector, multiregion general equilibrium model of the U.S. economy that encompasses energy technologies and land use change. It has been used to examine scenarios for economic growth, energy use, and emissions (both anthropogenic GHGs and conventional pollutants). Key outputs include gross domestic product (GDP), energy use, sectoral output and consumption, and GHG emissions ($CO_2$, $CH_4$, $N_2O$, etc.) estimated in five-year steps. In the base setting, the spatial resolution is at the state level with some aggregation. For this study, USREP was recalibrated to represent the 11 regions in this appendix.

USREP represents market interactions between profit-maximizing (cost-minimizing) producers and welfare (utility)-maximizing consumers. Producers use intermediate inputs from different sectors of economy and primary factors of production (i.e., capital, labor, natural resources) to provide goods and services to the economy. Consumers receive income from government transfers and from the supply of labor, capital, and resources to optimize their consumption patterns. Government collects taxes and provides subsidies and transfers.

## C.  Use of the Modeling Tools

SESAME provides pathway-level assessments for energy systems, but does not speak to the

---

1   E. Gençer, et al. 2020. "Sustainable Energy System Analysis Modeling Environment: Analyzing Life Cycle Emissions of the Energy Transition." *Appl. Energy 227.* https://doi.org/10.1016/j.apenergy.2020.115550.

2   MIT Energy Initiative. https://sesame.mit.edu.

3   M. Yuan, et al. 2019. "The MIT U.S. Regional Energy Policy (USREP) Model: The Base Model and Revisions." *Joint Program Technical Note.* https://globalchange.mit.edu/publication/17331.

## MODELING WORKFLOW

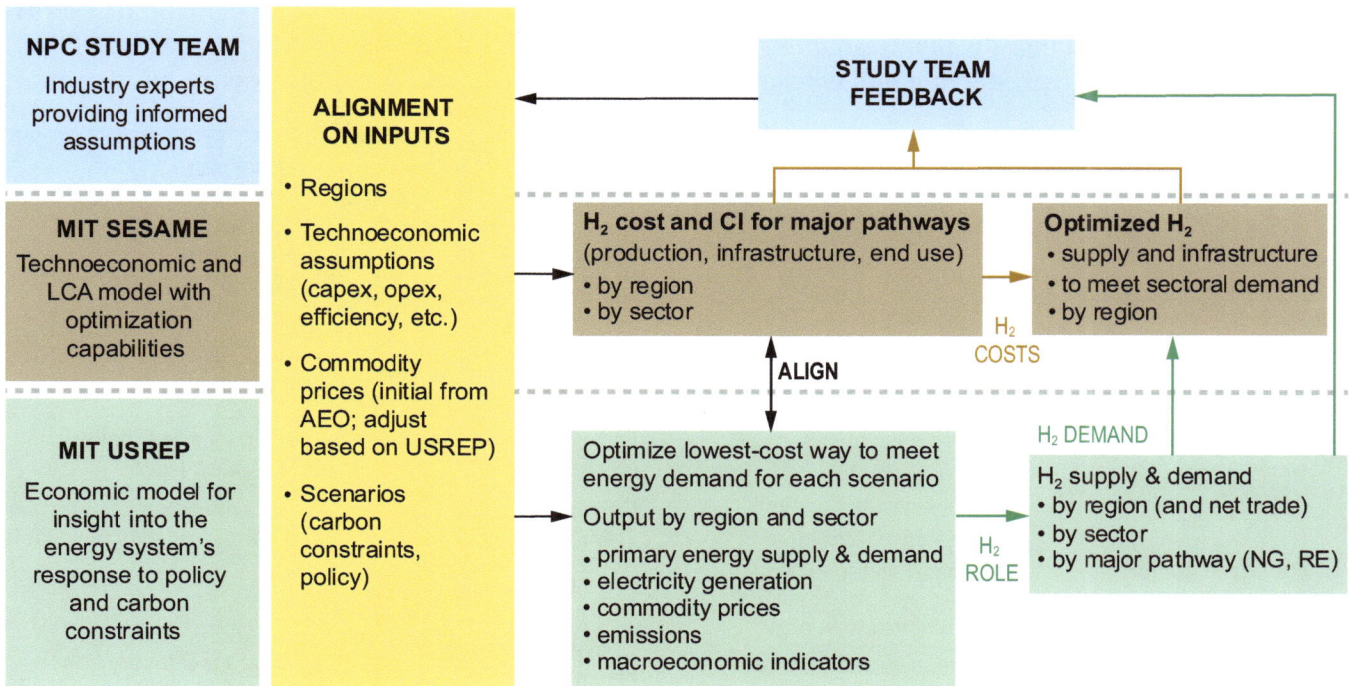

*Figure D-2. NPC-MIT Modeling Framework*

economy-wide impacts of technology adoption under different scenarios. USREP provides this higher-level view, but its technology resolution is limited. Therefore, the study used SESAME and USREP together to achieve a granular technology representation within the context of an economy-wide analysis. The result was an integrated assessment of pathways for LCI $H_2$ hydrogen deployment, which provided insights into the system-level cost and performance that LCI $H_2$ must deliver to become a substantial contributor to decarbonization at the national scale.

The interaction between SESAME and USREP is depicted in Figure D-2. SESAME provided information about cost and carbon intensity (CI). USREP provided the trajectory of the energy mix, including $H_2$ supply and demand, as well as the cost and emissions of commodity energy vectors (e.g., natural gas, grid electricity) by region. Table D-1 provides a breakdown of $H_2$ value chain elements included and not included in the modeling.

SESAME's technoeconomic analysis (TEA) and life cycle analysis (LCA) capabilities were used to

determine the cost and CI of each major step in the $H_2$ value chain, from production to end use. Three types of analysis were involved:

1. Supply pathway analysis, which covered the cost and CI of production and delivery

2. Regional $H_2$ supply chain optimization, conducted for three regions that represent a large fraction of the projected U.S. $H_2$ demand

3. End-use analysis, which focused on the Industrial, Transportation, and Power sectors

SESAME was also used to determine the cost and CI of competing fuels.

USREP was used to project $H_2$ supply and demand under the two U.S. emissions reduction scenarios adopted by the study.[4] In the model, different energy sector technologies are available with specific cost and CI characteristics that can vary by year. The set of technologies deployed evolves to meet the emissions constraint over

---

4    A reference scenario calibrated to the U.S. Energy Information Administration's *Annual Energy Outlook 2023* (https://www.eia.gov/outlooks/aeo/) was also examined.

time, which drives changes in the cost of goods and services. The reaction of producers and consumers to these changes is manifested in subsequent changes in the production and consumption activities in the various sectors of the economy, including the supply and demand of energy options like LCI $H_2$, which in turn affects GDP. This temporal progression occurs in five-year

| INCLUDED | NOT INCLUDED |
|---|---|
| **Supply Chain** | |
| Natural gas reforming with and without $CO_2$ capture and storage | Methane pyrolysis |
| Electrolytic water splitting powered by dedicated solar and/or wind renewable energy | Coal gasification |
| $H_2$ delivery by dedicated pipelines | Biomass gasification |
| $H_2$ delivery by trucking | Electrolytic water splitting powered by the grid |
| $H_2$ storage in compressed gaseous tanks | Electrolytic water splitting powered by nuclear or hydro renewable energy |
| $H_2$ storage in liquid tanks | $H_2$ storage in depleted reservoirs or saline aquifers |
| $H_2$ storage in salt caverns | $H_2$ conversion to methanol |
| $H_2$ conversion to ammonia | $H_2$ conversion to synthetic methane |
| **End Uses** | |
| Industry—refining | Transportation—light-duty vehicles |
| Industry—steel | Transportation—medium-duty trucks |
| Industry—cement | Transportation—marine |
| Industry—other (includes chemicals) | Transportation—rail |
| Transportation—heavy-duty trucks | Transportation—aviation |
| Power—use of $H_2$ for long-duration storage of renewable energy | Power—interaction between grid-connected electrolysis and Power sector cost, CI, scale |
| Res/Comm—blending up to 20% $H_2$ into natural gas networks | Res/Comm—unblended $H_2$ |
| Export—$H_2$ exported as ammonia | Export—$H_2$ exported in other forms |

Notes: The cost and CI of ammonia were modeled using SESAME because ammonia is a major end use for $H_2$. However, USREP includes ammonia production in the broad Other Industry category, for which adoption of LCI $H_2$ was modeled without consideration of those cost and CI results. Also, for simplicity, the study assumed a level of exports in the form of ammonia without consideration of those cost and CI results. "Res/Comm" is shorthand for the Residential & Commercial sector; i.e., buildings.

**Table D-1.** *$H_2$ Value Chain Elements Considered in the Study Modeling*

| Conventional Technologies | Low Emissions Technologies |
|---|---|
| Natural gas used by Industry | Renewable energy (solar, wind, hydro) |
| Natural gas used to generate electricity | Nuclear energy |
| Natural gas used by Res/Comm buildings | Carbon-neutral liquid fuels |
| Petroleum used to produce refined fuels | Electric vehicles (battery EVs, fuel cell EVs) |
| Refined fuels used for Transportation | Post-combustion CCS for natural gas power plants |
| Coal used by Industry | LCI $H_2$ used as a feedstock or fuel |
| Coal used to generate electricity | EAF for steel production |
| | $CO_2$ direct air capture and storage |

Notes: Carbon-neutral liquid fuels include second-generation biofuels and e-fuels made from $CO_2$ and RE $H_2$ as described in section VIII.A.1.a of this appendix. EV = electric vehicle. EAF = electric arc furnace using feedstocks including natural gas or $H_2$-based direct reduced iron and scrap steel. CCS = carbon capture and storage.

**Table D-2.** *Energy Pathways Included in USREP*

| Outputs Covering 2020–2050 in Five-Year Increments | Whole U.S. | Individual Regions |
|---|---|---|
| Primary energy mix by fuel | X | |
| Energy demand by sector and fuel mix | X | |
| Emissions by sector | X | |
| Shadow cost of carbon | X | |
| Implications of decarbonization on GDP | X | |
| $H_2$ supply by production pathway | X | X |
| $H_2$ demand by sector | X | X |
| Grid electricity CI | X | X |
| Grid electricity price | X | X |
| Natural gas price | X | X |
| Refined oil price | X | X |

Notes: USREP includes electricity in the fuel mix for demand. For this study, refined oil represents diesel.

**Table D-3.** *Key Outputs from USREP*

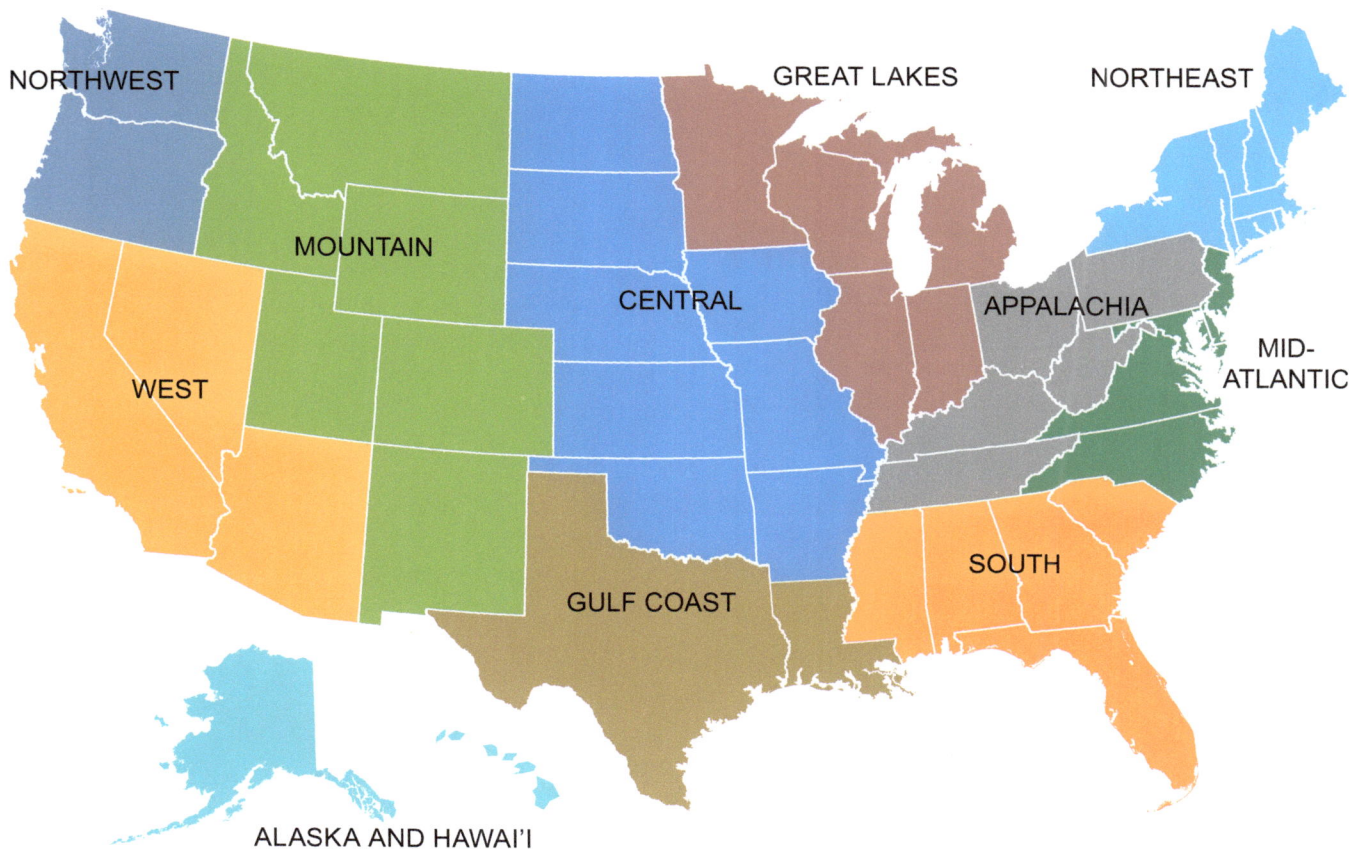

*Figure D-3. Map of NPC Study Regions*

steps, with calculations done at a regional level to build up to a national view.

The major inputs to USREP were:

- The national emissions trajectory defined for each scenario as shown in Figure D-1
- Cost and CI estimates for energy pathways described in Table D-2. Values for included elements from Table D-1 were provided by SESAME. Otherwise, USREP default values were used.

The key USREP outputs for the study are cataloged in Table D-3, including whether the metric is available at the regional level or only at the U.S. level.

## D. Regions

To develop insights into regional differences in the $H_2$ value chain and the future role of $H_2$ in the energy system, the study divided the United States into 11 regions as shown in Figure D-3.

## E. Technoeconomic Inputs

The study team agreed on key TEA inputs for the modeling based on publicly available data and the expertise of study participants, which included representatives from companies across the $H_2$ value chain as well as from academia, consulting, nongovernmental organizations, and several U.S. Department of Energy national labs. Costs for manufacturing, EPC (engineering, procurement, and construction), and operation were informed by companies actively scoping and developing projects. Actual project costs were not shared.

The TEA inputs used to describe $H_2$ production, infrastructure, and end uses are documented in this appendix. For technologies not covered here, default input values in the SESAME and USREP models were used.

To simplify the modeling, the study assumed constant capital and operating cost inputs across the United States. This is equivalent to asserting that actual regional cost differences (due to different labor rates, land costs, etc.) will be small enough to have a minor impact on results.

Also to simplify the modeling, capital and operating costs were assumed to remain constant in real terms during the modeling period (2025–2050) for most technologies. In reality, costs can increase or decrease over time in response to multiple drivers. For a new technology, however, it is generally observed that costs decrease in real terms as the technology scales up due to increasing economy of scale, learning by doing, and technology improvements. Therefore, the study team chose to explicitly model declining costs for a few less mature technologies, including electrolysis and wind and solar power generation.

## II. ECONOMIC ANALYSIS

### A. Levelized Cost Methodology

Most costs in this report are expressed on a levelized basis. A levelized cost is equivalent to the price that must be charged for a product or service, so the revenue stream is sufficient to both cover all expenses (capital and operating) and generate enough profit to meet the desired return on investment over a given timeframe. That is, it represents the break-even price for the product or service generated by a project to ensure the net present value (NPV) of the project is zero.[5] A levelized cost is independent of the future market price of the product or service.

The levelized cost of hydrogen (LCOH) is commonly expressed in $/kgH_2$, although other units are useful in certain contexts (e.g., on an energy basis when comparing to the cost of a fuel). Separate levelized costs can be calculated for the production, storage, transmission, and distribution steps along the supply chain. The sum of these is the LCOH seen by the end user. Using subscripts to distinguish the contributions from these steps, the total LCOH is:

$$LCOH = LCOH_p + LCOH_s + LCOH_t + LCOH_d$$
$$\text{end user} \quad \text{production} \quad \text{storage} \quad \text{transmission} \quad \text{distribution}$$

For this study, costs are expressed in real terms using 2020 as the reference year; i.e., in 2020$. The levelized cost identified with a particular year represents a fixed value (in real terms) for a project that starts production in that year. A real return on investment of 10% is assumed for all levelized cost calculations.[6]

Each contribution to LCOH is calculated using the following equation, which is based on a simplified discounted cash flow analysis with NPV set to zero:

$$LCOH_i = CRF_i \cdot \left(\frac{CAPEX_i}{cf_i \cdot c_i}\right) + FEED_i + V.OPEX_i + F.OPEX_i - \sum_n CLF_n CREDIT_n$$

where:

- The subscript $i$ represents a step in the supply chain
- $CRF$ is the capital recovery factor, which accounts for amortization of the return on investment, capital depreciation, and taxes (see equation on the next page)
- $CAPEX$ is the total installed capital cost for the project with capacity c on an overnight basis (i.e., by accounting for working capital, construction, and startup costs as if all were incurred in the year immediately prior to startup)
- $cf$ is the annual capacity factor, averaged over the capital recovery period
- $c$ is the production or throughput capacity on an annual basis
- $FEED$ is the cost of continuous feeds to the operation (e.g., energy inputs like natural gas and electricity) per unit of product, averaged over the capital recovery period
- $V.OPEX$ is the variable operating cost per unit of product not included in FEED, averaged over the capital recovery period
- $F.OPEX$ is the fixed operating costs per unit of product, averaged over the capital recovery period

---

5   This NPV is calculated using a discount rate equal to the desired rate of return on investment over the capital recovery period. The return on investment includes payback of the initial capital. The capital recovery period is the timeframe for the return on investment; it is a financial decision, which can be equal to or less than the physical lifetime of the plant.

6   That is, the weighted cost of capital is 10% for all projects.

- *CREDIT* is an available credit per unit of product
- *CLF* is the credit levelization factor for that credit (see equation below)
- *n* is an index if multiple credits are available

CRF is calculated using the following equation:

$$CRF = \frac{r(1+r)^L}{(1+r)^L - 1} \cdot \frac{1 - TR \sum_n^{L_d} \frac{d_n}{(1+r)^n}}{(1 - TR)}$$

where:

- *r* is the target rate of return
- *L* is the capital recovery period
- *TR* is the net tax rate on profits, before credits
- $L_d$ is the depreciation period
- $d_n$ is the depreciation fraction in year n (set by the depreciation schedule)

The credits available under the Inflation Reduction Act (IRA) are tax credits. To account for their impact on LCOH, such credits must be converted to a pretax basis since LCOH is a pretax cost metric. Moreover, the benefit of these credits must account for the fact that they are granted for a length of time (10 or 12 years) that may be less than the capital recovery period. The CLF is used to achieve both objectives. The formulation for CLF depends on whether the credit is an investment tax credit (ITC) or production tax credit (PTC):[7]

$$CLF_{ITC} = CRF$$

$$CLF_{PTC} = \frac{1}{(1 - TR)} \cdot \frac{\sum_n^{L_s} \frac{1}{(1+r)^n}}{\sum_n^{L} \frac{1}{(1+r)^n}}$$

where $L_s$ is the credit period in years.

## B. Financial Inputs

To simplify the modeling, the study used a single set of financial inputs to calculate levelized costs, shown in Table D-4. Only the capital recovery period was changed to reflect the specific technology being deployed. In reality, all these fac-

tors will be set on a project-by-project basis. The rate of return and financing structure are likely to vary by industry and over time, considering multiple drivers, including risk factors (technology, development, commercial, market) and business model. Taxes will vary by jurisdiction. The choice of depreciation schedule could be influenced by the expected lifetime of the asset.

| Variables | Values |
|---|---|
| Financing structure | 100% equity (no debt) |
| Investment rate of return | 10% (real) |
| Total income tax rate | 25% |
| U.S. Dollar reference year | 2020 |
| Depreciation schedule | 7-year MACRS |
| Capital recovery period | Asset specific |

Notes: The investment rate of return is equivalent to the weighted-average cost of capital. MACRS = Modified Accelerated Cost Recovery System.

*Table D-4. Financial Inputs for Levelized Cost Calculations*

## C. Emissions

### 1. No Explicit Penalty for Emissions

The study did not assume a national cost associated with GHG emissions, such as a carbon tax. Therefore, no direct financial penalty for GHG emissions was included in any levelized cost.

### 2. Cost of Avoided Emissions

The cost of avoided emissions was calculated as:

Cost of Avoided Emissions = (Cost of LCI option - Cost of reference )/(CI of reference - CI of LCI option)

where cost and CI are expressed on the same functional basis; e.g., per amount of $H_2$, per unit of energy, or per mile traveled (for transportation).

### 3. Shadow Price of Carbon

The USREP modeling methodology involved a calculation wherein energy pathways were penalized for their associated $CO_2$ emissions. This penalty served as a proxy for an unspecified set of policies that would drive adherence to the carbon budget set under each scenario. It was accounted for in the economic optimization, with the value

---

7    The production tax credit CLF also applies to the IRA 45Q credit for $CO_2$ capture and storage.

($/MT-CO_2$) in each modeling year adjusted until the projected energy sector emissions met the constraint dictated by the scenario for that year. This shadow price of carbon was not included in the reported cost of any energy product. Nevertheless, its value over time was an output of the USREP modeling for each scenario.

## 4. Negative Emissions Technology

SESAME was not used to model negative emissions technology for the study. Instead, it was accounted for using default inputs in USREP.

USREP considers a single negative emissions technology: $CO_2$ direct air capture (DAC). A cost of $600/MT-CO_2$ captured was assumed for an nth-of-a-kind plant.[8] USREP endogenously calculates first-of-a-kind costs and the decrease in costs over time as technology is deployed.

Under the Net Zero 2050 scenario, the cost of DAC was projected to be $750/MT-CO_2$ when it starts to be deployed at a material scale in 2040, and to decrease to $700/MT-CO_2$ by 2050. DAC was not observed to be deployed at a material scale by 2050 under the Stated Policies scenario.

## III. COMMODITY ENERGY CARRIERS

Several commodity energy products are relevant to the study: natural gas, grid electricity, and diesel fuel. Natural gas is used to make unabated and NG+CCS $H_2$. Grid electricity delivered to the Industrial sector was assumed to meet the electricity input demands for producing hydrogen from natural gas with carbon capture and storage (NG+CCS $H_2$) production and $H_2$ infrastructure (e.g., compression and liquefaction), while grid electricity delivered to the Transportation sector was assumed to meet the electricity demand for battery electric vehicles. Diesel is used by conventional trucks.

### A. Stated Policies Scenario

For the Stated Policies scenario, the study relied on the EIA 2023 "Annual Energy Outlook"

(AEO) for the future cost of grid electricity, natural gas, and diesel.[9] The AEO provided projections of prices for nine U.S. regions through 2050 in 2022$. These regions were mapped to the study's 11 regions using best efforts. Prices for each study region were calculated based on that mapping, and converted to 2020$. This yielded time series for the price of grid electricity, natural gas, and diesel in each study region through 2050, expressed in 2020$. The average cost (price) of a commodity fuel used in the study's levelized cost calculations was determined from these series as follows:

$$\bar{c} = \frac{\sum_{n=1}^{L} \frac{c_n}{(1+r)^n}}{\sum_{n=1}^{L} \frac{1}{(1+r)^n}}$$

where:

- $c_n$ is the cost (price) in year from the time series
- $\bar{c}$ is the average cost (price) over the project lifetime to be used in a levelized cost calculation for a project that starts in a given year, which is assigned
- $L$ is the capital recovery period in years
- $r$ is the discount factor (the same as the investment rate of return)

As calculated, the time series derived from the AEO data end at 2050. To calculate the average commodity fuel cost for a plant where the capital recovery period extends past 2050 (e.g., a plant that starts up in 2045), prices after 2050 were assumed to be fixed at the 2050 value.

The CI of the future electricity grid was estimated using EIA 2023 AEO data. The AEO provided projections for emissions from electricity generation and amount of electricity generated for 25 regions through 2050.[10] Annual emissions intensity (grid CI) values were estimated by dividing $CO_2$ emissions by electricity generated. The AEO regions were mapped to the study's 11

8 L. Desport, et al. 2024. "Deploying direct air capture at scale: How close to reality?" *Energy Economics* 129. https://doi.org/10.1016/j.eneco.2023.107244.

9 EIA. *Annual Energy Outlook 2023.* https://www.eia.gov/outlooks/aeo. Reference Case. Table 3 for Energy Prices of Industrial Natural Gas, Industrial Electricity, Transportation Electricity, and Transportation Diesel Fuel.

10 EIA. *Annual Energy Outlook 2023.* https://www.eia.gov/outlooks/aeo. Reference Case. Table 54 for Total Electricity Generation and Carbon Dioxide Emissions from the Electric Power Sector.

regions using best efforts, and grid CI values for each study region calculated based on that mapping. This yielded time series for grid CI in each study region through 2050.

The CI of diesel through 2050 was estimated based on work by the California Air Resources Board (CARB), which assessed contributions from upstream, refining, transport, and tailpipe emissions for ultra-low sulfur diesel.[11] For the study, the life cycle CI of diesel was assumed to be 85 $gCO_2e/MJ$ in 2025 and to decrease linearly over the study period to 36 $gCO_2e/MJ$ in 2050, inspired by the CARB objective for its Low Carbon Fuel Standard.[12] The diesel CI was assumed to be the same for all study regions.

The CI of natural gas in the future was estimated as described in Section IV.

## B. NZ2050 Scenario

For the NZ2050 scenario, the cost of grid electricity and diesel over time were determined endogenously within USREP, which models the evolution of the generation mix for the electricity grid at the regional level and the mix of conventional and advanced fuels in the diesel fuel pool at the national level. The cost of natural gas was also determined endogenously within USREP at the regional level. The CI of grid electricity was determined endogenously by USREP. The CI of diesel and natural gas were assumed to be the same as under the Stated Policies scenario. These costs and CI values were used by SESAME in levelized cost and CI calculations for NG+CCS $H_2$ production, $H_2$ infrastructure, and cost of ownership for heavy-duty (HD) trucks under the NZ2050 scenario.

## IV. CARBON INTENSITY OF NATURAL GAS SUPPLY CHAIN

The CI of the natural gas supply chain is an important input to the CI of $H_2$ produced via steam methane or autothermal reforming with carbon capture and storage (i.e., NG+CCS $H_2$). Therefore, the study undertook an analysis to 1) establish a credible reference for current GHG emissions from the natural gas supply chain for the 11 U.S. regions adopted by the study, and 2) develop an outlook on how the natural gas supply chain CI in these regions might evolve through 2050.

This work took place while NPC was also producing a report specifically on natural gas GHG emissions, titled *Charting the Course: Reducing GHG Emissions from the U.S. Natural Gas Supply Chain*, which included the potential for GHG emissions reduction across the U.S. natural gas supply chain.[13] One feature of *Charting the Course* was an LCA meta model based on studies published between 2016 and 2023 by organizations such as the Department of Energy (DOE) and its national labs, the Environmental Protection Agency (EPA), the Energy Information Administration (EIA), the International Energy Agency (IEA), and data from demonstration and commercial-scale projects.

Unfortunately, the timing of the two studies did not allow for *Charting the Course* output to be used as input for this study. Nevertheless, the two teams consulted while developing the work products, which ensured a reasonably consistent view on the future U.S. natural gas supply chain. A key difference between the studies was that the $H_2$ study focused on the natural gas supply chain specifically in the context of LCI $H_2$ production. The *Charting the Course* report took a broader view of the generic natural gas supply chain.

It is also important to emphasize that the CI of natural gas as discussed in this study covers only emissions resulting from the supply chain, i.e., from production to the end user's gate. It does not include emissions resulting from consumption (combustion or oxidation) of the natural gas by an end user.

## A. Key Sources of Data

The study team chose to source its natural gas supply chain CI data from two publications out

---

11 California Air Resources Board. "Technical Support Documentation for Lookup Table Pathways." https://ww2.arb.ca.gov/sites/default/files/classic/fuels/lcfs/ca-greet/lut_update_v12192023.pdf. Table B1.

12 California Air Resources Board. https://ww2.arb.ca.gov/resources/documents/lcfs-data-dashboard.

13 NPC. 2024. "Charting the Course: Reducing GHG Emissions from the U.S. Natural Gas Supply Chain." https://chartingthecourse.npc.org.

of the DOE's National Energy Technology Lab (NETL) that met several important criteria: were peer-reviewed studies based on LCA methodology; addressed both upstream and midstream segments of a supply chain representative of natural gas; pertained to natural gas delivered to an industrial-scale facility; and allowed for regional differentiation of the supply chain based on differentiated upstream and midstream characteristics. Specifically:

- **Upstream emissions** were sourced from a 2021 NETL report based on 2017 data.[14] Upstream includes production, gathering and boosting, and processing of natural gas. The study was conducted in partnership with the ONE Future Coalition and largely relies on ONE Future data, which are inclusive of, but not fully reliant upon, measured emissions data.

- **Midstream emissions** were sourced from the 2022 NETL *U.S. Natural Gas Delivery Pathways* report.[15] The results rely on the same 2017 upstream emissions data, but derive from a unique modeling approach, providing a nuanced estimate of natural gas midstream regional emissions. Midstream includes transmission (including pipeline blowdown) and storage.

*Harnessing Hydrogen* study members engaged with authors of the reports at DOE and NETL to ensure accurate interpretation and use of the data. The authors provided additional datasets to enable the study team to disaggregate the delivery pathways data from the NETL regional definitions to a state level, so that delivery emissions could be properly accounted for, and both upstream and delivery emissions could be reaggregated according to the study's regional definitions.[16]

## B. Methodology

### 1. Allocation of Associated Gas to NETL Supply Basins

Emissions data from the NETL study for upstream segments were provided at the basin level for nonassociated gas, while a single nationwide average emissions intensity was applied for associated gas.[17] Since associated gas emissions are generally higher than nonassociated gas emissions, the mix of these sources impacts the natural gas supply chain CI. To account for both associated and nonassociated gas, the study leveraged proprietary Wood Mackenzie gas production data, which include the percentage of production attributable to associated gas at the basin level in 2017. Aggregating the two datasets allowed a composite CI for each basin to be calculated using 1) the NETL basin-level nonassociated gas CI estimate, 2) the NETL U.S.-level associated gas CI estimate, and 3) the Wood Mackenzie share of production attributed to associated gas in each basin.[18]

### 2. Allocation of NETL Supply Basin Data to States

Assigning upstream emissions at the level of the study's 11 regions involved disaggregating these emissions from the basin level to the level of individual states. NETL supply basins were allocated to individual states using EIA state-level gas production data and supply basin maps. A weighted-average upstream CI for each supply state was calculated based on this supply basin allocation and the composite CI calculated in the previous step.

### 3. Definition of Delivery Pathways

NETL's *U.S. Natural Gas Delivery Pathways* study provided state-to-state supply delivery pathways, including delivered gas volume and $CO_2$ and $CH_4$ emissions for transmission, storage, and pipeline blowdown. The objective was to provide a detailed perspective on differences in GHG

---

14 Rai, S., et al. 2021. "Industry Partnerships and Their Role in Reducing Natural Gas Supply Chain Greenhouse Gas Emissions-Phase 2." *NETL Technical Report*. https://doi.org/10.2172/1765004.

15 Littlefield, J., et al. 2022. "Life Cycle GHG Perspective on U.S. Natural Gas Delivery Pathways." *Environ. Sci. Tech.* 56. https://doi.org/10.1021/acs.est.2c01205.

16 The analysis utilized additional data from NETL (provided by J. Littlefield) to disaggregate downstream emissions.

17 Associated gas is from wells that coproduce natural gas and crude oil; nonassociated gas is from wells that produce only natural gas.

18 Supply basin maps were leveraged on a best-effort basis to map NETL supply basin definitions to Wood Mackenzie supply basin definitions.

emissions based on where natural gas is produced and where it is delivered. Pathways were assigned using an algorithm that simplified the U.S. natural gas transmission network by inferring likely pathways between production and consumption. The inputs were natural gas production and delivery volumes for each state and the geographic distribution of processing and delivery facilities for each state. The outputs were state-level estimates of delivery emissions.[19]

## 4. NPC Regional Emissions Intensity

State-level estimates of total $CO_2$ and $CH_4$ emissions across the supply chain were obtained by combining the state-specific upstream emissions with delivery emissions within the demand state. The state data were then reaggregated to align with the study's regions. Finally, the $CO_2$ and $CH_4$ emissions were combined into $CO_2$ equivalent ($CO_2e$) emissions using the 100-year global warming potential (GWP100) for $CH_4$.[20]

## 5. Approach for Special Regions

The approach described thus far accounted for emissions estimates for gas produced and consumed in most study regions. The two exceptions were:

- **Alaska and Hawai'i:** Alaska was represented in the NETL publications from a supply perspective but not from a demand or delivery perspective. Hawai'i was not represented at all. The approach taken was to use data for Alaska from the 2021 NETL study for upstream emissions, and U.S. average midstream emissions for the rest. The resulting natural gas supply chain CI was applied for the combined Alaska and Hawai'i region.

- **Northwest:** The Northwest region was excluded from the NETL studies because it receives almost all of its gas from the Western Canadian Sedimentary Basin. The U.S. average

natural gas supply chain CI was used for the Northwest.

## C. Estimate of Current Natural Gas Carbon Intensity

Figure D-4 summarizes the outcomes of this analysis for each of the 11 NPC $H_2$ study regions. The regional analysis exposed a degree of clustering across the regions in terms of natural gas supply chain CI. To reflect the uncertainty inherent to the methodology used to estimate CI, the study team chose to create four tiers of natural gas CI as shown in Figure D-4. Figure D-5 provides a map summarizing how the regions were allocated across tiers. Note that seven of the 11 NPC $H_2$ study regions were allocated to Tier C, which is reflective of the U.S. average natural gas supply chain CI as defined in the NETL studies referenced for this analysis.

## D. Projected Reduction in Natural Gas Carbon Intensity

The NETL publications provide a credible source of data to estimate natural gas supply chain CI as of the year 2017. However, the study modeling required an outlook to 2050. A decrease over time was expected in response to two drivers:

1. Supply-side actions taken by industry, whether voluntarily or in response to policy

2. Demand-side incentives for low CI natural gas across end-use applications, including liquefied natural gas (LNG) exports, Power, Residential/Commercial (Res/Comm) building heat, and Industrial consumers

A qualitative analysis was performed to estimate the CI reduction potential from 2017 to 2050, although only the results for 2025–2050 were used for the study's modeling purposes. The process considered regulatory requirements, industry pledges, and interviews with NPC members and other industry participants. It also assumed that NG+CCS $H_2$ producers will source natural gas from the highest performing providers (which, in this context, means low CI natural gas), given that the overarching reason for adopting LCI $H_2$ is to decarbonize applications. As such, CI reduction assumptions were developed

---

19  For more details, see the NETL *U.S. Natural Gas Delivery Pathways* report and its Supporting Information.

20  To be consistent with the NETL publications, a GWP100 value of 36 was used for methane in this calculation, which is the value in the IPCC AR5 report, including contributions from methane oxidation and climate-carbon feedbacks. See Table 8.7 of https://www.ipcc.ch/site/assets/uploads/2018/02/WG1AR5_Chapter08_FINAL.pdf.

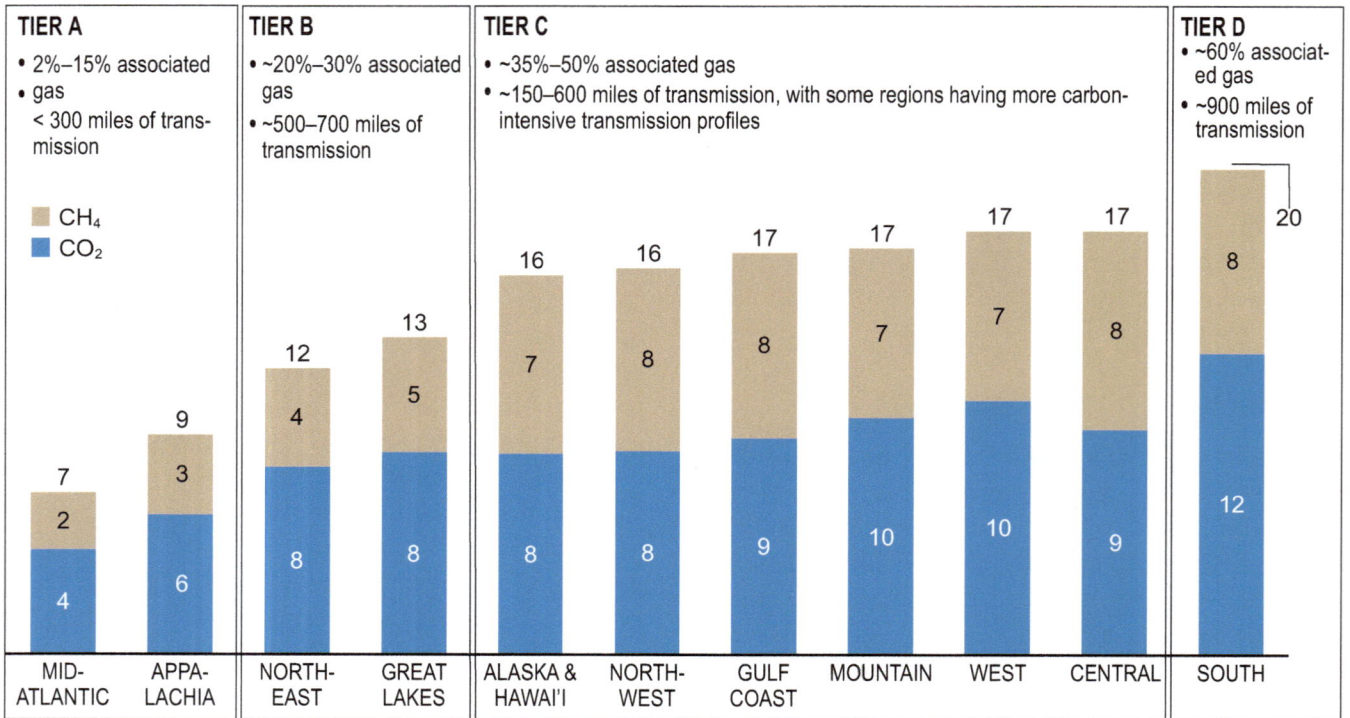

**Figure D-4.** *Natural Gas Supply Chain Carbon Intensity by Study Region*

Notes: CH$_4$ and CO$_2$ values are in units of gCO$_2$e/MJLHV. Values are for 2017, rounded for simplicity. Regions are grouped based on similar total emissions.

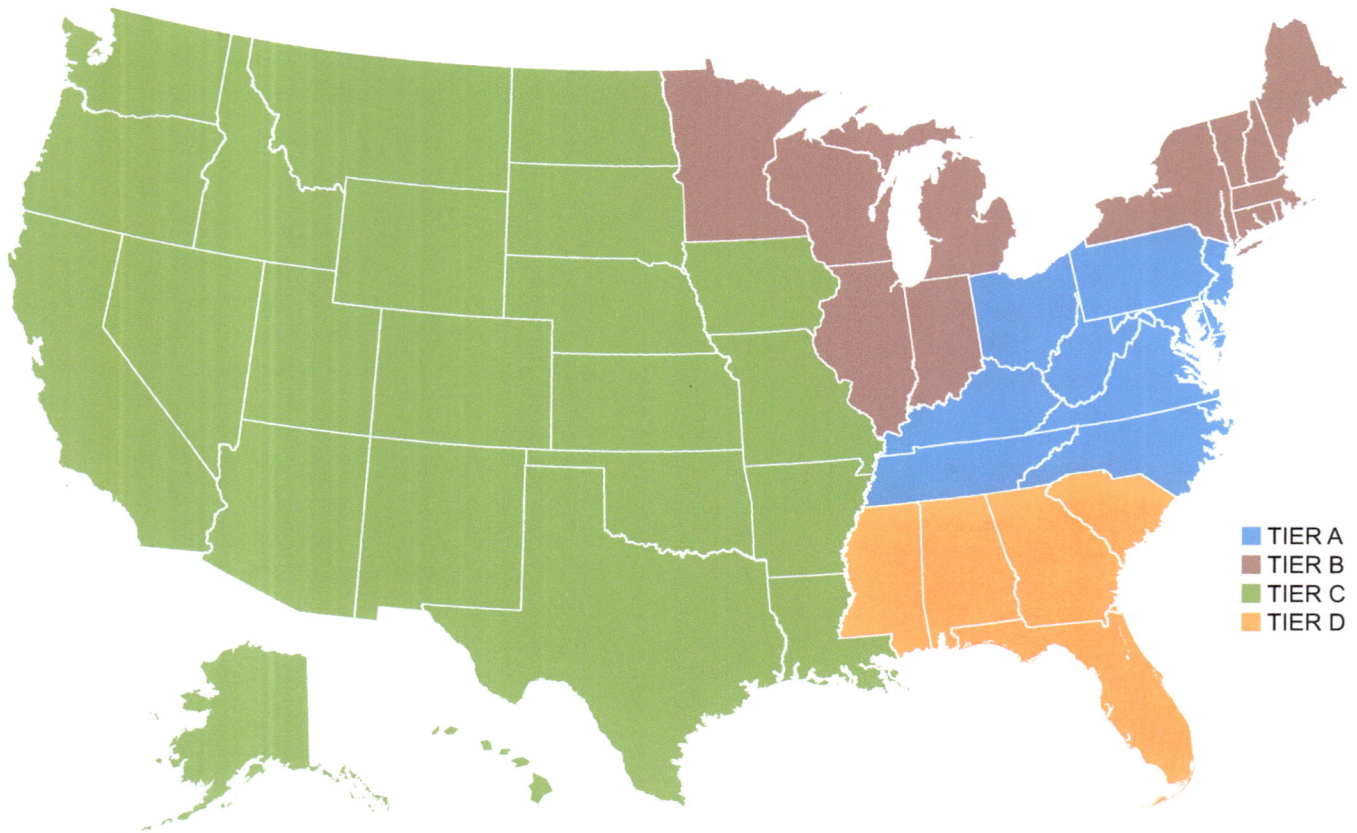

**Figure D-5.** *Map of Natural Gas Carbon Intensity Tiers by Study Region*

to reflect top performance in terms of CI reductions, not the average CI of the U.S. natural gas supply chain.

**Industry Actions:** Several midstream operators, including NPC members, shared that they had reduced methane emissions to the 0.1%–0.2% range in parts of their upstream operations. This performance is consistent with targets set by members of the Oil and Gas Climate Initiative, who have pledged to reduce methane emissions to 0.2%. Some operators have further pledged to achieve net zero emissions in their operations, which includes nonmethane emissions (primarily $CO_2$ and to a lesser extent $N_2O$) from flaring and combustion.[21]

**Regulatory Drivers:** Policies exist to reduce natural gas supply chain emissions in the United States. For example, the IRA sets methane emissions thresholds for oil and gas supply chains. Under section 136, methane emissions that exceed

specified thresholds will be penalized beginning in 2025.[22] Separately, the EPA finalized methane regulations in 2023 that are expected to reduce methane emissions from production, gathering, processing, transmission, and storage by 87% (relative to 2005 levels) by 2030.[23]

Based on these inputs, the NPC $H_2$ study assumed that the supply chain CI for natural gas used to make NG+CCS $H_2$ will achieve a methane emissions intensity of 0.1% in all regions by 2050, and a 75% reduction in $CO_2$ and $N_2O$ emissions in all regions by 2050.[24] Figure D-6 summarizes the net effect of these assumptions for the four regional tiers.

For context, Figure D-6 includes U.S. average emissions estimates from NETL and Argonne

---

21 The bulk of $CO_2$ and $N_2O$ emissions in the midstream are due to natural gas combustion to drive compressors. Technologies to reduce these emissions include electric drives, CCS, and using LCI $H_2$ as a fuel.

22 EPA. 2023. "Waste Emissions Charge." https://www.epa.gov/inflation-reduction-act/waste-emissions-charge.

23 The White House. 2022. "Delivering on the U.S. Methane Emissions Reduction Action Plan." https://www.whitehouse.gov/wp-content/uploads/2022/11/US-Methane-Emissions-Reduction-Action-Plan-Update.pdf.

24 IEA analysis supports that a 75% reduction in emissions intensity is achievable. https://www.iea.org/energy-system/fossil-fuels/methane-abatement.

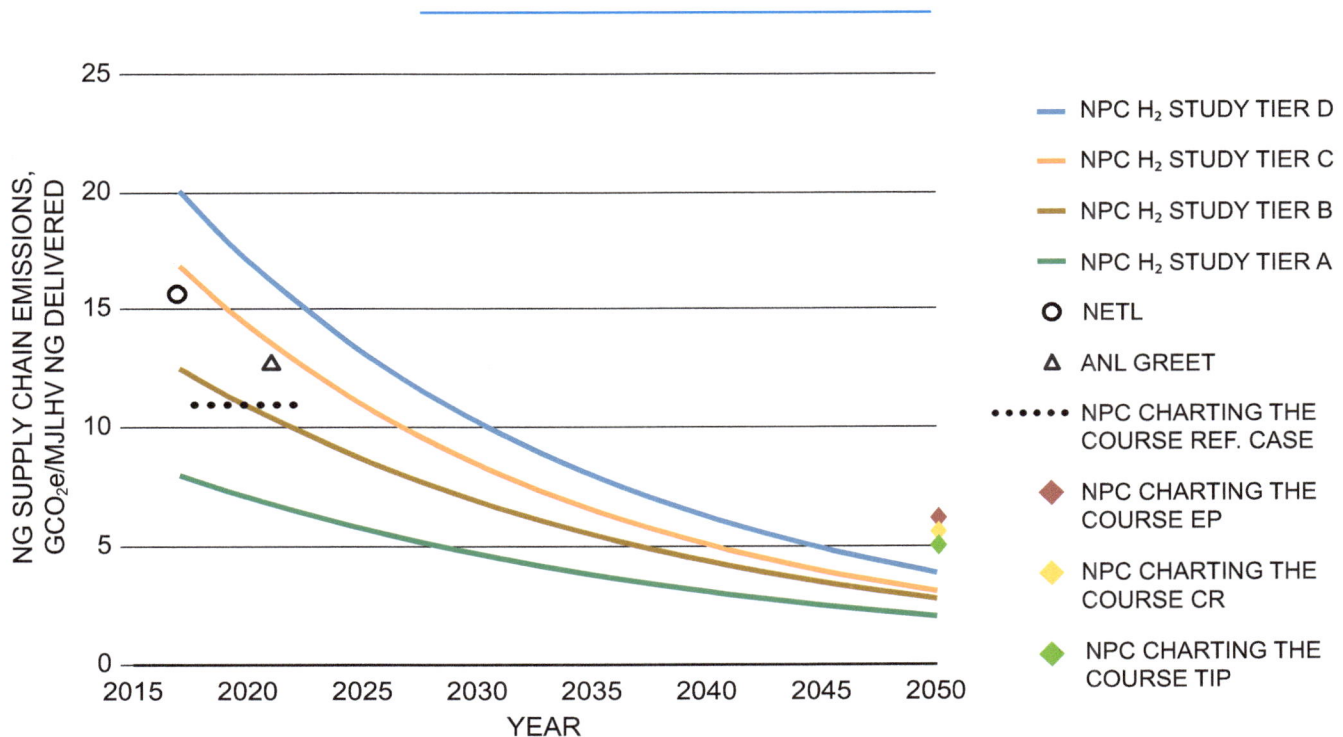

Notes: NPC $H_2$ Study tiers indicative of NG used by NG+CCS $H_2$ producers. See text for references to comparison values from NETL, ANL, and the NPC *Charting the Course* study. Pathways = Existing Policies (EP), Continued Reductions (CR), and Technology, Innovation, and Policy (TIP).

***Figure D-6.*** Harnessing Hydrogen *Study Outlook for U.S. Natural Gas Supply Chain Carbon Intensity*

National Lab (ANL).[25, 26] These align well with the study's Tier C, which reflects the majority of U.S. natural gas. The figure also includes results for the U.S. average natural gas supply chain from the *Charting the Course* study, including a reference case for current emissions and projections for 2050.[27] The values in 2050 are based on three scenarios that encompass increasingly aggressive emissions reductions: Existing Policies (EP), Continued Reductions (CR), and Technology, Innovation, and Policy (TIP). As shown in Figure D-6, the $H_2$ study finds slightly higher natural gas supply chain emissions in much of the country today compared to the *Charting the Course* view, and anticipates a stronger pace of reduction that yields somewhat lower total emissions in 2050. The difference is consistent with the study's assertion that NG+CCS $H_2$ producers will choose to use natural gas with a lower CI than the national average.

## E. Limitations of the Modeling Approach

Limitations of the methodology used to develop regional natural gas supply chain CI values for use in the study modeling include:

- Estimates of today's methane emissions were not derived from direct measurements. The NETL studies rely heavily on ONE Future data, which include measured data but are largely based on EPA emissions inventories. These inventories have been shown to underreport methane emissions by more than 60% in some cases. Consequently, the emissions estimates used could be biased low. Future studies should rely as much as possible on measured data, including from peer-reviewed publications covering U.S. production basins.[28, 29]

- The proposed reduction in methane emissions may not materialize. The study's assumption of 0.1% in 2050 represents a 90% reduction relative to the estimated level of 1% in 2017 (U.S. average). Where current emissions are higher, the percentage reduction is even larger. For example, the U.S. average methane emissions rate from oil and gas systems was estimated to be about 2.3% in 2017,[30] which would mean emissions must be reduced by 95% to meet the study's assumption for 2050.

- The assumption that NG+CCS $H_2$ producers would seek natural gas supplies with lower-than-average emissions intensities may not be realized. Recognizing differentiated natural gas would require an acceptable certification and verification system, including statistically valid sampling and the reconciliation of both source-level and site-level data. Even if these hurdles were overcome, system-level climate impacts must be considered. For example, higher-emissions gas might be simply diverted to other consumers with no change to the overall emissions intensity of the natural gas supply chain. Policy to ensure that this does not happen has yet to emerge.

## V. HYDROGEN PRODUCTION

The modeling assumptions and inputs for key $H_2$ production processes are described in this section.

## A. Natural Gas Reforming

Inputs for new-build steam methane reforming (SMR) and autothermal reforming (ATR) are from the 2022 NETL report on fossil-based hydrogen production technologies.[31]

- Plant size modeled by NETL: 200 MSCFD (483 metric tons per day) for SMR and 274 MSCFD (660 metric tons per day) for ATR.

- The SMR retrofit case was assumed to involve adding $CO_2$ capture to a fully depreciated plant.

25  Littlefield, J., et al. 2022. "Life Cycle GHG Perspective on U.S. Natural Gas Delivery Pathways. " *Environ. Sci. Tech.* 56. https://doi.org/10.1021/acs.est.2c01205.

26  ANL. Default case from GREET1 model, v.2022. https://greet.anl.gov/.

27  The *Charting the Course* reference case is the harmonized mean from its "meta model." The harmonization process involved accounting for differences in natural gas composition, heating values, and loss rates for each segment of the natural gas supply chain through delivery.

28  Omara, M., et al. 2022. "Methane emissions from US low production oil and natural gas well sites." *Nature Comm.* 13. https://doi.org/10.1038/s41467-022-29709-3.

29  Shen, L., et al. 2023. "National quantifications of methane Emissions from Fuel Exploitation using high resolution inversions of satellite observations." *Nature Comm.* 14. https://doi.org/10.1038/s41467-023-40671-6.

30  Alvarez, R.A., et al. 2018. "Assessment of methane emissions from the U.S. oil and gas supply chain." *Science* 361. https://doi.org/10.1126/science.aar7204.

31  Lewis, E., et al. 2022. "Comparison of Commercial, State-of-the-Art, Fossil-Based Hydrogen Production Technologies." *NETL Technical Report.* https://doi.org/10.2172/1862910.

| Parameters | Units | SMR Unabated (new build) | SMR with $CO_2$ Capture (retrofit) | SMR with $CO_2$ Capture (new build) | ATR with $CO_2$ Capture (new build) |
|---|---|---|---|---|---|
| Capital recovery period | years | 30 | 20 | 30 | 30 |
| **Plant capex** | | | | | |
| Total installed cost | M$/Mscfd-$H_2$ | 1.7 | 2.5 | 4.2 | 3.4 |
| | $/(kg$H_2$/yr) | 2.0 | 2.8 | 4.8 | 3.8 |
| **Plant opex** | | | | | |
| Fixed opex | % of capex | 3% | 3% | 3% | 3% |
| Variable opex, nonenergy | % of capex | 2% | 2% | 2% | 2% |
| **Efficiency** | | | | | |
| NG to $H_2$ efficiency (LHV) | -- | 72% | 68% | 68% | 71% |
| Total NG import | MBtuNG-HHV/kg$H_2$ | 0.175 | 0.186 | 0.186 | 0.178 |
| Electricity import | kWhe/kg$H_2$ | 0.6 | 2.0 | 2.0 | 4.0 |
| $CO_2$ capture | -- | 0% | 96% | 96% | 95% |
| Plant capacity factor | -- | 90% | 90% | 90% | 90% |

Note: All costs are expressed in 2020$ on a nameplate capacity basis.

*Table D-5. Technoeconomic Assessment (TEA) Inputs for Natural Gas-Based $H_2$ Production Plants*

The capex required was assumed to be the same as the difference between new-build SMRs with and without $CO_2$ capture. Other parameters were assumed to be the same as for the new-build SMR with $CO_2$ capture case, except a shorter capital recovery period.

- Electricity is assumed to be supplied by the local grid.

- Costs are assumed to remain constant in real terms to 2050.

- Energy import (natural gas and electricity) and $CO_2$ capture rates are assumed to be unchanged to 2050.

## B. Electrolysis

## 1. Renewable Electricity Generation Technologies

Cost projections are from the 2023 National Renewable Energy Laboratory (NREL) *Annual Technology Baseline* moderate innovation case.[32]

- The solar photovoltaic (PV) technology represents utility-scale, single-axis tracking with a capacity of 100 $MW_{DC}$. The onshore wind tech-

nology represents Class 1 through Class 7 turbines. The offshore wind technology represents Class 5 fixed bottom turbines.

- These inputs—along with regional capacity factors—were used to calculate the levelized cost of electricity (LCOE) in each region, which is an operating expense for electrolysis plants.

## 2. Renewable Electricity Capacity Factor

Renewable electricity supply profiles for solar and onshore wind were estimated for continental U.S. regions using the MIT ZEPHYR model.[33] This model leverages NREL assessments of solar and wind capacity installation potential (based on available land considerations) and hourly solar irradiation and wind speed over a one-year timeframe at high geographic resolution for the continental United States. The data allow hourly and annual capacity factors to be calculated for a given solar/wind mix in a given study region. The results represent a generation-weighted average of renewable resources for the region. While such weighted averages are dominated by contributions from the higher quality resources, they necessarily

---

32 NREL. "2023 Annual Technology Baseline v2." 20 July 2023. https://atb.nrel.gov/electricity/2023/data.

33 Brown, P.R., and A. Botterud. 2021. "The Value of Inter-Regional Coordination and Transmission in Decarbonizing the US Electricity System." *Joule* 5. https://doi.org/10.1016/j.joule.2020.11.013.

| Parameter | Units | 2025 | 2030 | 2040 | 2050 |
|---|---|---|---|---|---|
| **Solar, PV** | | | | | |
| Capital recovery period | years | 20 | 20 | 20 | 20 |
| Capex | $/kWe | 1,190 | 990 | 730 | 605 |
| Opex, fixed (nameplate capacity basis) | $/MWhe | 2.2 | 2.0 | 1.6 | 1.5 |
| Opex, variable | $/MWhe | 0.0 | 0.0 | 0.0 | 0.0 |
| **Wind, onshore** | | | | | |
| Capital recovery period | years | 20 | 20 | 20 | 20 |
| Capex | $/kWe | 1,210 | 1,100 | 990 | 880 |
| Opex, fixed (nameplate capacity basis) | $/MWhe | 3.1 | 2.9 | 2.7 | 2.5 |
| Opex, variable | $/MWhe | 0.0 | 0.0 | 0.0 | 0.0 |
| **Wind, offshore** | | | | | |
| Capital recovery period | years | 20 | 20 | 20 | 20 |
| Capex | $/kWe | 3,245 | 2,980 | 2,700 | 2,535 |
| Opex, fixed (nameplate capacity basis) | $/MWhe | 11.2 | 10.2 | 9.1 | 8.3 |
| Opex, variable | $/MWhe | 0.0 | 0.0 | 0.0 | 0.0 |

Notes: All costs are expressed in 2020$. Solar costs are on an AC basis.

***Table D-6.*** *TEA Inputs for Renewable Electricity Generators*

underrepresent the best possible resource opportunities that might be chosen first for solar/wind installations.

- For the Alaska and Hawai'i region, solar and onshore wind supply profiles were estimated as a weighted average of the data for the 10 other regions.

- Supply profiles for offshore wind data were estimated using average wind speeds at a 100-meter height within 50 nautical miles of the shoreline. Those average wind speeds were sourced from the NREL Wind Integration National Dataset (WIND) Toolkit,[34] and the power curve of a 6-MW rated wind turbine.[35] The offshore installation potential within 50 nautical miles

of the shoreline was estimated using the NREL Offshore Wind Energy Resource Assessment.[36]

### 3. Battery Technology

Battery technology costs and performance projections were taken from the 2023 NREL *Annual Technology Baseline* moderate innovation case for utility-scale 4-hour lithium-ion (Li-ion) batteries.[37]

| Parameter | Units | 2025 | 2030 | 2040 | 2050 |
|---|---|---|---|---|---|
| Capital recovery period | years | 20 | 20 | 20 | 20 |
| Capex | $/kWe | 1,370 | 1,150 | 970 | 795 |
| Opex, fixed (nameplate capacity basis) | $/MWhe | 3.9 | 3.3 | 2.8 | 2.3 |
| Opex, variable | $/MWhe | 0.0 | 0.0 | 0.0 | 0.0 |
| Roundtrip efficiency | % | 85% | 85% | 85% | 85% |

Note: All costs are expressed in 2020$.

***Table D-7.*** *TEA Inputs for Li-ion Batteries*

### 4. Electrolysis Technology

As discussed in Chapter 2: Production, there are multiple electrolysis technologies that are likely to find commercial success over the study's modeling period. The most advanced are alkaline, proton exchange membrane (PEM), and solid oxide electrolysis cell (SOEC). To avoid the modeling burden of carrying multiple electrolysis technologies in parallel, and to avoid the perception of picking one technology as the winning technology, the study team opted to define a hypothetical electrolysis technology to represent a market mix of the actual technologies likely to be deployed.

- The estimated capex of the stack and balance-of-plant (BOP) of the hypothetical electrolysis plant in 2025 was guided by literature

34 NREL. 2020. "2023 National Offshore Wind Data Set." https://doi.org/10.25984/1821404.

35 Stehly, T., et al. 2020. "2019 Cost of Wind Energy Review." *NREL Technical Report.* https://doi.org/10.2172/1756710.

36 Musial, W., et al. 2016. "2016 Offshore Wind Energy Resource Assessment for the United States." *NREL Technical Report.* https://doi.org/10.2172/1324533.

37 NREL. "2023 Annual Technology Baseline v2." 20 July 2023. https://atb.nrel.gov/electricity/2023/data.

| Parameter | Units | 2025 | 2030 | 2040 | 2050 |
|---|---|---|---|---|---|
| Capital recovery period | years | 20 | 20 | 20 | 20 |
| **Plant capex** | | | | | |
| Stacks | $/kWe | 600 | 460 | 280 | 170 |
| BOP+EPC | $/kWe | 1,400 | 1,300 | 1,130 | 980 |
| Total | $/kWe | 2,000 | 1,760 | 1,410 | 1,150 |
| **Plant opex** | | | | | |
| Stack replacement | $/kWe-yr | 15 | 12 | 7 | 4 |
| Fixed opex | $/kWe-yr | 50 | 50 | 50 | 50 |
| Variable opex | $/kWe-yr | 3 | 3 | 3 | 3 |
| **Plant efficiency** | | | | | |
| Electricity consumption | kWhe/kgH$_2$ | 56 | 53 | 48 | 44 |
| Efficiency on LHV basis | -- | 60% | 63% | 69% | 76% |

Notes: All costs are expressed in 2020$. Values for a representative market mix of electrolysis technologies. BOP = balance-of-plant; EPC = engineering, procurement, and construction.

*Table D-8. TEA Inputs for Electrolsis Plants*

references.[38, 39, 40] BOP includes equipment and utilities to produce H$_2$ at 30 bar and minimum 99.9% purity, but not substantial water cleanup (e.g., desalination). EPC costs in 2025 were estimated by consensus among study participants. EPC includes all indirect costs, such as owners' costs, construction and installation, and contingency.

- Costs were assumed to decrease by a fixed percentage per year in real terms through 2050: stack costs by 5% per year; BOP costs by 2% per year; and EPC costs by 1% per year. Stack costs remain above the expected floor associated with material costs.[41]

38  International Renewable Energy Agency. 2020. "Green Hydrogen Cost Reduction." https://www.irena.org/publications/2020/Dec/Green-hydrogen-cost-reduction.

39  Institute for Sustainable Process Technology. 2020. "Gigawatt green hydrogen plant." https://ispt.eu/media/ISPT-public-report-gigawatt-green-hydrogen-plant.pdf.

40  Bohm, et al. 2019. "Estimating future costs of power-to-gas – a component-based approach for technological learning." *Int. J. Hydrogen Energy* 44. https://doi.org/10.1016/j.ijhydene.2019.09.230.

41  Mayyas, A., et al. 2019. "Manufacturing Cost Analysis for Proton Exchange Membrane Water Electrolyzers." *NREL Technical Report.* https://www.nrel.gov/docs/fy19osti/72740.pdf.

- Opex elements were estimated by consensus among study participants. Stack replacement was amortized and treated as an operation and maintenance (O&M) cost that decreases 5% per year in real terms to 2050. Fixed opex and variable opex (including ~3 gal/kgH$_2$ water feed) were assumed to remain unchanged in real terms to 2050.

- In terms of efficiency, the electrolysis plant's electricity consumption in 2025 was estimated by consensus among study participants. It reflects an average value over the stack lifetime and was assumed to decrease 1% per year to 2050.

## 5. Electrolysis Capacity Factor

The study team chose to model electrolysis plants as directly powered by dedicated renewables; i.e., in a behind-the-meter configuration with no grid connection. Consequently, the capacity factor of a plant is determined by the availability of renewable electricity (RE), which is tied to the capacity factor of the RE generators being used. If the capacity of the RE generators equals the capacity of the electrolysis plant (e.g., both 500 MW$_e$), then the electrolysis plant capacity factor is the same as the capacity factor of the RE generators.

The capacity factor of the electrolysis plant can be increased by overbuilding renewable capacity or adding electrical energy (e.g., battery) storage.

## VI. INFRASTRUCTURE

After production, H$_2$ must be delivered to end users, which may involve transmission (large volumes over typically long distances) and/or distribution (small volumes over typically short distances) and some amount of storage. For the study, the H$_2$ distribution infrastructure needed for Industrial and Power sector customers was assumed to be minimal compared to transmission infrastructure, while both elements are material for the Transportation sector.

As such, the levelized cost of hydrogen (LCOH) for H$_2$ delivered to end users in the Industrial and Power sectors is the sum of the levelized costs of production, storage, and transmission. Likewise, the CI of H$_2$ delivered to end users in these sectors accounts for emissions related to production, storage, and transmission.

For NG+CCS $H_2$, the production facility was assumed to be colocated with the demand facility, providing a continuous stream of $H_2$. Storage and distribution requirements were assumed to be negligible. For hydrogen produced with renewable energy (RE $H_2$), the production facility can be far from the demand facility. In addition, storage is necessary to buffer the intermittent nature of production. As a result, the infrastructure for RE $H_2$ delivery involves substantial storage and transmission components.

For the study, $H_2$ use in the Transportation sector was limited to heavy-duty (HD) trucks. Getting $H_2$ to those vehicles was assumed to involve delivering it from centralized terminals to $H_2$ refueling stations via liquid $H_2$ ($LH_2$) delivery trucks. Hydrogen transmission to the terminal, which occurs by pipeline, has the same cost and CI as for Industrial and Power sector customers. The additional cost and CI of distribution include contributions from the terminal, the $LH_2$ delivery trucks, and the refueling station. These values do not depend on the type of $H_2$ being delivered.

The modeling assumptions and inputs for key infrastructure elements are described in this section.

## A. Hydrogen Storage

The study modeled large-scale, stand-alone $H_2$ storage.

- Costs and performance metrics were assumed to remain unchanged to 2050.

- *Max turnover frequency* represents the maximum number of working capacity volumes that can be discharged from the storage facility per year. It is determined by the maximum filling and emptying rates set by the facility design (e.g. size of compressors and pipes relative to size of storage). Increasing the turnover frequency increases capex. The maximum filling rate was assumed to be 20% of the maximum emptying rate.

- Compressed gaseous $H_2$ ($CGH_2$) was assumed to be stored in salt caverns or tanks. The capex

for salt cavern storage includes geological site prep, well drilling, and cushion gas.[42] Tank storage was modeled as a string of pipeline segments.[43] However, as this approach is unproven for $H_2$ storage, a contingency factor of ~1.3x was applied to the published capex. Compressor costs are based on the size needed to support the maximum filling rate.[44]

- Liquid $H_2$ ($LH_2$) storage capex is estimated for 10,000-$m^3$ insulated tanks.[45, 46, 47] The associated liquefier and regasifier (if needed) are sized to support the maximum $LH_2$ tank filling and emptying rates, respectively.[48] Boil-off is minimized by leveraging the liquefaction facilities.

- Derivation of total capex per throughput capacity:

$$C_{TOTAL} \text{ [units of \$/(kg/yr)]} = (V_S \cdot C_S + F_{C/L} \cdot C_{C/L} + F_R \cdot C_R)/(V_S \cdot f)$$

where $V_S$ is the storage working capacity [$kgH_2$], $C_S$ is the storage capex [\$/$kgH_2$], $F_{C/L}$ is the rated throughput of the compressor or liquefier [$kgH_2$/d], $C_{C/L}$ is the compressor or liquefier capex [\$/($kgH_2$/d)], $F_R$ is the rated throughput of the regasifer [$kgH_2$/d], $C_R$ is the regasifier capex [\$/($kgH_2$/d)], and $f$ is the nameplate number of storage capacity discharges per year [1/y].

42  Chen, F., et al. 2023. "Capacity assessment and cost analysis of geologic storage of hydrogen: A case study in Intermountain-West Region USA." *Int. J. Hydrogen Energy* 48. https://doi.org/10.1016/j.ijhydene.2022.11.292.

43  Papadias, D.D., and R.K. Ahluwalia. 2021. "Bulk storage of hydrogen." *Int. J. Hydrogen Energy* 46. https://doi.org/10.1016/j.ijhydene.2021.08.028.

44  Chen, F., et al. 2023. "Capacity assessment and cost analysis of geologic storage of hydrogen: A case study in Intermountain-West Region USA." *Int. J. Hydrogen Energy* 48. https://doi.org/10.1016/j.ijhydene.2022.11.292.

45  Papadias, D.D., and R.K. Ahluwalia. 2021. *Int. J. Hydrogen Energy* 46. Assumed a 2x installation factor and adjusted to 2020S.

46  ANL. "Hydrogen Delivery Infrastructure Analysis." https://hdsam.es.anl.gov. Adjusted to 2020S.

47  DOE. "DOE Technical Targets for Hydrogen Delivery." https://www.energy.gov/eere/fuelcells/doe-technical-targets-hydrogen-delivery. Used ultimate technical target with a 2x installation factor and adjusted to 2020S.

48  DOE. 2010. "Current Status of Hydrogen Liquefaction Costs." *Hydrogen and Fuel Cells Program Record* 19001. https://www.hydrogen.energy.gov/docs/hydrogenprogramlibraries/pdfs/19001_hydrogen_liquefaction_costs.pdf. Adjusted to 2020S.

| Parameters | Units | CGH$_2$ Salt Cavern | CGH$_2$ Pipe Farm | LH$_2$ Tank Farm |
|---|---|---|---|---|
| Typical working capacity | metric tons H$_2$ | 5,000 | 500 | 700 |
| Typical pressure when full | bar | 150 | 100 | <10 |
| Capital recovery period | years | 30 | 20 | 20 |
| Max turnover frequency, nameplate design basis | 1/yr | 12 | 36 | 36 |
| **Capex (total installed cost)** | | | | |
| Cavern | $/kgH$_2$ working capacity | 15 | -- | -- |
| Vessel | $/kgH$_2$ working capacity | -- | 750 | 35 |
| Compressor (incl. BOP) | $/(kgH$_2$/d) nameplate capacity | 200 | 200 | -- |
| Liquefier (incl. BOP) | $/(kgH$_2$/d) nameplate capacity | -- | -- | 2,700 |
| Regasifier (incl. BOP) | $/(kgH$_2$/d) nameplate capacity | -- | -- | 180 |
| Total (design basis) | $/(kgH$_2$/yr) nameplate capacity | 1.9 | 21.5 | 12.8 |
| **Opex** | | | | |
| Fixed O&M | % of capex | 2% | 2% | 2% |
| Compression | kWhe/kgH$_2$ | 2 | 1 | -- |
| Liquefaction | kWhe/kgH$_2$ | -- | -- | 10 |
| Loss rate | % per day | 0 | 0 | 0.03% |
| Utilization factor | -- | * | * | * |

Notes: All costs are expressed in 2020$.

*Table D-9. TEA Inputs for H$_2$ Storage*

- The compressor/liquefier and regasifier capacities are set to ensure the storage capacity can be filled in a minimum filling time $t_F$ [d] and emptied in a minimum emptying time $t_E$ [d], so that:

$$F_{C/L} = V_S/t_F \text{ and } F_R = V_S/t_E$$

Consequently:

$$C_{TOTAL} = (C_S + C_{C/L}/t_F + C_R/t_E)/f$$

Since $t_F + t_E = 365/f$ and the design yields a ratio of minimum filling-to-emptying times, $R = t_F/t_E$, then:

$$t_F = 365 \cdot R/f \cdot (R+1) \text{ and } t_E = 365/f \cdot (R+1)$$

- The utilization factor for a storage facility, which is the ratio of actual annual throughput (kg/yr) to the maximum annual throughput, depends on the actual usage profile. It is equal to 1 when annual throughput = (design annual capacity turnover frequency)·(storage capacity).

- The boil-off rate for the LH$_2$ delivery pathway was used to put costs on a discharged H$_2$ basis, but not used in calculating the CI of that H$_2$.

## B. Hydrogen Transmission by Pipelines

Regional costs are based on the ICF natural gas pipeline survey documented in Appendix N: ICF Report on Pipeline and Compression Costs.[49]

- Assumed a 10% premium for the capex and fixed opex of H$_2$ pipeline costs vs. natural gas pipeline.

- Assumed 36-in-diameter H$_2$ pipelines capable of transmitting 180 MT H$_2$/hr with an annual fixed opex of $46,200/mi.

- Assumed pipeline capacity and compression requirements from 2021 *Transition Accelerator* study.[50]

- Regions with similar capex were grouped in cost tiers labeled A to E. The ICF survey has no data for Alaska or Hawai'i, so cost Tier D was assumed.

49 ICF. 2023. "Pipeline and Compression Cost Study Prepared for the National Petroleum Council."

50 Khan, M.A., et al. 2021. "The Techno-Economics of Hydrogen Pipelines." *Transition Accelerator Technology Briefs* 1. https://transitionaccelerator.ca/reports/the-techno-economics-of-hydrogen-pipelines/.

- Costs for actual projects will depend on specific circumstances such as distance, design capacity, location, terrain conditions, and right of way.

- Costs are assumed to remain unchanged in real terms to 2050.

| Parameter | Units | Value | Region |
|---|---|---|---|
| Capital recovery period | years | 30 | All |
| Capex | $/(MT $H_2$/yr)-mile | 5.3 | Tier A: South, Central, Gulf Coast, Mountain |
| | | 7.4 | Tier B: Great Lakes |
| | | 9.3 | Tier C: Appalachia, Northwest, West |
| | | 11.4 | Tier D: Mid-Atlantic, Alaska & Hawai'i |
| | | 20.0 | Tier E: Northeast |
| Opex (fixed O&M) | $/MT $H_2$-mile | 0.03 | All |
| Electricity for compression | kWhe/MT $H_2$-mile | 1.7 | All |

Note: All costs are expressed in 2020$ on a nameplate capacity basis.

**Table D-10.** *TEA Inputs for $H_2$ Transmission by Pipelines*

### C. Characteristic Distances for $H_2$ Pipelines

The study assumed NG+CCS $H_2$ delivery pathways would involve minimal pipeline distances due to the proximity between production and demand (not modeled explicitly but assigned to be 25 miles universally). In contrast, RE $H_2$ required long pipeline distances since they were assumed to provide the connectivity between geographically separated production, storage, and end use—i.e., between regions of high-quality renewable energy, regions with low-cost storage in the form of salt caverns, and regions of high $H_2$ demand. Figure D-7 shows the approach taken to model RE $H_2$ transmission.

- **Salt cavern storage case:** Hydrogen produced at location A is sent to the storage site at location B. If the hourly flow exceeds demand, the excess goes into storage and the rest goes

to fulfill demand at location C. If the hourly flow is less than demand, it is augmented with $H_2$ from storage at location B and sent on to fulfill demand at location C. $H_2$ flows sporadically from A to B but constantly from B to C. The total length of pipeline is the sum of the distances for two legs of the triangle—i.e., (length of A to B) + (length of B to C).

- **Liquid $H_2$ storage case:** Hydrogen flows constantly from A to C since the storage is co-located with production at location A. The pipeline length is the distance for one leg of the triangle, A to C.

- **Characteristic $H_2$ pipeline distances** for the three legs of the triangle were assigned by estimating typical distances from subregions with high-quality renewables to high demand centers and to potential salt storage, validated through results from the intraregional optimization exercise described in Section VI.B of this appendix.

### D. Hydrogen Distribution by Trucks

All inputs were informed by ANL's *Hydrogen Delivery Scenario Analysis* Model.[51]

---

51  ANL. "Hydrogen Delivery Infrastructure Analysis." https://hdsam.es.anl.gov.

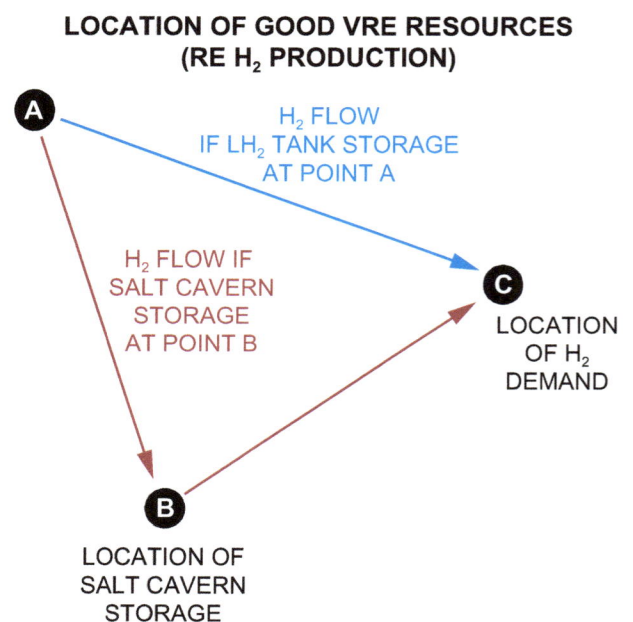

**LOCATION OF GOOD VRE RESOURCES (RE $H_2$ PRODUCTION)**

A

$H_2$ FLOW IF LH$_2$ TANK STORAGE AT POINT A

$H_2$ FLOW IF SALT CAVERN STORAGE AT POINT B

C — LOCATION OF $H_2$ DEMAND

B — LOCATION OF SALT CAVERN STORAGE

**Figure D-7.** *RE $H_2$ Transmission Scenarios*

| Region | A → C RE resource to demand | A → B RE resource to salt cavern storage | B → C Salt cavern storage to demand | Notes |
|---|---|---|---|---|
| | miles | miles | miles | |
| Northwest | 200 | No salt | No salt | No salt in region |
| West | 200 | 150 | 300 | Closest Salt: Western AZ<br>Production w/o salt: Central Valley<br>Production w/salt: near Western AZ |
| Mountain | 200 | 100 | 200 | Salt near renewable wind in Eastern CO |
| Central | 100 | 100 | 250 | Salt near renewable wind in ND, OK |
| Great Lakes | 150 | 300 | 250 | Closest salt: Eastern MI |
| Gulf Coast | 500 | 400 | 100 | Salt near demand |
| South | 350 | 500 | 500 | Closest salt: Western MS |
| Appalachia | 100 | 100 | 100 | Salt and RE close to demand |
| Mid-Atlantic | 100 | 200 | 200 | Closest salt: Western VA/WV |
| Northeast | 100 | 300 | 300 | Closest salt: Western NY |
| Alaska & Hawai'i | 100 | No salt | No salt | No salt in region |

*Table D-11. Characteristic $H_2$ Pipeline Distances for RE $H_2$ Transmission*

- **CGH$_2$ delivery:** Modeled as a 60-MTpd terminal with compressors, storage tanks, and 15 loading bays. The truck fleet consists of twice as many trailers as tractors, operating under a trailer drop and swap model. Each trailer holds 1 MT $H_2$ at ~500 bar. Each bay can load four trailers (4 MT $H_2$) per day. Trailer loads per day assumes a delivery distance of 50 miles roundtrip, with a ratio of stopped time (for loading and unloading at the terminal and stations) to driving time of about 3:1. Hydrogen losses are negligible for this delivery pathway.

- **LH$_2$ delivery:** Modeled as a 120-MTpd terminal with a liquefier, storage tanks, and six loading bays. The truck fleet consists of paired tractor-trailer units, which unload the LH$_2$ into tanks at the stations. Each trailer holds 4 MT $H_2$. Each bay can load five trailers (20 MT $H_2$) per day. Trailer loads per day assumes a delivery distance of 50 miles roundtrip, with a ratio of stopped time (for loading and unloading at the terminal and stations) to driving time of about 3:1. Boil-off is kept close to zero at the LH$_2$ terminal by leveraging the on-site liquefier, but can be as high as ~5% per LH$_2$ delivery. This loss is accounted for in the cost per delivered $H_2$, but not used in calculating the CI of delivered $H_2$.

- The size of the truck fleet depends on the number, size (MT $H_2$/day), and distance of stations serviced by the terminal. Longer delivery distances require longer delivery times, which increases both labor costs and fuel consumption per MT $H_2$ delivered. The number of trailer loads delivered per day is limited by the time needed for $H_2$ loading, unloading, and roundtrip driving.

- Costs are assumed to be unchanged to 2050 in real terms.

- Energy use (terminal electricity, truck fuel consumption) assumed unchanged to 2050.

- Operations and maintenance (O&M) includes all labor.

- The terminal and truck infrastructure was assumed to be utilized at 80% of its nameplate capacity for the purposes of estimating delivery costs for the study.

| Parameters | Units | CGH$_2$ Truck Delivery | LH$_2$ Truck Delivery |
|---|---|---|---|
| **Terminal** | | | |
| Capital recovery period | years | 25 | 25 |
| Capex, total installed cost | M$/(MT H$_2$/d) | 2.0 | 4.5 |
| compressors or liquefier | M$/(MT H$_2$/d) | 0.7 | 3.5 |
| storage | M$/(MT H$_2$/d) | 0.9 | 0.6 |
| rest of terminal | M$/(MT H$_2$/d) | 0.4 | 0.4 |
| O&M (excl. electricity) | $/(kgH$_2$/d) | 100 | 150 |
| Electricity | kWh/kgH$_2$ | 3 | 10 |
| **Delivery trucks** | | | |
| Capital recovery period | years | 12 | 12 |
| Capex (tractor + trailers) | $/(kgH$_2$/day) delivered | 500 | 150 |
| on trailer capacity basis | $/kgH$_2$ | 1,000 | 300 |
| avg trailer loads delivered per day by each tractor | trailer loads/day | 2 | 2 |
| O&M (not including fuel) | | | |
| distance independent | $/(kgH$_2$/d) | 30 | 20 |
| distance dependent | $/(kgH$_2$/d/mi-roundtrip) | 0.5 | 0.1 |
| Fuel for trucks | MJLHV/MT H$_2$/mi | 20 | 5 |

Note: All costs are expressed in 2020$ on a nameplate capacity basis.

**Table D-12.** *TEA Inputs for H$_2$ Distribution by Trucks*

## E. Heavy-Duty Truck H$_2$ Refueling Stations

Input values were informed by ANL's *Heavy-Duty Refueling Station Analysis* Model[52] and industry experience.

- H$_2$ refueling stations for HD trucks modeled assuming large stations (5–15 MTpd), with

dispensers delivering an average of 50 kgH$_2$ per fill at a dispensing rate of 3.6 kgH$_2$/min.

- CGH$_2$ stations include gas storage and dispensers fed by a cascade compressor system to fill 700-bar CGH$_2$ vehicle tanks. H$_2$ is supplied to stations by CGH$_2$ tube trailer deliveries. Capex is dominated by the compressor (~65% of total).

- LH$_2$ stations include liquid storage and dispensers fed by a liquid pump and vaporization system to fill 700-bar CGH$_2$ vehicle tanks; H$_2$ is supplied to stations by LH$_2$ trailer deliveries. Capex is dominated by the cryo-pump/evaporator system (~60% of total).

- Costs are assumed to remain unchanged in real terms to 2050.

- Refueling infrastructure was assumed to be utilized at 80% of its nameplate capacity for the purposes of estimating delivery costs for the study.

| Parameters | Units | CGH$_2$ Station | LH$_2$ Station |
|---|---|---|---|
| Capital recovery period | Years | 20 | 20 |
| Capex, total installed cost | M$/(MT H$_2$/d) | 3.2 | 1.2 |
| Opex | | | |
| O&M | $/kgH$_2$ | 0.35 | 0.25 |
| Electricity | kWhe/kgH$_2$ | 1.5 | 0.5 |

Note: All costs are expressed in 2020$ on a nameplate capacity basis.

**Table D-13.** *TEA Inputs for H$_2$ Refueling Stations*

## F. HD Truck Charging Stations

The cost of electricity at HD truck refueling stations was estimated using the NREL *Electric Vehicle Infrastructure Financial Analysis Scenario Tool.*[53]

- Inputs adjusted to be consistent with the financial assumptions made in the study.

- Costs assumed to be the same across the United States and remain unchanged in real terms to 2050.

52 ANL. "Hydrogen Delivery Infrastructure Analysis." https://hdsam.es.anl.gov.

53 NREL. "EVI-FAST: Electric Vehicle Infrastructure – Financial Analysis Scenario Tool." https://www.nrel.gov/transportation/evi-fast.html.

| Parameters | Units | Value |
|---|---|---|
| Charging station infrastructure cost | $/MWh | 200 |

Note: All costs are expressed in 2020$.

***Table D-14.** TEA Inputs for H$_2$ Refueling Stations*

## G. Electricity Transmission

Cost estimates for long-distance electricity transmission were informed by the NREL *ReEDS model*[54] and industry input to reflect a mix of long-distance and spur-line transmission and a mix of mostly high voltage AC (HVAC) with some high voltage DC (HVDC) lines.

- Regional variability is reflected in cost tiers.

- Costs are assumed to remain unchanged in real terms to 2050.

- Actual project costs will depend on specific circumstances (e.g., capacity, terrain, permitting) and can vary significantly (from less than $1,000/MW-mile to over $20,000/MW-mile).

## H. CO$_2$ Transport and Storage

Costs represent the levelized costs for a company that provides CO$_2$ transport and storage (T&S) services.

| Parameter | Units | Value | Region |
|---|---|---|---|
| Capital recovery period | years | 25 | All |
| | $/MW-mile | 1,500 | Tier A: Central, Great Lakes, South |
| | | 3,000 | Tier B: Alaska & Hawai'i, Appalachia, Gulf Coast, Mid-Atlantic, Mountain, Northwest |
| | | 4,500 | Tier C: Northeast, West |
| Opex (fixed O&M) | % of capex/yr | 1.5% | All |
| Losses | % per mile | 0.01% | All |

Note: All costs are expressed in 2020$ on a generated electricity basis (i.e., before transmission losses).

***Table D-15.** TEA Inputs for Electricity Transmission*

- Regional variability is expressed in cost tiers.

- Costs are assumed to stay unchanged in real terms to 2050.

- **CO$_2$ transport costs** were assigned by assuming a national-average cost of 0.15 $/MT-CO$_2$-mile, based on a combination of recent CO$_2$ trunkline projects of similar scale in North America, market research, and industry guidelines. Regional factors were applied based on the 2023 ICF natural gas pipeline survey[55]

54 Ho, J., et al. 2021. "Regional Energy Deployment System (ReEDS) Model Documentation: Version 2020." *NREL Technical Report.* https://www.nrel.gov/docs/fy21osti/78195.pdf.

55 See Appendix N: ICF Report on Pipeline and Compression Costs.

| Cost Tier | CO$_2$ Transport ($/MT-CO$_2$-mile) | CO$_2$ Storage ($/MT-CO$_2$) | Region | Characteristic Distance for Region (miles) |
|---|---|---|---|---|
| A1 | 0.10 | 8 | South<br>Gulf Coast | 250<br>100 |
| B1 | 0.15 | 8 | Great Lakes | 100 |
| C1 | 0.18 | 8 | Appalachia<br>West | 100<br>200 |
| D1 | 0.22 | 8 | Mid-Atlantic | 200 |
| E1 | 0.33 | 8 | Northeast | 300 |
| A2 | 0.10 | 12 | Central<br>Mountain | 600<br>200 |
| C2 | 0.18 | 12 | Northwest | 200 |
| D2 | 0.22 | 12 | Alaska & Hawai'i | 100 |

Note: All costs are expressed in 2020$.

***Table D-16.** TEA Inputs for CO$_2$ Transport & Storage*

with each region assigned to a pipeline transport cost tier (A, B, C, D, or E). Uncertainty estimated to be ±0.05 $/MT-$CO_2$-mile.

- **$CO_2$ storage costs** were assigned by assuming a national-average cost of 10 $/MT-$CO_2$ based on a combination of market research, industry guidelines, and the 2019 NPC Carbon Capture, Utilization, and Storage (CCUS) study (which found 7-11 $/MT-$CO_2$).[56] Regional factors were applied based on the same 2019 NPC CCUS study with each region assigned to a storage cost tier (1 or 2). Uncertainty estimated to be ±2 $/MT-$CO_2$.

- **Characteristic $CO_2$ pipeline distances** were assigned based on the approximate distance between the largest industrial cluster in a region and the nearest potential $CO_2$ storage location listed in the National Carbon Sequestration Database and Geographic Information System created by NETL.[57]

---

56  NPC. 2019. "Meeting the Dual Challenge: A Roadmap to At-Scale Deployment of Carbon Capture, Use, and Storage." https://dualchallenge.npc.org/.

57  NETL. "National Carbon Sequestration Database and Geographic Information System: Carbon Storage Atlas." https://www.netl.doe.gov/coal/carbon-storage/strategic-program-support/natcarb-atlas.

- Costs associated with actual projects will depend on specific circumstances, including distance, design capacity, location, terrain conditions, right of way, etc.

## VII. HYDROGEN INTEGRATED SUPPLY CHAIN

The SESAME modeling platform includes a Hydrogen Supply Chain (HSC) module for TEAs and LCAs of pathways that consider upstream, production, transmission, and storage steps. Figure D-8 summarizes the pathways components included in the HSC module, as well as key inputs and outputs.

The HSC module includes conventional pathway analysis capability, where specified elements of a supply chain are combined for TEA and LCA calculations. The module can also treat the supply chain as a multinodal system, where each node represents a different geographical region. It has an optimization function for identifying the supply chain structure that minimizes system costs. These costs include capital and operational expenditures, fuel costs, and, if applicable, the financial implications of emissions for all steps in the supply chain, including delivery. The delivery step accounts for transportation distances, required storage, and

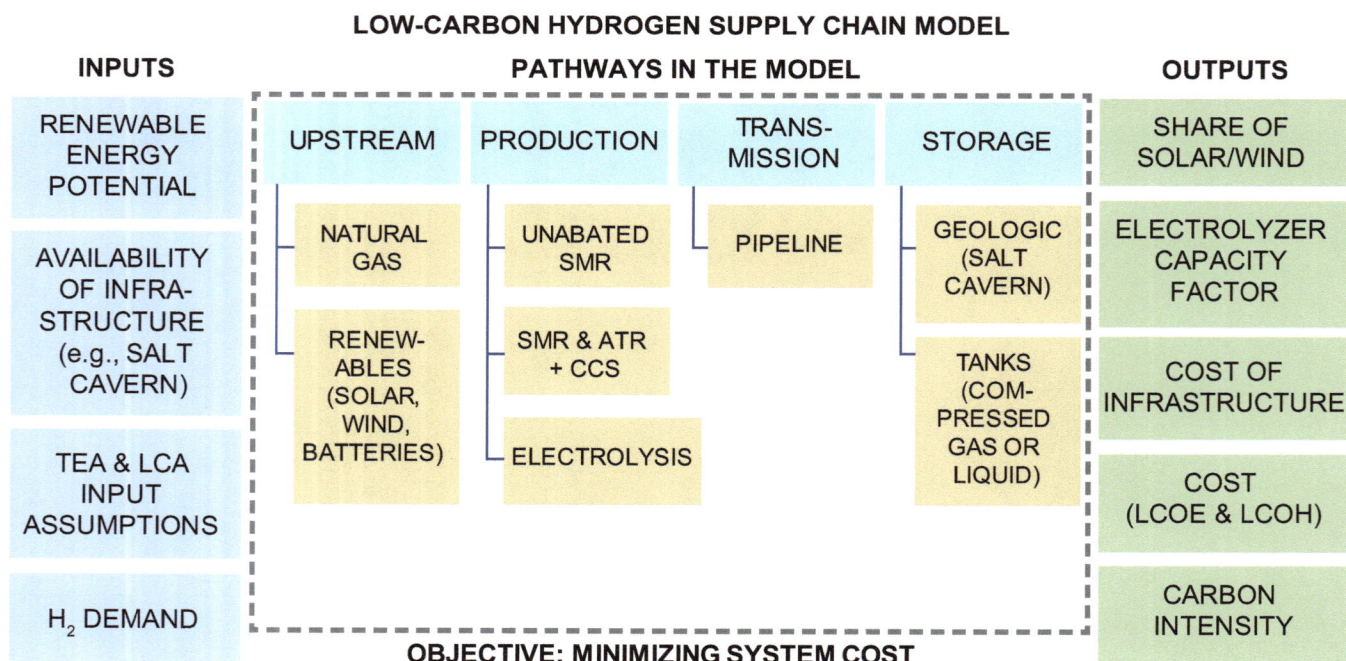

**LOW-CARBON HYDROGEN SUPPLY CHAIN MODEL**

*Figure D-8. SESAME Hydrogen Supply Chain Module*

delivery methods that depend on production sources and customer needs (e.g., delivery as a compressed gas or liquid).

For each region, the overall levelized cost (= sum of production, transmission, and storage costs) and overall CI (= sum of production, transmission, and storage CI) are estimated. Relevant credits are subsequently applied to the levelized cost.[58]

The SESAME modeling capabilities were utilized for TEA and LCA analysis of the two major LCI $H_2$ supply chains investigated in the study: NG+CCS $H_2$ and RE $H_2$. For both pathways, the study assumed $H_2$ would need to be delivered at a constant rate to the end user.

For NG+CCS $H_2$, the process was straightforward. SMR and ATR plants were assumed to run at an annual capacity factor in the 90%-100% range, with $H_2$ produced and delivered at a constant rate. The plant was assumed to include a small amount of on-site storage and $H_2$ delivered to customers via short pipelines. TEA and LCA results were obtained through the pathway analysis functionality of the SESAME HSC module; no optimization was required.

For RE $H_2$, the situation was more complex. The electricity used to produce $H_2$ is generated intermittently, and the electrolysis plants were assumed to be "behind the meter," without a grid connection. Delivering a constant supply of $H_2$ requires structuring the supply chain to bridge that intermittency. A number of options are available, including overbuilding wind/solar generation and/or electrolysis capacity and buffering the intermittency using batteries or $H_2$ storage. The SESAME HSC module's optimization functionality was used to determine the supply chain structure. The relative capacities of renewable electricity generation, electrolysis, and $H_2$ storage were sized to achieve a constant flow of $H_2$ supply.

- **Optimization objective function:** The optimization sought to minimize the total system

cost. These contributing costs at each individual step, made up from capex and opex, are calculated from the relevant TEA inputs. The capex contribution represents the levelized capital cost, which depends on the capacity factor of the asset. For electrolysis, the capacity factor was estimated as part of the optimization approach for RE $H_2$ production.

- **Electricity constraints:** Dedicated renewable energy generators (solar PV and wind turbines) were assumed to be the sole source of electricity for RE $H_2$ production plants (i.e., no grid connection). The RE $H_2$ production system consists of an electrolysis plant with an option of battery-based energy storage. Electricity stored in the batteries can be used to produce $H_2$ in a period of low renewable electricity generation. Any unused electricity was assumed to be curtailed. The optimization framework determined whether energy storage or electricity curtailment is optimal. The electricity generation profile was determined based on hourly electricity generation profiles for solar and wind.

- **Hydrogen constraints:** The hourly $H_2$ demand was assumed to be a constant. The supply to meet this demand is a sum of direct $H_2$ production (from the electrolysis plant) and $H_2$ pulled from storage.

## A. RE $H_2$ Regional Optimization

For regional optimization, each region is treated as a single node in SESAME. Energy transmission was limited to $H_2$ transmission (i.e., electricity transmission was not considered). Characteristic transmission distances were assumed for each region.

The study modeled $H_2$ production by electrolysis plants fed by variable renewable energy (VRE) generated using a mix of solar PV, wind, and batteries that varied by region.[59] The VRE facilities were assumed to be behind the meter (i.e., not grid connected), and constructed to provide dedicated renewable electricity to the electrolysis plant.

---

58 Example credits in the United States are the 45Q carbon storage tax credit, 45V clean hydrogen production tax credit, and 45Y clean energy production tax credit provisions of the Inflation Reduction Act.

59 Onshore wind was considered for all regions, and offshore wind was included for regions with coastlines.

The levelized cost of $H_2$ production was calculated for each region over 2025–2050 in five-year increments, based on:

1. Electrolyzer costs (capex and opex)

2. Electrolyzer efficiency (determines how much VRE is required to generate $H_2$)

3. VRE costs (capex and opex appropriate for the solar/wind/battery mix)

4. VRE availability (depends on the solar/wind/battery mix and quality of solar/wind resources)

5. VRE-to-electrolyzer capacity ratio (the "overbuild ratio")

The overbuild ratio is important for increasing the electrolyzer capacity factor, because VRE capacity factors can be much less than 50%, even for combined solar + wind. At an overbuild ratio of 1, the electrolyzer capacity factor matches that of the VRE supply, resulting in underutilization of an expensive electrolyzer and a high levelized cost of hydrogen production ($LCOH_p$). Overbuilding the VRE capacity (i.e., increasing the overbuild ratio) allows the electrolyzer to run at higher productivity during times of less-than-full VRE generation, thereby increasing electrolyzer utilization and decreasing $LCOH_p$. The downside is that the electricity consumed to make $H_2$ becomes more expensive, since more capex and opex is being spent on the VRE facilities and some electricity is wasted (curtailed) whenever the amount of electricity generated exceeds the electrolyzer capacity.[60] This disbenefit grows faster than the benefit from higher electrolyzer utilization as the overbuild ratio increases. Consequently, there is an optimum overbuild ratio (>1) that yields a minimum $LCOH_p$. At this optimum, the capacity factor of the electrolysis plant is greater than the capacity factor of the VRE supply.

On top of this dynamic, the study required RE $H_2$ to be delivered at a constant rate, to meet an assumed constant $H_2$ demand. Overcoming intermittent production involves adding electricity and/or $H_2$ storage.[61] The VRE and electrolysis capacity must also increase to allow the plant to generate excess $H_2$ at times of high VRE generation, which is used to fill the $H_2$ storage. Subsequently, when the VRE supply is insufficient, $H_2$ is drawn from storage to (partially or fully) meet demand. The cost of $H_2$ storage is captured in the levelized cost of $H_2$ storage ($LCOH_s$); it depends on how frequently the storage capacity is utilized, in addition to its capex and opex. Figure D-9 outlines the supply chain elements included in the optimization model to minimize the total cost of production and storage of RE $H_2$.

The total cost of $H_2$ from VRE-powered electrolysis plants is therefore $LCOH_p + LCOH_s$. The study employed an optimization process to determine this cost for each region over 2025–2050. Fixed inputs included solar and wind supply profiles for each region; cost for electrolysis, VRE generation, and battery facilities; electrolysis plant efficiency; and $H_2$ storage costs. The optimization minimized $LCOH_p + LCOH_s$ by varying the relative capacities of solar, wind, battery, and electrolysis facilities, as well as the $H_2$ storage capacity, under a constraint of constant $H_2$ delivery rate from the electrolyzer and/or $H_2$ storage.

To reflect a balance between minimizing levelized cost through a high overbuild ratio and reducing the capital risk associated with large VRE facilities, the optimization was then repeated at a progressively lower overbuild ratio until $LCOH_p + LCOH_s$ rose to 5% above the minimum value. The electrolyzer/solar/wind/battery/$H_2$ storage system at this point was used as to represent $H_2$ production by VRE-powered electrolysis, and the resulting $LCOH_p$ and $LCOH_s$ values adopted for each region and modeling year.

For $H_2$ produced electrolytically via renewable sources, hourly renewable generation capacity factor profiles were derived from the ZEPHYR[62]

---

60 The behind-the-meter assumption precludes selling this excess electricity to the grid.

61 Hydrogen storage would not be required for an electrolysis facility with a capacity factor of 1. But achieving this limit requires such extensive overbuild of renewables generation and batteries that it is more economic to add $H_2$ storage.

62 ZEPHYR stands for Zero-Emissions Electricity System Planning with Hourly Operational Resolution.

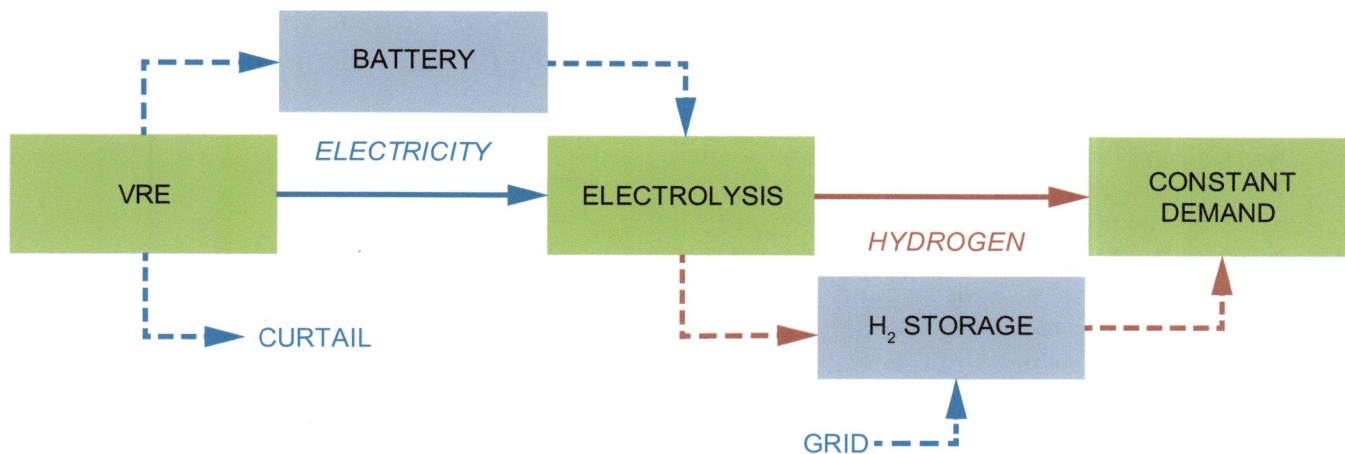

*Figure D-9. Supply Chain Elements Used in the RE H₂ Cost Optimization*

repository.[63] This database contains historical wind and solar irradiance data from sources like the NREL WIND Toolkit [64, 65, 66] and the NREL National Solar Radiation Database.[67] It assumes power output based on single-axis tracking PV solar systems with 1.3 DC-to-AC inverter ratios, and wind turbines with a 100-meter hub height. A curated set of capacity factor curves, representative of each region, was manually extracted spanning the years 2007–2013.

## B.  RE H₂ Intraregional Optimization

Optimization of the supply chain architecture for RE H₂ was performed for a few select regions using a specialized intraregional analysis. First, the region was subdivided into 11–12 subregions, which were chosen to reflect the geographical variability of natural resources (e.g., sun and wind intensity, subsurface salt for storage) and societal characteristics (e.g., industrial activity,

transportation corridors, population centers). Then a similar methodology as employed for the regional optimization was applied to these subregions, again to investigate how to bridge the gap between intermittent production and constant demand. The main difference is that flows of RE H₂ within the region (i.e., between subregions) were included in the model as a variable. The modeling considered the relative attributes of each subregion to determine where production and storage were advantaged, the distribution of demand, and the connections between them. Thus, the amount of RE H₂ and renewable electricity produced, stored, and delivered in each subregion was optimized to create the lowest cost supply chain that met regional demand constraints.

### 1.  Supply

The production of RE H₂ was assumed to use dedicated renewable energy production, with no grid connection, so the electrolysis plant only operates when electricity is provided. This placed a premium on high-quality renewable resources (i.e., high renewable capacity factors). The intraregional analysis utilized hourly solar and wind data over a model year for each subregion in the algorithm to determine the optimal location for RE H₂ production.

### 2.  Infrastructure

The motivation behind the intraregional analysis is a view on how infrastructure might develop

63  Brown, P.R., and A. Botterud. 2021. "The Value of Inter-Regional Coordination and Transmission in Decarbonizing the US Electricity System." *Joule* 5. https://doi.org/10.1016/j.joule.2020.11.013.

64  Draxl, C., et al. 2015. "The Wind Integration National Dataset (WIND) Toolkit." *Applied Energy* 151. https://doi.org/10.1016/j.apenergy.2015.03.121.

65  Musial, W., et al. 2016. "2016 Offshore Wind Energy Resource Assessment for the United States." *NREL Technical Report.* https://doi.org/10.2172/1324533.

66  Doubrawa, P., et al. 2017. "Offshore Wind Energy Resource Assessment for Alaska." *NREL Technical Report.* https://doi.org/10.2172/1417728.

67  NREL. "National Solar Radiation Database." https://nsrdb.nrel.gov/.

to connect RE $H_2$ supply and demand within a region.

Storage is needed to mitigate the inherent intermittency of RE $H_2$ production. The modeling framework included two $H_2$ storage options: underground storage (lower cost) and aboveground liquid storage (higher cost). Salt caverns were the only underground storage option considered by the study, so only subregions with subsurface salt were relevant for this $H_2$ storage option. In contrast, aboveground liquid tanks could be placed anywhere. Energy storage in batteries was also allowed as an option to mitigate the intermittency of renewable energy upstream of RE $H_2$ production.

Transmission is needed to connect subregions of high-quality wind and/or solar (where RE $H_2$ production is advantaged) to subregions of high RE $H_2$ demand. Both electricity and $H_2$ transmission between subregions were included in the optimization framework. Electricity transmission lines were assumed to be built such that they directly connected a production subregion with a demand subregion. Hydrogen pipelines were assumed to be built only between neighboring subregions, although movement to other regions was allowed via subsequent transmission through the network of regional pipelines.

## 3. Demand

The objective was to estimate how LCI $H_2$ demand would be distributed among subregions, since USREP did not provide results at that level of granularity. The intraregional optimization needed this information over time for each region of interest, under both scenarios.

A methodology was developed that leveraged the following results available from USREP for each region:

- Dataset A: $H_2$ demand by type (unabated $H_2$, NG+CCS $H_2$, and RE $H_2$)

- Dataset B: total $H_2$ demand by sector (Industrial, Power, Transportation, and Res/Comm)

Both sets of data were available in five-year increments over 2020–2050 for each scenario.

The following equation was used to estimate the demand for RE $H_2$ in each subregion:

$$\text{RE } H_2 \text{ demand in subregion } j = \text{RE } H_2 \text{ demand in region } j \times \sum_{i=1}^{4} w_{ij}^{energy} \times w_i^{H2}$$

where

- RE $H_2$ demand in region $j$ is obtained from USREP's Dataset A

- the index $i$ represents the demand sector

- $w_{ij}^{energy}$ = fraction of the regional energy demand in sector i that has been allocated to the subregion j using the proxies described below

- $w_{ij}^{H2}$ = fraction of the region's total $H_2$ demand allocated to sector i, taken from USREP's Dataset B

The last term in the equation represents the fraction of the region's total RE $H_2$ demand that is assigned to the subregion. As calculated, however, it is a weighted average of the fraction of total $H_2$ (not just RE $H_2$) demand by sector, where the weighting is by the relative subregional demand for energy (not $H_2$) in those sectors. Two major assumptions are involved:

1. For each sector, the fraction of $H_2$ demand in a subregion can be approximated by the fraction of energy demand in that subregion. This will break down if subregions use more or less $H_2$ than energy, relative to other subregions, or the adoption of $H_2$ does not scale with sectoral energy demand.

2. The distribution of RE $H_2$ can be approximated by the distribution of total $H_2$. This will break down if sectors or subregions adopt RE $H_2$ more or less than the adoption rate for RE $H_2$ in the $H_2$ mix projected by USREP.

The subregional distribution of energy demand by sector was assigned based on proxies that contained geographic information about energy use:

- **Industrial sector:** Energy demand was assumed to scale with 2021 $CO_2e$ emissions reported in the EPA FLIGHT database for the categories of Petroleum and Natural Gas Systems, Refineries, Chemicals, Cement and

Minerals, Metals, and Other Industry.[68] Point sources were assigned to the appropriate subregion and aggregated.

- **Power sector:** Energy demand was assumed to scale with 2021 $CO_2$e emissions reported in the EPA FLIGHT database for the categories of Natural Gas Power and Coal Power. Emissions for coal plants were put on a natural gas basis using emissions factors of 53 kg$CO_2$e/MBtu for natural gas and 96 kg$CO_2$e/MBtu for coal. Point sources were assigned to the appropriate subregion and aggregated.

- **Transportation sector:** Energy demand was assumed to scale with 2025 ton-miles traveled from the U.S. Department of Transportation Freight Analysis Framework (FAF).[69] Data were subdivided across counties in each FAF region and aggregated across each subregion. The total ton-miles traveled in a given subregion was assumed to be the sum of travel within each FAF zone plus travel outbound from the given FAF zone.

- **Residential and Commercial (Res/Comm) sector:** Energy demand was assumed to scale with population from the 2022 U.S. Census.[70] County level data were aggregated across each subregion.

The resulting subregional distribution of energy demand by sector for each region ($w_{ij}^{energy}$) was assumed to apply to both the NZ2050 and Stated Policies scenarios and to remain unchanged over 2025–2050. However, since the distribution of $H_2$ demand by sector ($w_i^{H2}$) varied with time and by scenario, the RE $H_2$ demand assigned to each subregion also varied with time and scenario.

This process resulted in a projection of RE $H_2$ demand (in MMTpa) in each subregion in five-year increments over 2025–2050 under each scenario. The intraregional optimization used these projections as input. To mimic infrastructure buildout, the optimization for a given modeling year considered only the incremental RE $H_2$ demand since the last modeling year, assuming the infrastructure developed up to that point would remain intact.

An analogous process was followed to estimate the subregional demands for NG+CCS $H_2$ in each region of interest under both scenarios.

An alternative $H_2$ demand allocation dataset was calculated to test the sensitivity of the optimized RE $H_2$ supply chain to this allocation. Specifically, it was assumed that the Cement and Minerals, Metals, and Other Industry categories within the Industrial sector would adopt little-to-no LCI $H_2$ to decarbonize operations.[71] Despite the importance of the Industrial sector for LCI $H_2$ demand, the impact of the modified subregional allocation was minor for all the cases examined. LCOH changed by a few cents per kg$H_2$ and subregional production and transmission flows changed slightly, while the supply chain architecture remained qualitatively unchanged.

## 4. Results for the Gulf Coast Region

| Sub-region | Industry | Power | Transportation | Res/Comm |
|---|---|---|---|---|
| 1 | 33.1% | 10.3% | 5.8% | 8.0% |
| 2 | 2.1% | 11.4% | 17.4% | 12.5% |
| 3 | 0.7% | 21.4% | 10.4% | 11.5% |
| 4 | 2.7% | 3.8% | 4.4% | 3.3% |
| 5 | 0.5% | 1.1% | 4.9% | 1.6% |
| 6 | 9.5% | 2.0% | 2.0% | 3.0% |
| 7 | 2.1% | 15.1% | 12.0% | 7.1% |
| 8 | 0.6% | 4.0% | 18.5% | 24.2% |
| 9 | 0.2% | 0.0% | 1.8% | 1.9% |
| 10 | 2.0% | 4.9% | 6.7% | 2.5% |
| 11 | 4.2% | 2.5% | 7.8% | 4.4% |
| 12 | 42.4% | 23.5% | 8.3% | 19.9% |

Note: Column sums may not add to 100% due to rounding.

*Table D-17. Subregional Energy Demand by Energy Sector for the Gulf Coast Region*

---

68 EPA. "Facility Level Information on Greenhouse Gases Tool (FLIGHT)." 2022 data year. http://ghgdata.epa.gov/ghgp.

69 Department of Transportation, Bureau of Transportation Statistics. 2024. "Freight Analysis Framework." v5.4.1. https://www.bts.gov/faf.

70 U.S. Census Bureau. "County Population Totals and Components of Change: 2020-2023." https://www.census.gov/data/tables/time-series/demo/popest/2020s-counties-total.html.

71 Operationally, this involved including 0% of Cement and Minerals emissions, 5% of Metal emissions, and 5% of Other Industry emissions from the EPA FLIGHT database in the Industrial energy demand proxy.

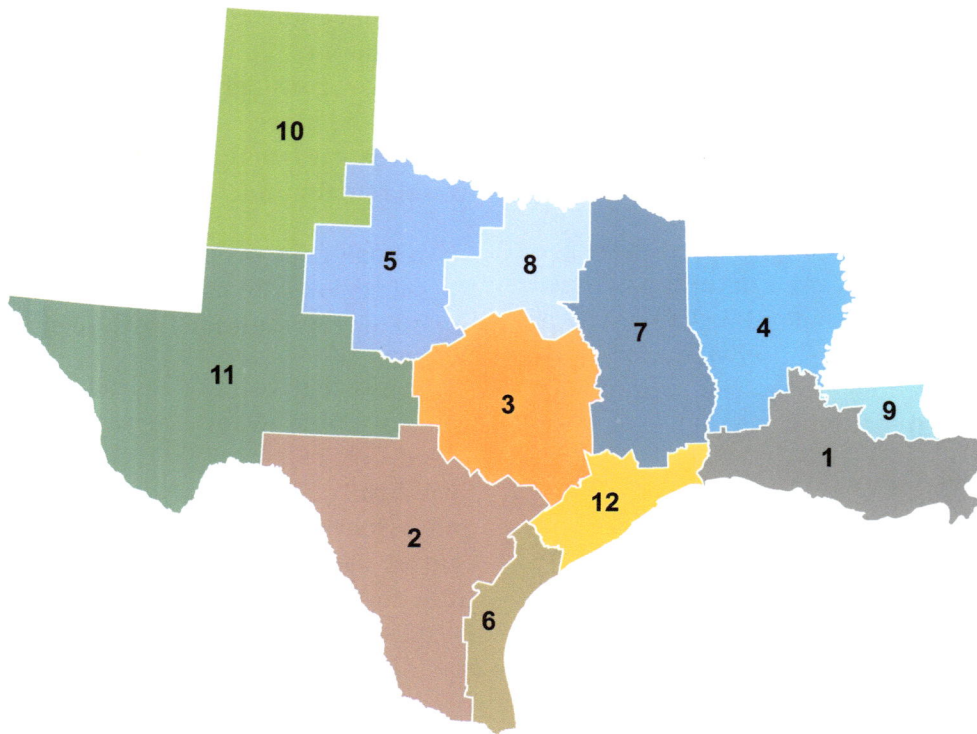

**Figure D-10.** Identification of Subregions within the Gulf Coast Region

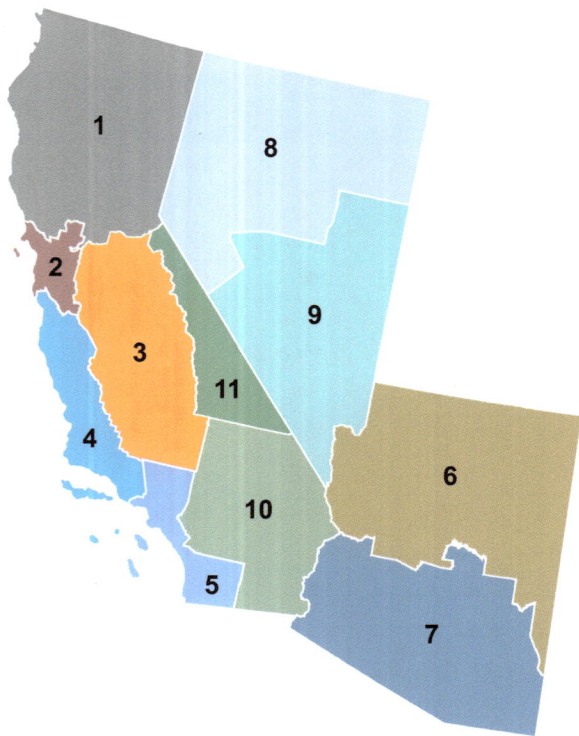

**Figure D-11.** Identification of Subregions within the West Region

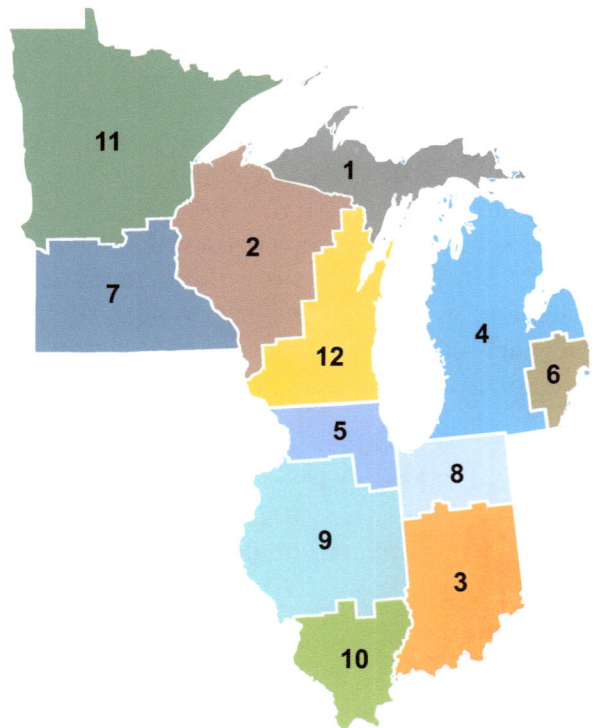

**Figure D-12.** Identification of Subregions within the Great Lakes Region

## 5. Results for the West Region

| Subregion | Industry | Power | Transpor-tation | Res/Comm |
|-----------|----------|-------|-----------------|----------|
| 1 | 1.6% | 6.6% | 14.9% | 8.6% |
| 2 | 25.1% | 8.7% | 10.5% | 13.9% |
| 3 | 17.0% | 7.2% | 9.0% | 9.1% |
| 4 | 2.0% | 3.6% | 12.6% | 4.7% |
| 5 | 37.7% | 11.6% | 20.7% | 32.6% |
| 6 | 1.9% | 15.2% | 1.2% | 1.6% |
| 7 | 2.2% | 25.5% | 7.6% | 13.2% |
| 8 | 2.7% | 5.4% | 2.5% | 1.5% |
| 9 | 2.6% | 10.8% | 2.8% | 4.8% |
| 10 | 7.3% | 5.4% | 16.5% | 9.8% |
| 11 | 0.0% | 0.0% | 1.7% | 0.1% |

Note: Column sums may not add to 100% due to rounding.

*Table D-18. Subregional Energy Demand by Energy Sector for the West Region*

## 6. Results for the Great Lakes Region

| Subregion | Industry | Power | Transpor-tation | Res/Comm |
|-----------|----------|-------|-----------------|----------|
| 1 | 0.7% | 0.0% | 1.7% | 0.8% |
| 2 | 1.1% | 2.7% | 8.3% | 3.3% |
| 3 | 9.3% | 25.1% | 10.2% | 11.3% |
| 4 | 4.2% | 12.3% | 9.0% | 11.0% |
| 5 | 9.2% | 6.3% | 12.8% | 23.0% |
| 6 | 5.4% | 12.3% | 6.8% | 12.8% |
| 7 | 9.9% | 8.1% | 11.7% | 11.3% |
| 8 | 34.8% | 3.7% | 6.1% | 5.1% |
| 9 | 12.9% | 5.8% | 11.7% | 5.6% |
| 10 | 8.3% | 6.9% | 5.7% | 2.2% |
| 11 | 1.6% | 2.2% | 6.7% | 2.5% |
| 12 | 2.7% | 14.5% | 9.4% | 11.2% |

Note: Column sums may not add to 100% due to rounding.

*Table D-19. Subregional Energy Demand by Energy Sector for the Great Lakes Region*

## VIII. HYDROGEN DEMAND

SESAME was used to investigate the cost and CI competitiveness of LCI $H_2$ vs. incumbent and other decarbonization options in the following demand sectors:

- Industrial—refining, steel, cement, and ammonia

- Transportation—long-haul HD trucks

- Power—turbines and $H_2$ fuel cells

The levelized cost and CI of delivered $H_2$ (and competitive fuels) from SESAME were combined with capital and operating costs for specific end uses in the demand sectors to develop demand-specific costs and CI comparisons.

### A. Industrial Sector

USREP divides the Industrial sector into four categories: Refining, Iron and Steel, Cement, and Other Industry (which includes chemicals such as ammonia).

The study assumed there would be no increase in the cost or CI of LCI $H_2$ due to using it as a replacement for unabated $H_2$ in feedstock applications. The study further assumed the same would be true for LCI $H_2$ used as a replacement for natural gas as a fuel for heat. Specifically, it was assumed that the cost associated with fuel switching (e.g., replacing furnace components) would be negligible when amortized over the capital recovery period of the project, that the heating efficiency would be unchanged, and that there would be no increase in the CI of $H_2$ due to fuel switching.

### 1. Refining

The representation of transportation fuels in USREP influenced how the study modeled LCI $H_2$ in the refining industry. The following provides relevant context for the nexus between the Transportation sector and refining in USREP.

#### a. Final Energy in the Transportation Sector

USREP accounts for final energy consumption in the Transportation sector using three categories: liquid fuels, electricity, and $H_2$.

Liquid fuels are used by internal combustion engine vehicles (ICEVs) of any type, from conventional gasoline or diesel engines to jet turbines. The broad range of liquid fuels are simplified into just two classes—Conventional Liquid Fuels and Carbon-Neutral Liquid Fuels—which are tracked separately. Hydrogen demand to make these fuels is also tracked. The refining industry refers to the collection of refineries that make just

Conventional Liquid Fuels (i.e., oil refineries and first-generation biofuel refineries).

- **Conventional Liquid Fuels** include those made by refineries with crude oil as the main input, and first-generation biofuels made by biorefineries with biomass as the main input. For USREP, first-generation biofuels are not carbon neutral (e.g., corn ethanol and renewable diesel).

- **Carbon-Neutral Liquid Fuels** include second-generation (e.g., cellulosic) biofuels made by biorefineries with biomass as an input, and e-fuels made from carbon recycled from the atmosphere (i.e., from biomass or DAC) and renewable $H_2$ (i.e., from electrolysis powered by renewable electricity).

Electricity is used by battery electric vehicles (BEVs), obtained from the grid. Hydrogen is used by fuel cell electric vehicles (FCEVs).[72]

## b. Transportation Fleets in USREP

USREP categorizes all vehicles as belonging to one of two fleets:

1. The **Passenger Vehicle Fleet** includes light-duty cars and trucks. The study assumed negligible demand for $H_2$ into this fleet, on the basis that electrification will be the primary approach to decarbonizing the light-duty vehicles. Therefore, energy demand by this fleet was assumed to be met entirely by Liquid Fuels and Electricity.

2. The **Commercial Vehicle Fleet** includes trucks (medium-duty, HD, off-road), rail, marine, and aviation. All three final energy options were assumed to be used to meet the energy demand by this fleet. However, the study assumed the only material demand for direct use of $H_2$ as a transportation fuel over 2025–2050 would be by HD trucks.[73] Still, $H_2$ was indirectly consumed by all ICEVs because $H_2$ was used in the production of Liquid Fuels.

## c. Ways to Reduce Transportation Emissions

USREP considers five ways to reduce emissions from the Transportation sector:

1. Increase the efficiency of vehicles, so they consume less fuel for a given level of demand for transportation services.

2. Lower the emissions intensity from ICEVs. Since the vast majority of emissions from liquid fuels today are from combustion (i.e., tailpipe emissions), the most effective way to reduce overall ICEV emissions is to increase the fraction of carbon-neutral fuels in the liquid fuels mix.[74]

3. Increase the adoption of BEVs that use low CI electricity.

4. Increase the adoption of FCEVs that use LCI $H_2$.

5. Reduce the demand for transportation services. The demand is determined endogenously within USREP.

The costs and emissions for different vehicle classes were provided by SESAME. These values were used by USREP, along with Transportation-related policies, to project the ICEV/BEV/FCEV mix in the passenger vehicle and commercial vehicle fleets, and the demand for energy sources (conventional fuels, carbon-neutral fuels, electricity, and hydrogen).

## d. Refining Industry Direct Emissions

Currently, USREP does not explicitly model the technologies utilized by the refining industry, therefore it does not project how the industry will decarbonize. For the study, the emissions trajectory for the refining industry was an input to USREP. To develop this trajectory, study participants assumed the refining industry would implement three approaches in concert:

1. Efficiency: implement changes to reduce energy consumption

---

72 If there is any $H_2$ used by $H_2$-fueled ICEVs, it would be included here.

73 Evaluation of the potential demand into other commercial transportation was beyond the scope of the modeling in this study. See Chapter 5: Demand for a discussion of the role $H_2$ may play in rail, marine, aviation, and off-road vehicles.

74 Decreasing fuel emissions from fuel production will also help reduce transportation-related emissions, albeit to a smaller extent. However, USREP attributes these emissions to the Industrial sector. Emissions associated with inputs to refineries (energy and feedstocks) are also not included in the Transportation sector.

2. CCS: install $CO_2$ capture on select point sources (e.g., fluid catalytic cracking for oil refineries and fermenters for biofuel refineries) and sequester the $CO_2$

3. Fuel switching: convert from hydrocarbon fuels to LCI $H_2$ for heat

The anticipated applicability of these approaches is outlined in Table D-20.

| Approaches to Decarbonization | Addressable Emissions |
|---|---|
| Efficiency | 10% |
| CCS | 20% |
| Fuel Switching to LCI $H_2$ | 70% |

**Table D-20.** *Assumed Steps to Reduce Refining Industry Direct Emissions*

Fuel switching involves burning LCI $H_2$ instead of hydrocarbon fuels for heat. Most of the LCI $H_2$ used for this purpose was assumed to be produced within the refinery. An oil refinery utilizes fuel gas for the majority of its heat duty (boilers, furnaces, cogens, etc.); the rest is met by imported natural gas. Adding new steam reformer capacity (SMR or ATR) to the refinery would allow the fuel gas and natural gas to be converted to $H_2$

plus $CO_2$, with a high fraction (90+%) of the $CO_2$ captured and sequestered, ensuring the $H_2$ has a low CI. Since the refinery was originally in energy balance, additional imported fuel would be needed to generate the process heat required by the new reformer. The resulting LCI $H_2$ would be used as the fuel to meet the existing heat duty of the refinery. The net effect would be adding a precombustion CCS pathway to decarbonize the refinery.

The imported fuel, which would include any original natural gas imports plus new fuel to drive the reformer, could be either natural gas sent to the reformer to generate LCI $H_2$ or externally sourced LCI $H_2$ (NG+CCS $H_2$ or RE $H_2$). In the modeling described below and represented schematically in Figure D-13, the imported fuel is assumed to be natural gas.

### e. Emissions and $H_2$ Demand Modeling

The regional split of total U.S. refining sector emissions and $H_2$ demand was derived from state and Refining District data published by EIA.[75]

---

75 EIA. "Refining Capacity Report." https://www.eia.gov/petroleum/refinerycapacity. 2021 data were used for the analysis (https://www.eia.gov/petroleum/supply/annual/volume1/archive/2021/psa_volume1_2021.php).

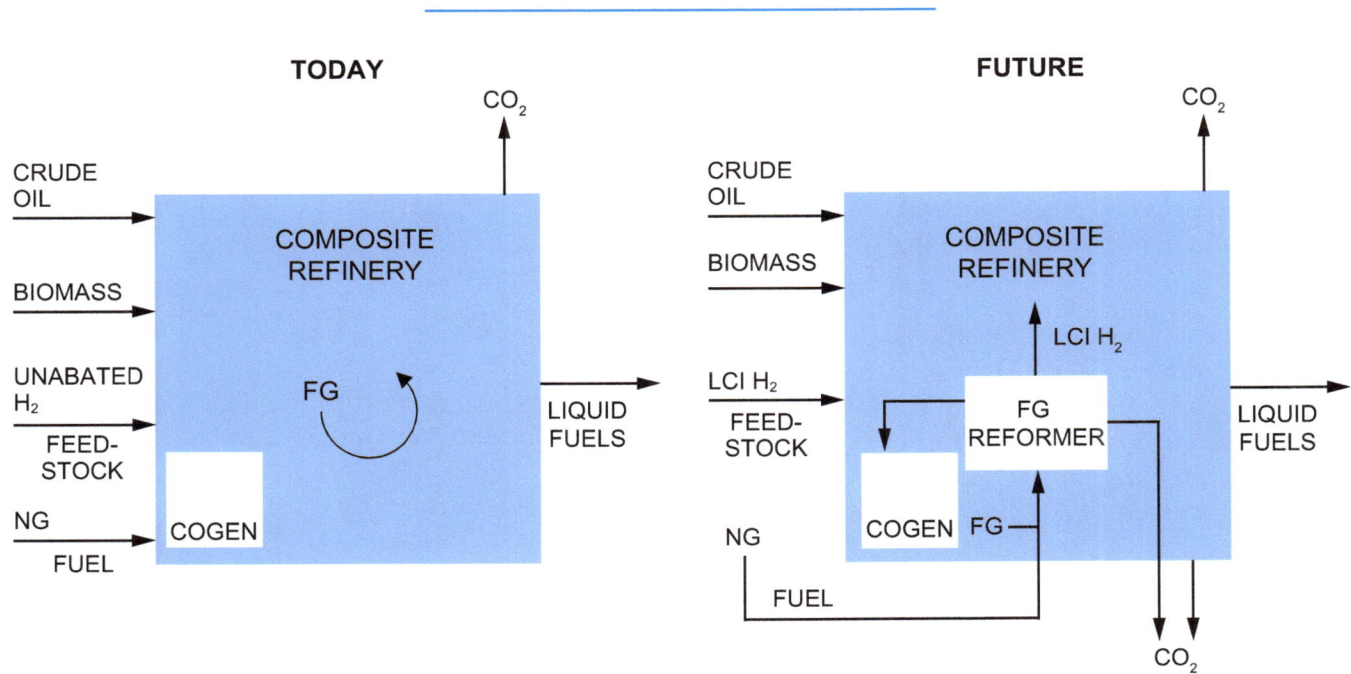

Notes: The lefthand diagram represents the basic configuration of an oil refinery today. The righthand diagram represents a future configuration. FG = fuel gas, Cogen = heat and power cogeneration unit.

**Figure D-13.** *$H_2$ Utilization in Modeled Refinery Configurations*

Emissions from the production of $H_2$ are tracked separately within USREP. For refineries that make on-purpose $H_2$ internally today (e.g., by unabated SMR), there is the potential for double counting when those emissions are included in the refinery direct emissions reported by EIA. However, the potential impact of this error on total emissions was judged to be small.

Two levels of decarbonization were envisioned:

1. **Partial decarbonization**, where only efficiency improvements and use of post-combustion CCS were assumed. This level of decarbonization was assumed to be aligned with the Stated Policies.

2. **Deep decarbonization**, where additional fuel switching to LCI $H_2$ was assumed to be deployed. This level of decarbonization was assumed to be aligned with the NZ2050 scenario.

Table D-21 shows the emissions intensity per unit of conventional liquid fuels in 2050 for each level of decarbonization. To generate an emissions trajectory, decarbonization of the refining industry was assumed to progress linearly from 2025 to 2050, with results given in Table D-22.

Table D-21 also provides the $H_2$ demand in 2050 broken down by feedstock $H_2$ and fuel $H_2$.

- Feedstock $H_2$ represents the conventional use of $H_2$ for hydrocracking and hydrotreating. This demand was assumed to remain constant through 2050.[76]

- Fuel $H_2$ represents a new demand for LCI $H_2$ as a fuel to generate heat, replacing fuel gas and natural gas.

For both partial decarbonization and deep decarbonization, the feedstock $H_2$ was assumed to be imported LCI $H_2$. The production pathway for this LCI $H_2$ was not specified, but rather determined by USREP, and any emissions associated with it were not included in refining emissions. Table

D-22 provides the $H_2$ demand trajectory corresponding to the assumption of a linear decarbonization progression over time.

| | Current Status | Partial Decarbonization | Deep Decarbonization |
|---|---|---|---|
| **Direct Emissions**, MMT-$CO_2$e/$EJ_{LHV}$-fuels | 5.6 | 4.0 (-28% vs current) | 0.4 (-93% vs current) |
| **$H_2$ Demand**, MMT-$H_2$/$EJ_{LHV}$-fuels | | | |
| Feedstock $H_2$ (imported) | 0.15 | 0.15 | 0.15 |
| Fuel $H_2$ (internally generated) | 0.00 | 0.00 | 0.75 |
| Total $H_2$ | 0.15 | 0.15 | 0.90 |

Notes: Key assumptions: $CO_2$ capture rate for CCS applied to large point-source emitters = 90%; Emissions factor for FG/NG blend = 64 MT-$CO_2$e/EJLHV; $H_2$ demand as feedstock = 1.15 kgH2/bbl liquid fuels. Conversion factor: 1 bbl = 5.4 GJLHV. Reformer efficiency and capture rate = same as ATR+CCS cited elsewhere in study.

*Table D-21. Key Metrics for Refining in 2050 under Decarbonization*

| | 2025 | 2030 | 2040 | 2050 |
|---|---|---|---|---|
| **Direct Emissions**, MMT-$CO_2$e/$EJ_{LHV}$-fuels | | | | |
| Stated Policies Scenario | 5.6 | 5.3 | 4.7 | 4.0 |
| Net Zero Scenario | 5.6 | 4.6 | 2.5 | 0.4 |
| **Feedstock $H_2$ Demand**, MMT-$H_2$/$EJ_{LHV}$-fuels | | | | |
| Stated Policies Scenario | 0.15 | 0.15 | 0.15 | 0.15 |
| Net Zero Scenario | 0.15 | 0.15 | 0.15 | 0.15 |
| **Fuel $H_2$ Demand**, MMT-$H_2$/$EJ_{LHV}$-fuels | | | | |
| Stated Policies Scenario | 0.00 | 0.00 | 0.00 | 0.00 |
| Net Zero Scenario | 0.00 | 0.15 | 0.45 | 0.75 |
| **Total $H_2$ Demand**, MMT-$H_2$/$EJ_{LHV}$-fuels | | | | |
| Stated Policies Scenario | 0.15 | 0.15 | 0.15 | 0.15 |
| Net Zero Scenario | 0.15 | 0.30 | 0.60 | 0.90 |

Notes: Feedstock $H_2$ is produced outside of the refinery and imported into the refinery. Fuel $H_2$ is produced inside the refinery by reforming + CCS.

*Table D-22. Projected Evolution of Refining Emissions and $H_2$ Demand*

## f. Cost Modeling for Conventional Liquid Fuels

Based on the approach to modeling Transportation fuels and the refining industry described above, the costs used by USREP to represent decarbonizing conventional liquid fuels were estimated as follows. The results are summarized in Table D-23.

---

76 Hydrogen demand from first-generation biofuel refineries is assumed to be negligible compared to the demand from oil refineries over the modeling period, for two reasons. First, while $H_2$ is required for some first-generation biofuels (e.g., renewable diesel), others require none (e.g., ethanol), so the average demand is modest. Second, the fraction of first-generation biofuels in the liquid fuels mix is projected to remain small, even if there is a rise over the medium term before carbon-neutral biofuels are scaled up.

| | Units | 2025 | 2030 | 2040 | 2050 |
|---|---|---|---|---|---|
| **Stated Policies Scenario** | | | | | |
| Efficiency | M$/EJ$_{LHV}$-fuel | 0 | 0 | 0 | 0 |
| CCS | M$/EJ$_{LHV}$-fuel | 0 | 24 | 72 | 120 |
| Total | M$/EJ$_{LHV}$-fuel | 0 | 24 | 72 | 120 |
| **Net Zero Scenario** | | | | | |
| Efficiency | M$/EJ$_{LHV}$-fuel | 0 | 0 | 0 | 0 |
| CCS | M$/EJ$_{LHV}$-fuel | 0 | 24 | 72 | 120 |
| Fuel Switching | M$/EJ$_{LHV}$-fuel | 0 | 240 | 720 | 1,200 |
| Total | M$/EJ$_{LHV}$-fuel | 0 | 264 | 792 | 1,320 |

Notes: Switching the feedstock $H_2$ to LCI $H_2$ will also increase the cost of conventional liquid fuel production, by $DH_2$ cost M$/MMT-$H_2$ x 0.15 MMT-$H_2$/EJ$_{LHV}$-fuel. For context, adding 1,120 M$/EJ$_{LHV}$-fuel is equivalent to adding $0.18/gallon to the production cost of conventional liquid fuels (assuming 136 MJLHV/gallon for diesel). All costs are expressed in 2020$.

*Table D-23. Additional Cost to Produce Conventional Liquid Fuels*

- **Cost of efficiency improvements:** The net cost impact of efficiency improvement projects was assumed to be negligible.

- **Cost of post-combustion CCS:** The cost of installing $CO_2$ capture on select point-source emitters and sequestering the $CO_2$ was assumed to be $120/MT-$CO_2$ based on previous analysis by the NPC.[77] Once fully implemented in 2050, the CCS approach would sequester ~1.0 MMT-$CO_2$/EJ$_{LHV}$-fuel (20% of refinery direct emissions, at 90% capture rate). Therefore, for a deeply decarbonized refining industry, CCS would add 120 M$/EJ$_{LHV}$-fuel to the cost of conventional liquid fuels.

- **Cost of feedstock $H_2$:** No additional costs for switching to LCI $H_2$ as a feedstock were assumed, beyond the potentially higher cost of the $H_2$ itself.

- **Cost of fuel $H_2$:** The fuel gas/natural gas-fed reformer was assumed to be an ATR with $CO_2$ capture with the same performance and cost structure as the natural gas-fed ATR modeled elsewhere in the study. The ATR was sized to make sufficient LCI $H_2$ to meet the heating duty previously met by fuel gas and imported natural gas. The extra energy needed to run the ATR was assumed to be met by imported natural gas. Additional capital costs relative to a stand-alone ATR were assumed to be: a 15% increase to account for pretreatment, compression, and other facility changes to accommodate fuel gas;

a 10% increase to account for fuel gas piping to the reformer and $H_2$ piping from the reformer; and a 5% increase to account for burner retrofits. The resulting levelized cost of LCI $H_2$ made by the refinery for use as heat was found to be ~1,600 M$/MMT-$H_2$ (range of ~1,400-1,800 M$/MMT-$H_2$).[78] In the case of a deeply decarbonized refining industry that consumes 0.75 MT of LCI $H_2$ per EJ$_{LHV}$ of liquid fuels produced, this would add ~1,200 M$/EJ$_{LHV}$-fuel to the cost of conventional liquid fuels.[79]

### g. Carbon-Neutral Liquid Fuels

Carbon-neutral liquid fuels can be second-generation biofuels or e-fuels made from captured $CO_2$.

- For second-generation biofuels, the ratio of hydrogen-to-carbon atoms in biomass is insufficient to produce drop-in liquid fuels for conventional engines (e.g., diesel or jet fuel). Therefore, the production process must either reject excess carbon (as $CO_2$) or add hydrogen (as $H_2$ or via $H_2O$ through a water-gas shift reaction). The oxygen in biomass is rejected as $H_2O$, which increases the demand for $H_2$.

- For e-fuels, all the $H_2$ needed for both the fuel and to reject oxygen as $H_2O$ must be sourced externally. Carbon rejection is not an option; it is just an inefficiency.

77 NPC. 2019. "Meeting the Dual Challenge: A Roadmap to At-Scale Deployment of Carbon Capture, Use, and Storage." https://dualchallenge.npc.org/files/CCUS-Chap_2-030521.pdf. See Table 2-7.

78 Range based on $3-6/MBtu-NG, $50-70/MWh electricity, and $15-30/MT-$CO_2$ for $CO_2$ T&S.

79 With 45Q tax credits of $85/MT-$CO_2$ sequestered for the first 12 years of a 30-year capital recovery period, the added cost for making and using LCI $H_2$ for heat is reduced to ~$600 M$/EJ$_{LHV}$-fuel.

- The diversity of possible process configurations and feedstocks to make carbon-neutral liquid fuels results in a range of potential $H_2$ demand, from zero (for a biofuel where all the excess carbon is rejected) to 0.5 MT-$H_2$/MT-fuel (for an e-fuel).

- For the study, a value of 0.15 MT-$H_2$/MT-fuel was assumed. This corresponds to 3.5 MMT-$H2/EJ_{LHV}$-fuel using the heating value of diesel (42.4 $MJ_{LHV}$/kg).

## 2. Steel and Cement

Steel and cement production were explicitly represented in USREP. The TEA inputs are presented here in terms of the incremental cost and performance for low-carbon production (based on emerging technology) relative to a reference production pathway (based on existing technology). For these industries, USREP endogenously modeled cost reductions for the new technologies with increasing adoption over time. The extent of the decrease was parameterized in terms of the higher cost for a first-of-a-kind (FOAK) plant versus an nth-of-a-kind (NOAK) plant. The ratio of FOAK/NOAK costs was assumed to apply to both capex and nonenergy opex.

**Steel:** The USREP modeling adopted for the study was based on prior MIT work on decarbonizing steel production.[80] It included four options:

1. Conventional BF-BOF (blast furnace and basic oxygen furnace)

2. Conventional EAF (electric arc furnace) = EAF fed by scrap iron/steel or unabated NG-DRI (natural gas-based direct reduced iron)

3. Advanced EAF, CCS-based = EAF fed by scrap iron/steel or NG-DRI with 90% of the $CO_2$ captured and sequestered

4. Advanced EAF, $H_2$-based = EAF fed by $H_2$-DRI ($H_2$-based direct reduced iron)

The advanced technologies represent low-carbon production methods that could be adopted under the study's decarbonization scenarios. The option of adding CCS to BF-BOF for low-carbon production was not included. Steel imports and exports were not modeled. The reference production technology was assumed to be a conventional EAF plant that consumes 11.5 $GJ_{HHV}$ (10.9 $MBtu_{HHV}$) of natural gas for heat per t-steel produced and emits 0.65 MT-$CO_2$/t-steel. The USREP modeling found a FOAK/NOAK cost ratio of 2.4 for advanced EAF steel plants.

- Inputs for NG-DRI+CCS pathway: The incremental capex and opex for a NOAK plant were taken from the prior MIT work. $CO_2$ T&S is an additional cost not included here.

- Inputs for $H_2$-DRI pathway: The incremental capex and opex for a NOAK plant was based on the prior MIT work, except that the $H_2$ demand was revised down slightly based on input from study participants.

**Cement:** The USREP modeling adopted for the study was based on prior MIT work on decarbonizing cement production.[81] It included three options:

1. Conventional plant (i.e., unabated)

2. Advanced plant that uses CCS to mitigate $CO_2$ emissions with 95% capture of the total plant $CO_2$ emissions (i.e., both $CO_2$ from the chemistry and $CO_2$ from fuel combustion)

3. Advanced plant that uses LCI $H_2$ for heat, where 40% of the plant's heat duty is met by LCI $H_2$, resulting in a ~12% reduction in emissions

In practice, both low-carbon options may be deployed together. The reference production technology was assumed to be a conventional plant that consumes 3.5 $MBtu_{LHV}$ fuel for heat per metric ton of cement produced[82] and emit 0.75 MT-$CO_2$/MT-cement produced.[83] The previous

80  Benavides, K., et al. 2022. "Emission Mitigation in the Global Steel Industry: Representing CCS and Hydrogen Options in Integrated Assessment Modeling." *GHGT-16 Conference Proceedings.* https://papers.ssrn.com/sol3/papers.cfm?abstract_id=4271699.

81  Paltsev, S., et al. 2021. "Hard-to-Abate Sectors: The role of industrial carbon capture and storage (CCS) in emissions mitigation." *Appl. Energy* 300. https://doi.org/10.1016/j.apenergy.2021.117322.

82  Portland Cement Association. 2021. "Roadmap to Carbon Neutrality." https://www.cement.org/docs/default-source/roadmap/pca-roadmap-to-carbon-neutrality_10_10_21_final.pdf.

83  Close to the median direct emissions intensity for U.S. cement plants, according to EPA. 2021. "U.S. Cement Industry Carbon Intensities." https://www.epa.gov/system/files/documents/2021-10/cement-carbon-intensities-fact-sheet.pdf.

MIT modeling found a FOAK/NOAK cost ratio of 1.6 for decarbonized cement plants.

- **Inputs for CO$_2$ capture pathway:** The incremental capex and opex were based on the mid-range investment cost and energy required to add 90% CO$_2$ capture from the 2019 NPC CCUS study.[84] CO$_2$ T&S is an additional cost not included here.

- **Inputs for LCI H$_2$ pathway:** The incremental capex was estimated by study participants for a 1 MMTpa cement plant retrofit so that 40% of the heat duty could be met by H$_2$.

## 3. Other Industry

USREP does not explicitly model the technologies that may be deployed in Other Indus-

---

try, which represents a collection of very different manufacturing activities. Therefore, it does not project how these individual industries will decarbonize. For the study, the emissions trajectory for Other Industry was an input to USREP. To develop this trajectory, the study assumed a mix of approaches will be taken:

1. Efficiency: implement process changes to reduce energy consumption

2. Clean electricity: electrify processes where possible and leverage low-carbon electricity

3. CCS: install CO$_2$ capture where feasible, and sequester the CO$_2$

4. Biofuel switching: convert from hydrocarbon fuels to bio-based fuels

5. LCI H$_2$ fuel switching: convert from hydrocarbon fuels to LCI H$_2$ for heat

---

84  NPC. 2019. "Meeting the Dual Challenge A Roadmap to At-Scale Deployment of Carbon Capture, Use, and Storage." https://dualchallenge.npc.org. See Tables 2-4 and 2-6, assumed to be for a NOAK plant.

| Parameter | Units | NG-DRI+CCS Pathway | | H$_2$-DRI Pathway | |
|---|---|---|---|---|---|
| | | FOAK Plant | NOAK Plant | FOAK Plant | NOAK Plant |
| Capital recovery period | years | 25 | 25 | 25 | 25 |
| Incremental capex | M$/MMTpa-steel | 340 | 140 | negligible | negligible |
| Incremental opex | | | | | |
| Change in NG demand | GJ$_{HHV}$/MT-steel | negligible | negligible | -9.6 | -9.6 |
| Change in H$_2$ demand | GJ$_{HHV}$/MT-steel MT-H$_2$/MT-steel | -- -- | -- -- | +10.9 +0.077 | +10.9 +0.077 |
| Change in electricity demand | MWh$_e$/MT-steel | +0.16 | +0.16 | negligible | negligible |
| Change in nonenergy O&M | $/MT-steel | +12.5 | +5.2 | negligible | negligible |

Notes: FOAK = first-of-a-kind, NOAK = n$^{th}$-of-a-kind, steel = crude steel. All costs are expressed in 2020$ on a nameplate capacity basis.

*Table D-24. TEA Inputs for the Steel Industry*

| Parameter | Units | H$_2$ Pathway | | CO$_2$ Capture Pathway | |
|---|---|---|---|---|---|
| | | FOAK Plant | NOAK Plant | FOAK Plant | NOAK Plant |
| Capital recovery period | years | 30 | 30 | 30 | 30 |
| Incremental capex | M$/MMTpa cement | +1.2 | +0.75 | +320 | +200 |
| Incremental opex | | | | | |
| Change in fossil fuel demand | MBTU$_{LHV}$/MT-cement | -1.4 | -1.4 | +2.0 | +2.0 |
| Change in H$_2$ fuel demand | MBTU$_{LHV}$/MT-cement kgH$_2$/MT-cement | +1.4 +12 | +1.4 +12 | -- -- | -- -- |
| Change in electricity demand | MWh$_e$/MT-cement | negligible | negligible | 0.12 | 0.12 |
| Change in nonenergy O&M | $/MT-cement | 0.05 | 0.05 | +16 | +10 |

Notes: FOAK = first-of-a-kind, NOAK = n$^{th}$-of-a-kind. All costs are expressed in 2020$ on a nameplate capacity basis.

*Table D-25. TEA Inputs for the Cement Industry*

| Industry Segments with Significant Emissions | Main Sources of Emissions | Emissions from Fuel Combustion, Electricity, and Process CO$_2$ | | Emissions from H$_2$ Production |
|---|---|---|---|---|
| | | MMTpa CO$_2$e (in 2021) | Addressable by H$_2$ Fuel Switching | MMTpa CO$_2$e (in 2021) |
| **Chemicals** | | | | |
| Natural gas processing | process CO$_2$ and electricity | 83 | 0% | |
| Ammonia | H$_2$ production and high-temp heat | 18 | 100% | 28 |
| Ethylene Steam Cracking | high-temp heat | 41 | 90% | |
| Chlor-alkali | Electricity | 26 | 0% | |
| Other Chemicals | high-temp heat | 119 | 67% | |
| Food & Beverage | low-temp heat and electricity | 85 | 0% | |
| Pulp & Paper | mixed-temp heat and electricity | 48 | 0% | |
| Aluminum | high-temp heat, electricity, and process CO$_2$ | 16 | 0% | |
| Glass | high-temp heat, electricity, and process CO$_2$ | 11 | 0% | |
| **Total** | | **447** | **30%** | **28** |

*Table D-26. Inventory of Other Industry Emissions and Applicability of H$_2$ Fuel Switching*

Data in the DOE *Industrial Decarbonization Lift-off* report[85] was used to characterize the emissions landscape for five industry segments found to contribute the most to industrial emissions (outside of refining, steel, and cement). Table D-26 gives a breakdown of sources and quantities of emissions in 2021. It also shows the percentage of non-H$_2$ production emissions that the study assumed would be addressed by H$_2$ fuel switching. Notably, LCI H$_2$ fuel switching was only anticipated for chemical production processes that rely on high-temperature heat and were judged to be difficult to retrofit with CO$_2$ capture.

Using this approach, the study estimated that a maximum of 30% of Other Industry emissions (excluding H$_2$ production emissions) could be addressed using LCI H$_2$ fuel switching. Emissions from H$_2$ production within Other Industry are attributed entirely to ammonia production, where H$_2$ is used as a feedstock. These emissions were assumed to be reduced or eliminated by moving from unabated H$_2$ to LCI H$_2$.

Table D-27 gives the applicability and cost of the five decarbonization approaches assumed by the study based on the results in Table D-26 and additional information in the DOE *Industrial Decarbonization Liftoff* report.

| Approach | Addressable Emissions | Average Cost to Implement ($/MT-CO$_2$ avoided) |
|---|---|---|
| 1. Efficiency | 10% | 0 |
| 2. Clean electricity | 40% | 150 |
| 3. CCS | 10% | 150 |
| 4. Biofuel switching | 10% | 150 |
| 5. H$_2$ fuel switching | 30% | 200 |

*Table D-27. Assumed Steps to Reduce Other Industry Emissions*

As was the case for refining, two levels of decarbonization were considered:

1. Partial decarbonization that accomplishes 40% decarbonization (vs. 2020) of Other Industry by 2050. It was assumed that the first four decarbonization approaches would be deployed. This level of decarbonization was assumed to be aligned with the Stated Policies scenario.

2. Deep decarbonization that accomplishes 90% decarbonization (vs. 2020) of Other Industry by 2050. It was assumed that all five decarbonization approaches would be deployed, including LCI H$_2$ fuel switching. This level of

---

85 DOE. 2023. "Pathways to Commercial Liftoff—Industrial Decarbonization." https://liftoff.energy.gov/wp-content/uploads/2023/10/LIFTOFF_DOE_Industrial-Decarbonization_v8.pdf. Non-CO$_2$ emissions from the Chemicals sector were assigned to the natural gas processing segment (see Figure 2a.4).

decarbonization was assumed to be aligned with the NZ2050 scenario.

Table D-28 shows the cost to implement each level of decarbonization, on a $/MT-$CO_2$ avoided basis, calculated as the weighted average over the approaches in Table D-26. To generate an emissions trajectory, decarbonization of Other Industry was assumed to follow a linear trajectory from today to 2050, with results given in Table D-29.

Also as done for the refining industry, the $H_2$ demand trajectory for Other Industry was broken down feedstock $H_2$ and fuel $H_2$ as summarized in Table D-27.

- Feedstock $H_2$ represents the $H_2$ required for the chemical reaction to make ammonia. U.S. ammonia production was estimated at 17 MMTpa $NH_3$ in 2021 by the U.S. Geological Survey.[86] Making that amount of ammonia requires 3.0 MMTpa $H_2$ on a stoichiometry basis.

- Fuel $H_2$ represents a new demand for $H_2$ as a low-carbon fuel to generate heat—for example, to replace natural gas. The maximum demand (20 MMTpa in 2050 under the NZ2050 scenario) was calculated by assuming that 30% of the Other Industry emissions cataloged in Table D-27 were generated by combusting natural gas (with an emissions factor of 50 MT-$CO_2$/$EJ_{LHV}$). This yields the energy that must be provided by $H_2$ (0.12 $EJ_{LHV}$/MT-$H_2$) instead.

For USREP, it was assumed that both Feedstock $H_2$ and Fuel $H_2$ could be either NG+CCS $H_2$ or RE $H_2$.

| Approach | Emissions Reduction in 2050 | Average Cost to Achieve That Emissions Reduction ($/MT-$CO_2$ avoided) |
|---|---|---|
| Partial decarbonization | 40% | 90 |
| Deep decarbonization | 90% | 150 |

*Table D-28. Assumed Cost to Achieve Decarbonization of Other Industry*

| | 2025 | 2030 | 2040 | 2050 |
|---|---|---|---|---|
| Emissions reduction, vs. 2020 | | | | |
| Stated Policies scenario | 0% | 8% | 24% | 40% |
| Net Zero scenario | 0% | 18% | 54% | 90% |
| $H_2$ Demand, MMTpa $H_2$ *based on current production levels* | | | | |
| Stated Policies scenario | | | | |
|     Feedstock $H_2$ | 3 | 3 | 3 | 3 |
|     Fuel $H_2$ | 0 | 0 | 0 | 0 |
|     Total $H_2$ | 3 | 3 | 3 | 3 |
| Net Zero scenario | | | | |
|     Feedstock $H_2$ | 3 | 3 | 3 | 3 |
|     Fuel $H_2$ | 0 | 4 | 13 | 22 |
|     Total $H_2$ | 3 | 7 | 16 | 25 |

Notes: $H_2$ demand is based on the scale of production for the composite Other Industry segment in 2021. $H_2$ demand is assumed to nearly unchanged by 2025, but would scale proportionally as Other Industry grows or shrinks to 2050.

*Table D-29. Assumed Emissions and $H_2$ Demand Trajectories for Other Industry*

## 4. Ammonia

While USREP embeds ammonia production in Other Industry along with other chemicals manufacture, the study examined the cost and emissions of ammonia pathways since LCI $H_2$ exports were represented as occurring via ammonia. Unabated ammonia is made using natural gas with no $CO_2$ capture via SMR integrated with a colocated Haber-Bosch unit. Low carbon intensity ammonia is made either by an integrated plant based on ATR+CCS with a colocated Haber-Bosch unit, or a stand-alone plant that purchases RE $H_2$ as a feedstock for a Haber-Bosch unit. The CI of ammonia production accounts for emissions through production only.

- Capex was estimated based on study participant input and recent public announcements[87, 88] and assumes a plant with nameplate capacity of 1.1 million metric tons $NH_3$ per annum.

- Other inputs were based on study participant input.

86 U.S. Geological Survey. 2019. "Nitrogen (Fixed) Ammonia." *Mineral Commodity Summaries.* https://pubs.usgs.gov/periodicals/mcs2022/mcs2022-nitrogen.pdf.

87 BASF. 2018. "Yara and BASF open world-scale ammonia plant in Freeport, Texas." https://www.basf.com/us/en/media/news-releases/2018/04/P-US-18-044.html.

88 OCI Global. 2022. "OCI N.V. Breaks Ground on 1.1 MTpa Blue Ammonia Site in Texas, USA." https://oci-global.com/news-stories/press-releases/oci-n-v-breaks-ground-on-1-1-mtpa-blue-ammonia-site-in-texas-usa/.

| Parameters | Units | NH₃ Unabated SMR (new build) | LCI NH₃ Integrated ATR+CCS | LCI NH₃ Externally Supplied RE H₂ |
|---|---|---|---|---|
| Capital recovery period | Years | 30 | 30 | 30 |
| Plant capex (total installed cost) | $/(kg-NH₃/day) | 760 | 865 | 330 |
| Plant opex (fixed and nonenergy variable) | $/(kg-NH₃) | 0.07 | 0.085 | 0.09 |
| Electricity demand | kWh/kg-NH₃ | ~0.01 | 0.6 | 0.5 |
| Natural gas demand | MJ$_{NG-LHV}$/kg-NH₃ | 30.5 | 30.6 | 0 |
| CO₂ capture rate | -- | -- | 95% | -- |
| Plant capacity factor | -- | 90% | 90% | 90% |

Notes: All costs are expressed in 2020$.

**Table D-30.** *TEA Inputs for Ammonia Industry*

## B. Transportation Sector

Only long-haul HD trucks were explicitly modeled in the study. The three types considered were:

1. Diesel trucks powered by an internal combustion engine running on diesel fuel

2. Fuel cell trucks powered by a fuel cell running on LCI H₂

3. Battery electric trucks powered by a battery charged using grid electricity

The total cost of ownership (TCO) and well-to-wheel (WTW) emissions were estimated using SESAME. The TCO is the sum of the levelized capital cost; costs for fuel; maintenance, repair, and general operation; and—for battery electric trucks—opportunity costs for lost cargo capacity and excess refueling dwell time compared to a diesel truck. The study assumed diesel trucks and fuel cell trucks would have the same cargo capacity, while battery electric trucks would have reduced cargo capacity due to the excess weight of the batteries. As a result, the battery electric trucks were assessed a payload cost. The dwell time cost represents the cost associated with the operational time lost while charging the battery.

• Capex: Vehicle initial cost reflects the purchase price of a new truck. Return on investment cal-

culated on net cost to original owner. Assumes a representative of market mix of possible powertrain configurations, based on variety of sources and industry knowledge.[89, 90, 91, 92, 93, 94, 95, 96]

89 Islam, E.S., et al. 2022. "A Comprehensive Simulation Study to Evaluate Future Vehicle Energy and Cost Reduction Potential." *ANL Technical Report.* https://doi.org/10.2172/2204856.

90 Ballard. 2020. "High Performance Fuel Cell Stack, Innovations in Proton Exchange Membrane Fuel Cell Stack Design." https://www.ballard.com/docs/default-source/default-document-library/high-performance-fuel-cell-stack-white-paper-14-september-2020.pdf.

91 Kurtz, J., et al. 2019. "Fuel Cell Electric Vehicle Durability and Fuel Cell Performance." *NREL Technical Report.* https://www.nrel.gov/docs/fy19osti/73011.pdf.

92 International Council on Clean Transportation. 2023. "Purchase Costs of Zero-Emission Trucks in the United States to Meet Future Phase 3 GHG Standards." https://theicct.org/wp-content/uploads/2023/03/cost-zero-emission-trucks-us-phase-3-mar23.pdf.

93 Clean Air Task Force. 2023. "Zero Emissions Long-Haul Heavy-Duty Trucking." https://www.catf.us/resource/zero-emission-long-haul-heavy-duty-trucking/.

94 North American Council for Freight Efficiency. 2022. "Electric Trucks Have Arrived: The Use Case for Heavy-Duty Regional Haul Tractors." https://nacfe.org/wp-content/uploads/edd/2022/05/HD-Regional-Haul-Report-FINAL.pdf.

95 Hsieh, I-Y.L., et al. 2019. "Learning only buys you so much: Practical limits on battery price reduction." *Applied Energy* 239. https://doi.org/10.1016/j.apenergy.2019.01.138.

96 Hunter, C., et al. 2021. "Spatial and Temporal Analysis of the Total Cost of Ownership for Class 8 Tractors and Class 4 Parcel Delivery Trucks." *NREL Technical Report.* https://www.nrel.gov/docs/fy21osti/71796.pdf.

| Parameter | Units | 2025 | 2030 | 2040 | 2050 |
|---|---|---|---|---|---|
| Capital recovery period | years | 10 | 10 | 10 | 10 |
| Annual mileage, average | miles/yr | 135,000 | 135,000 | 135,000 | 135,000 |
| **Fuel cell HD trucks** | | | | | |
| Capex (net after resale) | $/mile/yr | 3.33 | 2.67 | 1.67 | 1.67 |
| Vehicle initial cost | $ | 500,000 | 400,000 | 250,000 | 250,000 |
| Vehicle residual value (assume 10%) | $ | 50,000 | 40,000 | 25,000 | 25,000 |
| Opex (total excluding fuel) | $/mile | 1.09 | 1.09 | 1.09 | 1.09 |
| General operations | $/mile | 0.95 | 0.95 | 0.95 | 0.95 |
| Maintenance & repair | $/mile | 0.14 | 0.14 | 0.14 | 0.14 |
| Fuel economy | MPDGE | 10.0 | 10.6 | 11.9 | 13.3 |
| **Battery electric HD trucks** | | | | | |
| Capex (net after resale) | $/mile/yr | 2.42 | 1.91 | 1.76 | 1.67 |
| Vehicle initial cost | $ | 363,000 | 286,000 | 264,000 | 250,000 |
| Vehicle residual value (assume 10%) | $ | 36,300 | 28,600 | 26,400 | 25,000 |
| Opex (total excluding fuel) | $/mile | 1.62 | 1.41 | 1.23 | 1.09 |
| General operations | $/mile | 0.95 | 0.95 | 0.95 | 0.95 |
| Maintenance & repair | $/mile | 0.14 | 0.14 | 0.14 | 0.14 |
| Penalty for lost payload capacity | $/mile | 0.03 | 0.02 | 0.02 | 0.00 |
| Penalty for charging dwell time | $/mile | 0.50 | 0.30 | 0.12 | 0.00 |
| Fuel economy | MPDGE | 14.8 | 15.5 | 16.9 | 18.5 |
| **Diesel HD trucks** | | | | | |
| Capex (net after resale) | $/mile/yr | 1.10 | 1.10 | 1.10 | 1.10 |
| Vehicle initial cost | $ | 165,000 | 165,000 | 165,000 | 165,000 |
| Vehicle residual value (assume 10%) | $ | 16,500 | 16,500 | 16,500 | 16,500 |
| Opex (total excluding fuel) | $/mile | 1.18 | 1.18 | 1.18 | 1.18 |
| General operations | $/mile | 0.95 | 0.95 | 0.95 | 0.95 |
| Maintenance & repair | $/mile | 0.23 | 0.23 | 0.23 | 0.23 |
| Fuel economy | MPDGE | 6.7 | 7.1 | 8.0 | 9.0 |

Notes: MPDGE = miles per diesel gallon equivalent. All costs are expressed in 2020$.

*Table D-31. TEA Inputs for HD Transportation*

- Opex: General operations includes driver costs, insurance, permits, and tolls[92]

- Fuel economy: Based on a variety of sources and industry knowledge[97]

- Fuel cost varies by the type of truck: Refined fuel from USREP for diesel trucks, LCI $H_2$ at the refueling station from SESAME for fuel cell trucks, and grid electricity from USREP for battery electric trucks

- Battery electric trucks: Payload penalty assumes one-third of trucks conduct missions that are weight-limited, and the cost of lost payload capacity for these trucks is $0.09/mile. Dwell time penalty calculated from the charging time required to accomplish a 500-mile mission, which decreases as battery size and charging rates increase; assumes $75/hr for the driver's time.[89, 90, 92]

The WTW emissions intensity for each type of HD truck is a sum of the CI of the fuel as delivered to the truck and tailpipe emissions associated with consuming the fuel to power the truck. TCO and WTW life cycle emissions were put on a per-mile basis using the efficiency of the appropriate truck type.

## C. Power Sector

Hydrogen demand in the Power sector was assumed to derive from two applications. The first is as a fuel to generate low carbon intensity electricity within the mix of electricity generation options that make up the grid mix. The second is for seasonal storage of electricity generated by variable renewable generators like solar and wind when such generators made up a large fraction of total electricity generation.

### 1. Hydrogen in the Grid Mix

Electricity generation from LCI $H_2$ competed with incumbent pathways within USREP to establish the mix of grid generators over time in each region under each study scenario, which

---

97 Ledna, C., et al. 2022. "Decarbonizing Medium- & Heavy-Duty On-Road Vehicles: Zero-Emissions Vehicles Cost Analysis." *NREL Presentation.* https://www.nrel.gov/docs/fy22osti/82081.pdf.

determined the cost and CI of grid electricity.[98] SESAME was used to model the levelized cost and CI of electricity produced from turbines and fuel cells fueled by LCI $H_2$ or natural gas-fired turbines using the inputs given here. USREP provided the cost and CI of other pathways.[99]

### a. Natural Gas and Hydrogen Turbines

Both combustion turbines (CT) and combined cycle gas turbines (CCGT) were modeled.

- Natural gas turbines, new build: Capex, efficiency (heat rate), and nonfuel opex were taken from the NREL 2023 *Annual Technology Baseline* moderate innovation case for F-frame turbines.[100] Capacity factors were derived from EIA 2023 AEO data.[101] The average capacity factor for natural gas CTs was assumed to remain constant at the 2020 value (12%) through 2050. The average capacity factor for natural gas CCGTs was then calculated using AEO projections for natural gas CT and CCGT capacity and total natural gas electricity generation.

- Natural gas turbines, retrofitted to handle $H_2$: Capex values were based on study participant consensus. Efficiency, nonfuel opex, and capacity factors assumed to be the same as for new-build turbines.

- $H_2$ turbines: Capex was assumed to be 25% higher than natural gas versions in 2025, with the gap closing over time to reach parity by 2050. Efficiency was assumed to be ~15% lower than natural gas versions in 2025 with the gap closing over time to reach parity by 2050. Nonfuel opex was to be the same percentage of capex as for natural gas turbines. Capacity factors were assumed to be the same as for natural gas turbines.

---

98 The other generation options in the USREP grid mix were coal, nuclear, hydro, solar, and wind.

99 The cost of electricity generated by solar or wind was based on the same inputs as used for RE $H_2$. Default USREP parameters were used to calculate the cost and CI for electricity from coal, nuclear, and hydro.

100 NREL. "2023 Annual Technology Baseline v2." July 20, 2023. https://atb.nrel.gov/electricity/2023/data.

101 EIA. *Annual Energy Outlook 2023.* https://www.eia.gov/outlooks/aeo. Reference Case. Tables 8 and 9.

| Parameter | Units | 2025 | 2030 | 2040 | 2050 |
|---|---|---|---|---|---|
| Capital recovery period—new build | years | 30 | 30 | 30 | 30 |
| Capital recovery period—retrofit | years | 20 | 20 | 20 | 20 |
| **NG combustion turbine (peaker)** | | | | | |
| Capex—new build | $/kWe | 1,045 | 1,005 | 920 | 835 |
| Capex—retrofit for NG/$H_2$ blend up to 30% $H_2$ | $/kWe | 150 | 150 | 150 | 150 |
| Capex—retrofit for 100% $H_2$ | $/kWe | 200 | 200 | 200 | 200 |
| Nonfuel opex—fixed (nameplate capacity basis) | $/MWhe | 2.6 | 2.5 | 2.4 | 2.2 |
| Nonfuel opex—variable | $/MWhe | 6.2 | 6.2 | 6.2 | 6.2 |
| Efficiency—fueled by NG or NG/$H_2$ blend | HHV basis | 35% | 35% | 35% | 35% |
| **NG combined cycle gas turbine** | | | | | |
| Capex—new build | $/kWe | 1,160 | 1,110 | 1,015 | 925 |
| Capex—retrofit for NG/$H_2$ blend up to 30% $H_2$ | $/kWe | 150 | 150 | 150 | 150 |
| Capex—retrofit for 100% $H_2$ | $/kWe | 200 | 200 | 200 | 200 |
| Nonfuel opex—fixed (nameplate capacity basis) | $/MWhe | 3.3 | 3.1 | 2.8 | 2.6 |
| Nonfuel opex—variable | $/MWhe | 1.8 | 1.8 | 1.6 | 1.5 |
| Efficiency—fueled by NG or NG/$H_2$ blend | HHV basis | 54% | 55% | 55% | 55% |
| **NG combined cycle gas turbine with $CO_2$ capture** | | | | | |
| Capex—new build | $/kWe | 2,395 | 2,155 | 1,800 | 1,585 |
| $CO_2$ capture rate | -- | 95% | 95% | 95% | 95% |
| Nonfuel opex—fixed (nameplate capacity basis) | $/MWhe | 6.6 | 5.9 | 4.9 | 4.4 |
| Nonfuel opex—variable | $/MWhe | 4.2 | 3.9 | 3.4 | 3.2 |
| Efficiency—fueled by NG or NG/$H_2$ blend | HHV basis | 48% | 49% | 50% | 50% |

Notes: All costs are expressed in 2020$.

***Table D-32.*** *TEA Inputs for Natural Gas (NG) Turbines*

## b. Hydrogen Fuel Cells

The study assumed a hypothetical $H_2$ fuel cell technology representing a mix of three technologies: proton exchange membrane, phosphoric acid, and solid oxide.

- Capex was informed by DOE-sponsored analysis.[102] Efficiency in 2025 was estimated from published vendor materials and assumed to be 5% points higher by 2030 then improve 5% points per decade to 2050. The nonfuel opex was estimated to be 5% of capex. The capacity factor was assumed to be 30% based on the MIT *Future of Energy Storage* report.[103]

## 3. Hydrogen for Energy Storage

Under the study scenarios, the fraction of grid electricity generated by solar and wind grows over time. The intermittency and seasonal variability of such resources drive an increasing demand for energy storage to ensure reliability and resiliency of the grid. Some of this energy storage demand can be met by LCI $H_2$, which can be converted to electricity when renewables generation is low.

The demand for LCI $H_2$ for electrical energy storage was estimated using results from a 2021 NREL report on energy storage for low-carbon grids.[104] NREL projected the demand for energy storage (on an electricity discharge basis) as a function of the penetration of renewables for seven U.S. grid independent system operators (ISOs) representing ~65% of total U.S. electricity demand. Energy storage needs were divided into short-duration, long-duration, and seasonal. The study assumed LCI $H_2$ would be utilized to meet the seasonal energy storage needs, and the LCI $H_2$ used would be exclusively RE $H_2$.[105] The quantity of RE $H_2$ required was calculated assuming an

| Parameter | Units | 2025 | 2030 | 2040 | 2050 |
|---|---|---|---|---|---|
| Capital recovery period—new build | years | 30 | 30 | 30 | 30 |
| **$H_2$ combustion turbine (peaker)** | | | | | |
| Capex—new build | $/kWe | 1,320 | 1,205 | 1,000 | 835 |
| Nonfuel opex—fixed (nameplate capacity basis) | $/MWhe | 3.3 | 3.0 | 2.6 | 2.2 |
| Nonfuel opex—variable | $/MWhe | 7.8 | 7.4 | 6.7 | 6.2 |
| Efficiency | HHV basis | 30% | 31% | 33% | 35% |
| **$H_2$ combined cycle gas turbine** | | | | | |
| Capex—new build | $/kWe | 1,465 | 1,340 | 1,115 | 925 |
| Nonfuel opex—fixed (nameplate capacity basis) | $/MWhe | 4.2 | 3.8 | 3.1 | 2.6 |
| Nonfuel opex—variable | $/MWhe | 2.3 | 2.1 | 1.8 | 1.5 |
| Efficiency | HHV basis | 45% | 47% | 51% | 55% |
| **$H_2$ fuel cell (market mix of technologies)** | | | | | |
| Capex—new build | $/kWe | 2,165 | 1,930 | 1,830 | 1,740 |
| Nonfuel opex—fixed (nameplate capacity basis) | $/MWhe | 7.4 | 6.6 | 6.3 | 6.0 |
| Nonfuel opex—variable | $/MWhe | 4.9 | 4.4 | 4.2 | 4.0 |
| Efficiency | HHV basis | 46% | 49% | 52% | 54% |

Notes: All costs are expressed in 2020$.

**Table D-33.** *TEA Inputs for Hydrogen Turbines and Fuel Cells*

efficiency of 66% for generating electricity from $H_2$. Figure D-14 shows the resulting total RE $H_2$ demand, normalized by total electricity demand, along with the following fit to the data:

$$y = 115 \times 10^{-9}(x - 80\%)^5$$

where

- x = the share of grid electricity generated by all renewable sources after subtracting the electricity generated by nuclear plants

- y = RE $H_2$ demand normalized by the grid electricity load, in units of metric tons of $H_2$ per exajoule of electricity

---

102 Contini, V., et al. 2017. "Manufacturing Cost Analyses of Fuel Cell Systems for Primary Power and Combined Heat and Power Applications." *Battelle Presentation.* https://www.energy.gov/sites/prod/files/2017/05/f34/fcto_bop_workshop_contini.pdf.

103 MIT. "Future of Energy Storage." https://energy.mit.edu/research/future-of-energy-storage.

104 Guerra, O.J., et al. 2021. "Optimal energy storage portfolio for high and ultrahigh carbon-free and renewable power systems." *Energy Environ. Sci.* 10. https://doi.org/10.1039/D1EE01835C.

105 NREL assumed other technologies, such as Li-ion batteries, pumped hydro, and flow batteries would be used to satisfy short-duration and long-duration energy storage needs.

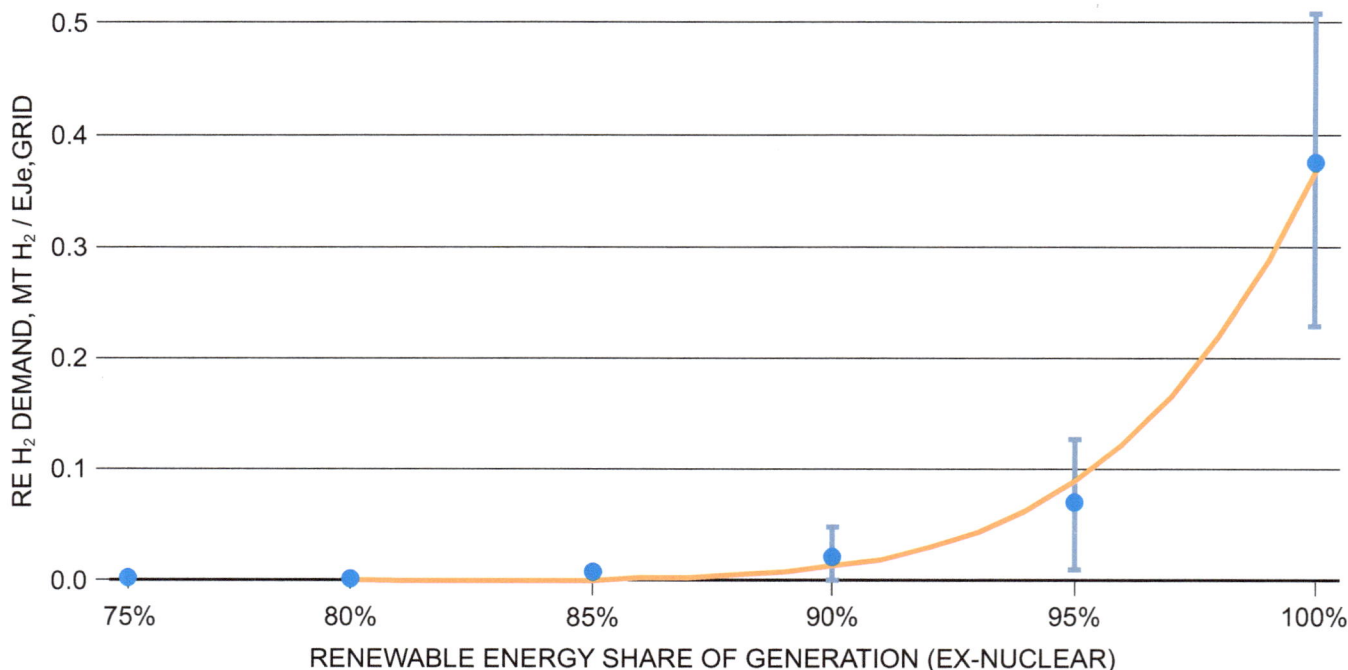

Notes: See text for descriptions of the x- and y-axes and the fit to the data (line). The whiskers represent the range of values for different grid ISOs. MT = metric tons, $EJ_e$ = exajoules of electricity (1 $TWh_e$ = 0.0036 $EJ_e$).

**Figure D-14.** *RE $H_2$ Demand for Seasonal Energy Storage*

---

This functional relationship was used by USREP to calculate, for every modeled year in each region under both study scenarios, the amount of RE $H_2$ needed specifically to satisfy energy storage needs. Those needs were based on two endogenously determined values: 1) total electricity demand and 2) penetration of renewables on the grid.

### D. Residential and Commercial Sector

Hydrogen was allowed to be blended into a natural gas network for use in the residential and commercial sector for heating, at zero cost, up to a blending level of 20 vol% $H_2$. Blend levels higher than 20 vol% were not considered in the study.

## IX. POLICY

Several policies were explicitly represented in the modeling.

### A. IRA Tax Credits

The relevant tax credits included in the IRA were considered. All values in this section are in 2020S.

**45Q Carbon Oxide Sequestration Tax Credit:** The credit amount depends on whether criteria related to the capture facility are met. It is granted over the first 12 years of $CO_2$ capture and storage. The study assumed a credit of $85/$MT-CO_2$ would be available for projects starting up in modeling years 2025 and 2030. The ATR + 95% $CO_2$ capture production pathway sequesters 9 $kgCO_2/kgH_2$, which translates to a tax credit of $0.77/kgH_2$ on a $H_2$ basis. The levelized impact is to reduce $LCOH_p$ by $0.74/kgH_2$ for plants that start before the credit expires. Projects modeled to start up in 2035 or later receive no 45Q credit.

**45V Clean Hydrogen Production Tax Credit:** The credit amount depends on the CI of the production route, the project startup year, and whether criteria related to the production facility are met.[106] It is granted over the first 10 years of

---

106 Internal Revenue Service. 2023. "Section 45V Credit for Production of Clean Hydrogen; Section 48(a)(15) Election to Treat Clean Hydrogen Production Facilities as Energy Property." https://www.federalregister.gov/documents/2023/12/26/2023-28359/section-45v-credit-for-production-of-clean-hydrogen-section-48a15-election-to-treat-clean-hydrogen.

production. The study assumed the credit would be available for projects starting up in modeling years 2025 and 2030 with the following incentive structure.

| Tier | $CI_p$ (kgCO$_2$e/kgH$_2$) | Tax Credit ($/kgH$_2$) |
|---|---|---|
| I | 4 – 2.5 | 0.60 |
| II | 2.5 – 1.5 | 0.75 |
| III | 1.5 – 0.45 | 1.00 |
| IV | <0.45 | 3.00 |

For RE H$_2$, levelization of the Tier IV tax credit of $3/kgH$_2$ leads to a reduction in LCOH$_p$ by $2.89/kgH$_2$ for plants that start up before the credit expires. Projects modeled to start up in 2035 or later receive no 45V credit.

**45Y Clean Electricity Production Tax Credit:** The credit amount depends on the project startup year and whether criteria related to the production facility are met. It is granted over the first 10 years of production. The study assumed $24.30/MWh$_e$ would be available for projects starting up in modeling years 2025 and 2030, with the credit droping to $11.50/MWh$_e$ for projects starting up in modeling year 2035.[107] Using the electrolysis plant efficiency, which improves over time, the tax credit on a H$_2$ basis is $1.35/kgH$_2$, $1.29/kgH$_2$, and $0.58/kgH$_2$ for modeling years 2025, 2030, and 2035, repectively. These translate to reduction in LCOH$_p$ of $1.17/kgH$_2$ in 2025, $1.12/kgH$_2$ in 2030, and $0.50/kgH$_2$ in 2035. Projects modeled to start up after 2035 receive no 45Y credit.

RE H$_2$ production was assumed to receive the maximum 45V credit of $3/kgH$_2$. This production route was also assumed to receive the 45Y credit for the renewable energy generated to make H$_2$ since the IRA allows these credits to be stacked.[108]

NG+CCS H$_2$ projects were assumed to take the 45Q credit instead of the 45V credit. (IRA rules do not allow 45V and 45Q credits to be stacked.)

The 45Q credit is more valuable since in the study CI$_p$ was projected to be greater than 1.5 kgCO$_2$e/kgH$_2$, limiting the 45V credits to Tier II at best.

## B. Low Carbon Fuel Standard

California's Low Carbon Fuel Standard (LCFS) policy provides a subsidy based on the WTW CI of a transportation fuel (i.e., considering cumulative emissions from production through end use by the vehicle). The amount of the credit depends on the extent of reduction in WTW CI vs. the relevant reference fuel. For HD trucks, the reference fuel is diesel. The intent of granting LCFS credits is to encourage a reduction in the WTW CI of the fuel pool over time, which would occur through increasing adoption of low CI fuels.[109] To promote continuous improvement, the WTW CI of the reference fuel also decreases over time. For the study, the impact is a narrowing of the WTW CI benefit of switching to LCI H$_2$.

LCFS credits were calculated using a calculator developed by the California Air Resources Board[110] with the following inputs:

- WTW CI for the reference fuel: The current LCFS target is a linear trajectory to a 20% reduction in WTW CI by 2030 vs. 100 gCO$_2$e/MJ$_{LHV}$ for conventional diesel in 2010.[111] The study assumed slightly more aggressive reduction targets, specifically: 15% lower by 2025, 25% lower by 2030, and then to decrease at a rate of 20% per decade thereafter.

- WTW CI for LCI H$_2$: The value assigned was the CI calculated using SESAME for LCI H$_2$ delivered at the station, since there are no subsequent tailpipe carbon emissions.[112]

- Carbon prices: Carbon prices are determined by the market, which makes them difficult to predict. Therefore, a simplifying assumption of $160/MT-CO$_{2e}$ was assumed for all modeling years.

107 Calculated from a tax credit of $27.50, $27.50, and $13.00 (all 2022$) per MWh$_e$ generated for plants that start up in 2025, 2030, and 2035, respectively, based on DOE guidance in https://www.energy.gov/eere/solar/federal-solar-tax-credits-businesses and converted to 2020$ assuming CPI inflation.

108 The 45Y credit was included for renewable electricity used to generate H$_2$. Any curtailed renewable electricity was not credited.

109 This is consistent with USREP modeling for the study.

110 California Air Resources Board. 2023. "The LCFS Credit Price Calculator v.1.3." https://ww2.arb.ca.gov/sites/default/files/2022-03/creditvaluecalculator.xlsx.

111 On a H$_2$ basis, this 2010 baseline value is equivalent to 12 kgCO$_2$e/kgH$_2$.

112 Using H$_2$ in an internal combustion engine can lead to NO$_x$ emissions, but this pathway is not included in the study.

- Energy economy ratio: A value of 1.9 was adopted from the lookup table for $H_2$ used in a HD fuel cell truck.

The LCFS credits thus calculated were assumed to only apply to the West region.

## C. Advanced Clean Trucks and Advanced Clean Fleets

California's Advanced Clean Trucks (ACT) regulation requires truck manufacturers of Class 2b–8 trucks to sell an increasing percentage of zero emission vehicles (ZEVs) per year (either FCEVs or BEVs).[113, 114] By 2035, 55% of Class 2b–3 truck sales, 75% of Class 4–8 straight truck sales, and 40% of truck tractor sales must be ZEV. Eleven states have adopted California's ACT standards, including Colorado, Maryland, Massachusetts, New Jersey, New Mexico, New York, Oregon, Rhode Island, Vermont, Virginia, and Washington.[115] In the USREP modeling, all these states were assumed to adopt ACT regulations.

The Advanced Clean Fleets (ACF) regulation requires certain vehicle fleets that operate in California to replace their existing vehicles with ZEVs according to a specified timetable.[116] Qualifying box trucks, vans, buses with two axles, yard tractors and light-duty package delivery vehicles must be 100% ZEV by 2035. Qualifying work trucks, day cab tractors, and buses with three axles must be 100% ZEV by 2039. Qualifying sleeper cab tractors and specialty vehicles must be 100% ZEV by 2042. Currently, qualifying vehicles represent 12% of Class 2b–3 vehicles, 52% of Class 4–8 vocational vehicles, and 67% of Class 7–8 tractor vehicles.

113 California Air Resources Board. "Advanced Clean Trucks." https://ww2.arb.ca.gov/our-work/programs/advanced-clean-trucks.

114 California Air Resources Board. 2021. "Advanced Clean Trucks Fact Sheet." https://ww2.arb.ca.gov/sites/default/files/2021-08/200625factsheet_ADA.pdf.

115 DOE Alternative Fuels Data Center. "Adoption of California's Clean Vehicle Standards by State." https://afdc.energy.gov/laws/california-standards.

116 California Air Resources Board. "Advanced Clean Fleets Regulation Summary." https://ww2.arb.ca.gov/resources/fact-sheets/advanced-clean-fleets-regulation-summary.

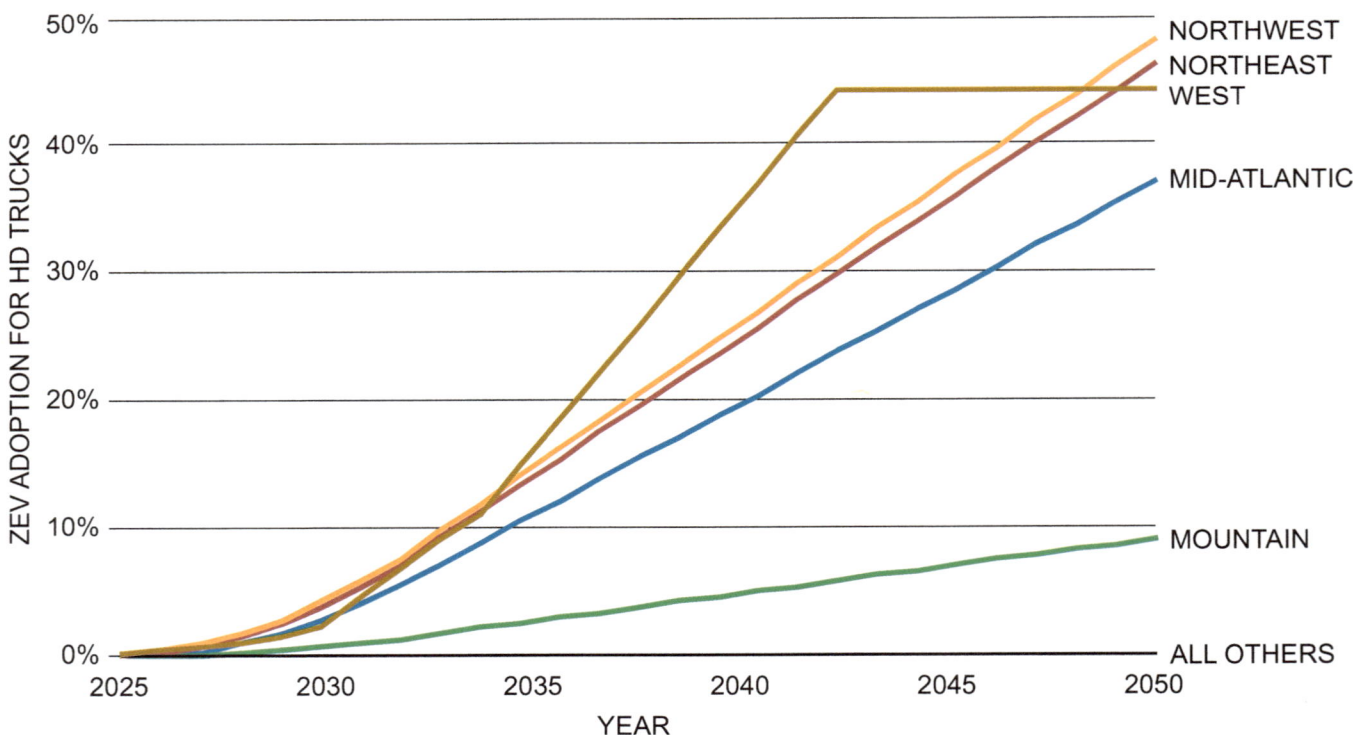

*Figure D-15. Assumed Regional ZEV Adoption Rates for HD Trucks*

Figure D-15 shows the adoption rate for ZEV HD trucks by region assumed for USREP. These rates assume compliance with both ACT and ACF regulations, and were weighted across regions with varying ACT/ACF adoption according to number of vehicle registrations in each state.[117]

## X. PHYSICAL PROPERTIES

Key physical properties used in the modeling are provided.

| H₂ Properties | Values | Units |
|---|---|---|
| **Density** | | |
| Specific volume at 60°F and 1 atm | 415.3 | SCF/kg |
| Specific volume at 0°C and 1 atm | 11.1 | Nm³/kg |
| Density liquid H₂ at -273°C and 1 atm | 70.9 | kg/m³ |
| **Heating Values** | | |
| Lower heating value | 113,725 | Btu/kg |
| Lower heating value | 120.0 | MJ/kg |
| Lower heating value | 33.33 | kWh/kg |
| Higher heating value | 134,510 | Btu/kg |
| Higher heating value | 141.9 | MJ/kg |
| Higher heating value | 39.42 | kWh/kg |
| Ratio of higher to lower heating value | 1.183 | |

Notes: SCF = standard cubic feet; Nm³ = normal cubic meter.

**Table D-34.** *Physical Properties of $H_2$*

| Properties | Value | Unit |
|---|---|---|
| **Heating Values** | | |
| Lower heating value | 44,700 | Btu/kg |
| Lower heating value | 13.1 | kWh/kg |
| Lower heating value | 47.2 | MJ/kg |
| Higher heating value | 49,500 | Btu/kg |
| Higher heating value | 14.51 | kWh/kg |
| Higher heating value | 52.2 | MJ/kg |
| Ratio of higher to lower heating value | 1.1 | |
| **Carbon content** | | |
| Mass fraction of carbon | 0.72 | kgC/kg |
| $CO_2$ emissions with complete oxidation | 2.65 | $kgCO_2$/kg |
| $CO_2$ emissions with complete oxidation | 56.3 | $gCO_2$/MJ$_{LHV}$ |
| $CO_2$ emissions with complete oxidation | 59.3 | $kgCO_2$/MBTU$_{LHV}$ |

**Table D-35.** *Physical Properties of Natural Gas*

| Property | Value | Unit |
|---|---|---|
| Lower heating value of ammonia | 18.6 | MJ/kg |
| Higher heating value of ammonia | 22.5 | MJ/kg |

**Table D-36.** *Physical Properties of Ammonia*

| Property | Value | Unit |
|---|---|---|
| Lower heating value of diesel | 128,450 | Btu/gallon |

**Table D-37.** *Physical Properties of Diesel*

| Physical Units Conversions | Value | Unit |
|---|---|---|
| Energy | 1,055 | MJ/Million Btu |
| Energy | 3.6 | MJ/kWh |

**Table D-38.** *Energy Unit Conversion Factors*

117 DOT Federal Highway Administration. "Truck and Truck-Tractor Registrations–2019." https://www.fhwa.dot.gov/policyinformation/statistics/2019/pdf/mv9.pdf.

# *Appendix E*

# CONTEXTUALIZATION OF MODELING RESULTS WITH OTHER PUBLISHED REPORTS

The National Petroleum Council employed a Modeling approach that leveraged MIT's methodology, used expert-informed and publicly available data for inputs, and provided regional granularity for a more detailed potential outlook of the U.S. hydrogen economy. The expert-informed inputs were aligned across companies representing interests throughout the $H_2$ value chain, from manufacturing, engineering, and construction to project operation. Additionally, the inputs were tested and challenged by the study members, including academia, government, and nonprofits. The outputs of this Modeling effort are unique from the outputs of other studies in the public domain. Table E-1 and Table E-2 provide comparisons between the outputs of this study and select other recently published studies. Due to the complexity of Modeling efforts, a detailed comparison between Model input assumptions for this study and other published studies has not been conducted. However, the study authors think it's likely that differences observed between the outputs of this study and other reports are due to the following key elements:

- **Expert-informed capital and operating costs:** The Modeling includes costs for manufacturing, engineering, procurement, construction, and operation that are informed by companies that are scoping and developing projects. Due to anticompetitive concerns, actual project costs have not been shared but real-world feedback on development costs has been incorporated.

- **Role of LCI $H_2$ in Industrial heat:** The study authors believe the Modeling accounts for a relatively larger share of low carbon intensity hydrogen (LCI $H_2$) use in Industrial heat in

the Net Zero by 2050 (NZ2050) scenario than other studies—a belief informed by companies that have begun to further evaluate carbon emissions-reduction opportunities for their existing industrial facilities. Specifically, these evaluations are showing that installing carbon capture on existing industrial facilities may be more difficult than initially anticipated in some cases, driven primarily by plot space constraints for carbon capture equipment adjacent to existing process equipment. The Modeling still assumes large-scale deployment of carbon capture to address carbon emissions from industrial facilities, but the carbon is captured precombustion through reformation rather than postcombustion. Performing carbon capture precombustion leads to an increase in use of LCI $H_2$ for Industrial heat, driving additional deployment of LCI $H_2$ in the Industrial sector in the NZ2050 scenario.

- **Carbon intensity:** The Modeling leveraged publicly available data, along with industry-informed greenhouse gas (GHG) emissions reductions assumptions, to calculate carbon intensity (CI) reductions over time for natural gas that could be the feedstock for hydrogen produced from natural gas using carbon capture and storage technology (NG+CCS $H_2$). The reductions assumed for the Modeling are well aligned with the assumptions in the parallel *Charting the Course*[1] study.

- **Delivered costs of LCI $H_2$:** The Modeling considers the full value chain for LCI $H_2$,

1   National Petroleum Council. 2024. "Charting the Course: Reducing GHG Emissions from the U.S. Natural Gas Supply Chain." https://chartingthecourse.npc.org/.

including the costs to deliver to the consumer. This detailed Modeling accounts for regional transportation distances, required storage, and delivery method, based on operational considerations for the production source and customer needs for the demand centers.

| Report (Scenario Name) | Years | Total Domestic Demand | Industrial Demand | Transport Demand | Power Demand | Export Demand | Production – NG+CCS | Production – RE |
|---|---|---|---|---|---|---|---|---|
| Units | | MMTpa | MMTpa | MMTpa | MMTpa | MMTpa | % | % |
| NPC (Stated Policies) | 2025 | 11 | 11 | <1 | 0 | <1 | 6 | 1 |
| | 2030 | 12 | 10 | 1 | <1 | 2 | 20 | 5 |
| | 2040 | 14 | 10 | 3 | <1 | 2 | 52 | 19 |
| | 2050 | 18 | 10 | 6 | 1 | 3 | 63 | 28 |
| DOE Liftoff (Base) | 2030 | 5 | 5 | 0 | 0 | N/A | 20-30 | 70-80 |
| | 2040 | 14 | 7 | 7 | 0 | N/A | 60-70 | 30-40 |
| | 2050 | 27 | 13 | 14 | 0 | N/A | 70-80 | 20-30 |
| FCHEA (Base)[3] | 2030 | 14 | 13 | 0 | 0 | N/A | N/A | N/A |
| | 2050 | 27 | 13 | 14 | 0 | N/A | N/A | N/A |
| NPC (Net Zero) | 2025 | 11 | 11 | <1 | <1 | 1 | 12 | 2 |
| | 2030 | 19 | 15 | 2 | 1 | 5 | 41 | 28 |
| | 2040 | 40 | 27 | 8 | 4 | 7 | 46 | 54 |
| | 2050 | 66 | 37 | 17 | 9 | 10 | 32 | 68 |
| DOE Liftoff (Net Zero) | 2030 | 11 | 11 | 0 | 0.3 | N/A | 0-5 | 95-100 |
| | 2040 | 27 | 13 | 14 | 0 | N/A | 50-60 | 40-50 |
| | 2050 | 50 | 15 | 26 | 8 | N/A | 40-50 | 50-60 |
| FCHEA (Ambitious)[3] | 2030 | 17 | 14 | 1 | 1 | N/A | N/A | N/A |
| | 2050 | 63 | 23 | 27 | 4 | N/A | N/A | N/A |
| H₂ Council – Global Trade Flows 2022 | 2030 | 25 | N/A | N/A | N/A | N/A | 35 | 19 |
| | 2040 | 60 | N/A | N/A | N/A | N/A | 68 | 20 |
| | 2050 | 100 | N/A | N/A | N/A | 20 | 59 | 41 |
| IRENA[4] | 2020 | 11 | N/A | N/A | N/A | N/A | 85-100 | 0-15 |
| | 2050 | 36-56 | 11 | 19 | 9 | 5-15 | 10-60 | 40-90 |

Notes: (1) Residential/Commercial data of the Modeling for the Stated Policies and Net Zero scenarios are not presented to be consistent with other studies. (2) Total domestic demand data do not include hydrogen demand for exports. (3) Data excerpted from "Road Map to a U.S. Hydrogen Economy," published by the Fuel Cell & Hydrogen Energy Association. (4) Data from two IRENA reports ("Accelerating Hydrogen Deployment in the G7" and "Global Hydrogen Trade to Meet the 1.5°C Climate Goal") have been excerpted.

**Table E-1.** *Detailed Comparison of LCI H₂ Demand and Production Projections in the United States*

| | Units | LCOH Production – NG+CCS $/kg-H_2$ | LCOH Production – RE $/kg-H_2$ | Note |
|---|---|---|---|---|
| | Years | | | |
| **NPC (this study)** | 2025 | 1.89-3.22 | 5.89-9.49 | Transmission cost excluded |
| | 2030 | 1.92-3.17 | 4.75-7.72 | Transmission (low-end): 0.09 |
| | 2040 | 1.98-3.24 | 3.79-6.32 | Transmission (high-end): 0.15 |
| | 2050 | 1.96-3.16 | 3.02-5.15 | |
| **DOE Liftoff** | 2025 | 1.6 | 2.5 | |
| | 2030 | 1.2 | 1.6 | |
| | 2040 | 1.2 | 1.4 | |
| | 2050 | 1.2 | 1.2 | |
| **FCHEA[1]** | 2030 | 1.28-1.95 | 1.87-3.04 | |
| **IRENA** | 2021 | N/A | 7.6-11.7 (solar only) 5.2-7.3 (wind only) | |
| | 2050 | N/A | 0.8-1.5 | |
| **DNV Hydrogen Forecast 2022-2050** | 2025 | 2.4 | 5.3 / 5.5 / 3.1 | Solar only/wind only/ grid connected |
| | 2030 | 1.8 | 3.2 / 3.2 / 2.8 | |
| | 2040 | 1.8 | 2.9 / 2.9 / 2.9 | |
| | 2050 | 1.7 | 2.2 / 2.2 /1.5 | |
| **PWC Green Hydrogen Economy** | 2025 | N/A | 4.25-4.5 | |
| | 2030 | N/A | 2.5-2.75 | |
| | 2040 | N/A | 1.5-1.75 | |
| | 2050 | N/A | 1-1.25 | |

Notes: (1) Data excerpted from "Road Map to a U.S. Hydrogen Economy," published by the Fuel Cell & Hydrogen Energy Association.

*Table E-2. Comparison of Published Values of Levelized Cost of H₂ in the United States*

# *Appendix F*

# TABLE OF HARD-TO-ABATE APPLICATIONS WITH POTENTIAL LCI H$_2$ USE

| Sector | Industrial | Transportation | Power | Residential/ Commercial |
|---|---|---|---|---|
| **Existing Applications** | • Oil refining<br>  – Feedstock<br>  – Ammonia production (e.g., fertilizer, plastics, synthetic fibers, resins)<br>  – Methanol production (e.g., plastics, formaldehyde)<br>  – Other chemicals (e.g., hydrogen peroxide) | • Material-handling equipment<br>  – Forklifts<br>• Light- and medium-duty vehicles<br>  – Passenger vehicles<br>  – Buses | • Distributed generation<br>  – Primary and backup power<br>  – Critical facilities (e.g., hospitals, data centers)<br>  – Remote locations (e.g., microgrids, telecommunications towers)<br>• Renewable grid integration and other ancillary services<br>  – Time shifting<br>  – Firming and dispatchable capacity<br>  – Avoiding transmission buildout | • Low-percentage hydrogen blending in limited regions |
| **Emerging Applications** | • Steel production<br>  – Reductant in iron ore refining<br>• Industrial heat<br>• Bio/synthetic fuels<br>• Cement | • Medium- and heavy-duty vehicles<br>  – Large bus fleets<br>  – Long-range coaches<br>  – Trucks<br>• Rail<br>• Maritime<br>  – Bunker fuels (e.g., hydrogen, ammonia, methanol)<br>  – Marine vessels<br>  – Ports (e.g., drayage trucks, shore power)<br>• Aviation<br>  – Sustainable aviation fuels (e.g., biofuels and power-to-liquid fuels)<br>  – Short duration/uncrewed aerial vehicles<br>  – Small passenger flight<br>• Offroad equipment<br>  – Mining<br>  – Construction<br>  – Agriculture | • Long-duration energy storage<br>• Hydrogen low nitrogen-oxides combustion<br>• Direct/reversible fuel cells<br>• Nuclear-hydrogen hybrids<br>• Fossil/waste/biomass hydrogen hybrids with carbon capture and storage | • Mid- to high-percentage hydrogen blending in regions with limited alternatives<br>• Building/district heating<br>  – Combined heat and power with fuel cells |

Note: The applications listed in the table may not be exhaustive.
Source: Table excerpted from "U.S. National Clean Hydrogen Strategy and Roadmap" by DOE, 2023.

*Table F-1. Existing and Emerging Applications in Demand for Hydrogen*

# *Appendix G*

# COMPENDIUM OF MODELING RESULTS

This appendix contains the MIT SESAME and USREP modeling results for the NPC *Harnessing Hydrogen* Report. Due to its size and to enhance its ease of use, Appendix G is only available digitally via the NPC report's website, https://harnessinghydrogen.npc.org, and is not included in the printed version of the report.

# *Appendix H*

# RELATIVE MERITS OF HYDROGEN TRANSPORTATION AND DELIVERY PATHWAYS

Table H-1 evaluates the relative merits of different modes and states of hydrogen. Given the relative advantages and disadvantages across the evaluated pathways, it is evident that a balanced mix of multiple hydrogen carrier infrastructure types are needed to address the different elements of the transport and delivery value chain.

| Carrier | Advantages | Disadvantages |
|---|---|---|
| **Compressed Gas Hydrogen** | • Mature and commercial, safe, reliable pathway with low technological complexity<br>• Highly versatile carrier and cost effective over short distances<br>• Pipelines can be used to transport long distances when delivering large volumes<br>• Potential to blend in existing natural gas pipelines | • Expensive to transport over longer distances when delivering large volumes<br>• Existing pipeline facilities must be evaluated for embrittlement potential<br>• Requires higher utilization for cost-effective pipeline transport<br>• Constraints with permitting and acquiring rights-of-way when using pipelines<br>• High capital cost and long lead times to construct new pipelines<br>• Existing natural gas pipelines must first be evaluated and, if deemed appropriate, upgraded for $H_2$ transport |
| **Liquid Hydrogen** | • Transport using liquid $H_2$ tank trucks is a commercial pathway and well established at a smaller scale<br>• Can transport more $H_2$ compared to compressed gas trailers<br>• Requires no reconversion at the point of receipt<br>• High purity $H_2$ in liquid state | • High energy requirements for liquefaction<br>• Transport cost can be expensive for shorter distances<br>• Boil-off losses during shipping and storage<br>• High capital cost due to cryogenic operating temperatures<br>• Transport involves higher operational complexities compared to compressed gas |
| **Ammonia** | • Globally traded and produced<br>• Can be easily liquefied<br>• Mature multimodal ammonia transportation value chain with low transport losses<br>• Packs high energy density and $H_2$ content<br>• Has multiple end-user applications (e.g., power generation, maritime fuel) | • High energy consumption for ammonia synthesis and cracking<br>• High temperature requirement for ammonia synthesis<br>• Highly toxic, corrosive, and flammable under heat, requiring rigorous safety management<br>• Ammonia cracking at large scale still to be proven |
| **Methanol** | • Methanol produced with LCI $H_2$ can be used directly as a fuel or fuel supplement for ships, rail, or other maritime applications | • Methanol, with its low flash point, is highly flammable and is classified as a hazardous material. The lower and higher explosive limits are 6.7% and 36%, respectively, requiring rigorous safety management.<br>• Methanol vapors can be ignited by a spark or flame, and the vapors can travel a considerable distance to an ignition source and flash back<br>• Methanol is a toxic chemical and can be harmful if ingested or inhaled |
| **Liquid Organic Hydrogen Carriers (LOHC)** | • Can be transported using existing oil infrastructure<br>• Suitable for multimodal transport<br>• Offers low toxicity and nonexplosive characteristics | • High energy consumption and high temperatures required for dehydrogenation<br>• Requires further purification of the $H_2$ after dehydrogenation<br>• Degradation of $H_2$ binding capacity after multiple cycles; carrier losses (0.1% per cycle) for every cycle<br>• LOHC conversion at-scale is still to be proven |

*Table H-1. Relative Comparison of Hydrogen Carriers*

# *Appendix I*

# RELATIVE COMPARISON OF HYDROGEN STORAGE PATHWAYS

Table I-1 provides the relative advantages and disadvantages across the major storage pathways.

| Pathway | Advantages | Disadvantages |
|---|---|---|
| **Salt Caverns** | • Potential to repurpose existing fields<br>• Commercially demonstrated to store $H_2$<br>• Can offer large volumes of storage, including seasonal (weeks to months)<br>• Offer tight and chemically inert environment for $H_2$ storage<br>• High purity after withdrawal and low losses during storage | • Has geographic siting constraints<br>• Removal of brine during salt cavern mining<br>• High water requirements for solution mining to dissolve salt (7–8 $m^3$ of freshwater injected into the cavity to dissolve 1 $m^3$ of halite salt)[1]<br>• Due to geographic constraints, additional infrastructure costs might be necessary for pipeline and electric interconnection to operate salt caverns<br>• Potential for cavern space to shrink over time |
| **Depleted Hydrocarbon Fields** | • Potential to repurpose existing fields<br>• Offers large storage volumes (weeks to months)<br>• Incremental costs to repurpose can be low<br>• Geologic formations are well understood and proven to be safe | • Has geographic siting constraints<br>• Potential for microbial reactions (methanogenesis, hydrogen sulfide formation), which can initiate at 10% blend<br>• Potential for diffusion losses<br>• Need for postwithdrawal processing to ensure $H_2$ purity<br>• Hydrogen storage in depleted reservoirs still to be proven technology at-scale<br>• Hydrocarbon fields are large storage formations. Charging and discharging cycling may be infrequent (compared to smaller storage sites). Infrequent cycling and usage could impact the cost economics of storage. |
| **Rock Caverns** | • Smaller surface footprint when compared to other geologic formation types<br>• Can be lined to prevent any losses from subsurface reaction<br>• High purity after withdrawal in lined caverns | • Has geographic siting constraints<br>• Hydrogen storage in rock caverns still to be proven technology at-scale<br>• Potential for microbial reactions and losses in unlined caverns<br>• Cost of storage in lined caverns might be higher than other geologic formation types<br>• Expensive relative to salt caverns |
| **Pressurized Containers** | • Offers high cycling rates of stored $H_2$<br>• Highly flexible storage and can be mobile and decentralized<br>• High purity after withdrawal<br>• Commercially proven and widely adopted | • May not be suitable for large-scale storage<br>• Higher capital costs<br>• Inconsistent global regulations on pressurized container standards |

***Table I-1.*** *Relative Comparison of Hydrogen Storage Pathways*

| Pathway | Advantages | Disadvantages |
|---|---|---|
| **Liquid Hydrogen** | • Offers higher energy density compared to gaseous storage<br>• High purity after withdrawal<br>• No geographic/locational storage constraints | • High energy demand for liquefaction<br>• Higher costs for liquid conversion<br>• Potential for boil-off losses<br>• Low temperatures and high flammability characteristics require complex operational handling |
| **Ammonia** | • Mature storage technology with well-developed supply chain of large storage tanks and transport vessels<br>• Offers high hydrogen density relative to other storage pathways. The volumetric hydrogen density in ammonia is about 45% higher than that of liquid hydrogen.[2]<br>• No geographic or locational storage constraints | • Requires rigorous safety management due to its toxic, corrosive, flammable, and odorous properties<br>• High energy requirements to store ammonia in liquid state<br>• Potential for conversion losses after cracking |
| **Liquid Organic Hydrogen Carriers (LOHC)** | • Liquid at normal operating conditions<br>• Easy to transport using trucks and ships<br>• Compatible with existing petroleum storage infrastructure<br>• Easy to store when compared to ammonia or liquid hydrogen | • Technology is still nascent and needs to be proven at-scale<br>• Requires high energy for dehydrogenation<br>• Can pose health and safety risks if handled improperly<br>• LOHC compounds can be flammable and/or toxic based on the type of chemical used |
| **Metal Hydrides** | • Storage medium operation under low operating pressures<br>• High purity of $H_2$ after release<br>• Storage medium does not pose regulatory or jurisdictional constraints when compared to other storage pathways | • Technology is still nascent, needs to be proven at-scale<br>• Storage medium degradation due to cycling loss<br>• Storage can be very heavy due to the associated weight of the metal hydride<br>• Can be highly flammable and pose safety risks |
| **Methanol[3]** | • Mature storage technology with well-developed supply chain<br>• Liquid handling and storage are easier when compared to gaseous compounds<br>• Biodegradable | • Not proven in a large supply chain network as an energy carrier with cracking at-scale to obtain hydrogen back from methanol<br>• Toxic and corrosive<br>• Burns with nonluminous flame |
| **Emerging Technologies: Metal-Organic Frameworks (MOFs)** | • Potential to provide cost-competitive $H_2$ storage options<br>• The sponge-like MOFs have a high surface area for the $H_2$ molecule to adsorb to the surface of the cavities<br>• Simple charge and discharge mechanism, which is favorable for several end-use applications<br>• Does not require high temperatures to discharge the $H_2$, making it less energy intensive | • Emerging technology that requires further RDD&D for commercialization<br>• High fabrication costs, poor selectivity, low capacity, and difficulties in recycling/regeneration |

Sources: (1) "Solution Mining and Salt Cavern Usage," SaltWork Consultants, 2016. (2) "Potential Roles of Ammonia in a Hydrogen Economy," DOE, 2006. (3) McNicol, B.D., Rand, D.A.J., and Williams, K.R. 2001. "Fuel Cells for Road Transportation Purposes - Yes or No?" *Journal of Power Sources* 100 47-59. Information from Table 3 on page 53.

*Table I-1. Relative Comparison of Hydrogen Storage Pathways (continued)*

# *Appendix J*

# CURRENT HYDROGEN INFRASTRUCTURE LANDSCAPE IN THE UNITED STATES

States in Table J-1 are listed in descending order of total hydrogen infrastructure miles.

| State | Intrastate (miles) | Interstate (miles) | Total (miles) |
|---|---|---|---|
| Texas | 535 | 483 | 1,018 |
| Louisiana | 108 | 369 | 477 |
| Alabama | 31 | | 31 |
| California | 26 | | 26 |
| Indiana | 12 | | 12 |
| Ohio | 9 | | 9 |
| Utah | 6 | | 6 |
| Washington | 3 | | 3 |
| Oklahoma | 2 | | 2 |
| New York | 1 | | 1 |
| **Total (miles)** | | | **1,585** |

Source: U.S. DOT PHMSA Portal Data, Gas Transmission Pipeline Miles: https://portal.phmsa.dot.gov/analytics/saw.dll?Portalpages.

***Table J-1.*** *Hydrogen Pipeline Miles by State*

# *Appendix K*

# LIST OF FEDERAL AGENCIES REGULATING HYDROGEN TRANSPORTATION AND STORAGE

| Agency | Agency Full Name | Principal Mission | Hydrogen Regulation |
|--------|------------------|-------------------|---------------------|
| BSEE | Bureau of Safety and Environmental Enforcement | Regulates offshore energy industry | No current offshore $H_2$ pipelines |
| FAA | Federal Aviation Administration | Safe and efficient aerospace system | Storage of liquid $H_2$ at aerospace facilities |
| FERC | Federal Energy Regulatory Commission | Reliable, safe, secure, and economically efficient energy services | Interstate pipeline transportation of oil and natural gas |
| STB | Surface Transportation Board | Economic regulation of various modes of surface transportation | Has congressional authority to regulate pipeline infrastructure, even though they have not yet exercised jurisdiction for $H_2$ |
| FHWA | Federal Highway Administration | Regulates construction, maintenance, and preservation of nation's highways, bridges, and tunnels | Highway safety, including hazardous materials |
| OSHA | Occupational Safety & Health Administration | Sets and enforces workplace standards to ensure safe and healthful working conditions | Safety of structural components and operations of gaseous and liquid $H_2$ storage and delivery |
| PHMSA | Pipeline & Hazardous Materials Safety Administration | Safe transportation of energy and other hazardous materials | Extensive safety regulation of HazMat transport via road, rail, and water |
| USCG | U.S. Coast Guard | Maritime safety, security, and environmental stewardship | Movement of hazardous materials on marine vessels in inland and coastal waters |
| FMCSA | Federal Motor Carrier Safety Administration | Prevents commercial vehicle-related fatalities and injuries | Motor carrier safety and HazMat regulation |

Source: "Federal Oversight of Hydrogen Systems," Sandia National Laboratories, 2021, Table 3.1.

***Table K-1.** Federal Agencies Regulating Hydrogen Transportation and Storage*

# Appendix L

# LIST OF HYDROGEN PIPELINE OPERATORS IN THE UNITED STATES

States in Table L-1 are listed in descending order of total hydrogen infrastructure miles.

| Operator | Intrastate (miles) | Interstate (miles) | Total (miles) |
|---|---|---|---|
| Air Products | 79 | 514 | 593 |
| Linde | 121 | 338 | 459 |
| Air Liquide | 369 | | 369 |
| Equistar Chemicals | 24 | | 24 |
| Flint Hills Resources | 23 | | 23 |
| INEOS USA | 21 | | 21 |
| US Amines | 20 | | 20 |
| Philips 66 | 17 | | 17 |
| Citgo | 9 | | 9 |
| Total (miles) | | | 1,535 |

Source: PHMSA, 2022, https://portal.phmsa.dot.gov/analytics/saw.dll?Go (last accessed on September 18, 2023).

**Table L-1.** *Hydrogen Pipeline Miles—Top 9 Operators*

# *Appendix M*

# ECONOMICS OF LCI HYDROGEN TRANSPORTATION, STORAGE, AND DELIVERY

| Parameter | Compressed Gaseous Hydrogen (CGH$_2$) | Liquefied Hydrogen (LH$_2$) |
|---|---|---|
| **Terminal** | | |
| Capital expenditures (capex), total installed cost, M$/(MTH$_2$/day) | 2.0 | 4.5 |
|     Compressors or liquefier | 0.7 | 3.5 |
|     Storage | 0.9 | 0.6 |
|     Rest of terminal | 0.4 | 0.4 |
| Operations and maintenance (O&M), excluding electricity, $/(kgH$_2$/day) | 100 | 150 |
|   Electricity consumption, kWh/kgH$_2$ | 3 | 10 |
| **Delivery trucks** | | |
|   CAPEX, tractor + trailers, $/(kgH$_2$/day) | 500 | 150 |
|     On-trailer capacity basis, $/kgH$_2$ | 1,000 | 300 |
|     Trailer loads delivered per day per tractor | 2 | 2 |
| **O&M, excluding fuel costs** | | |
|   Distance independent, $/(kgH$_2$/day) | 30 | 20 |
|   Distance dependent, $/(kgH$_2$/day/mile) | 0.5 | 0.1 |
| O&M, truck fuel, MJ$_{LHV}$/MTH$_2$/mile | 20 | 5 |

*Table M-1. Modeling Parameters for Truck Delivery*

| Parameter | Units | Value |
|---|---|---|
| **Nominal Pipe Size** | Inches | 36 |
| **Capacity** | GW$_{H2-LHV}$ | 6 |
| | MTH$_2$/day | 4,300 |
| | mmcf per day | 1,800 |
| | billion Btu per day | 0.5 |
| **Compression Power** | MW$_e$/GW$_{H2-LHV}$-mile | 0.05 |
| | kWh$_e$/MTH$_2$-mile | 1.7 |

*Table M-2. Capacity and Compression Power Requirements for NPS 36-Inch Pipeline*

| Parameter | Units | Value | Region |
|---|---|---|---|
| **Capital Recovery Period** | Years | 25 | All |
| **Capital Expenditures (Capex)** | $/MW-mile | 1,500 | South, Great Lakes, Central |
| | | 3,000 | Mid-Atlantic, Appalachian, Gulf Coast, Mountain, Northwest, Alaska & Hawai'i |
| | | 4,500 | Northeast, West |
| **Operational Expenses (Opex), Fixed** | % of Capex/yr | 1.5% | All |
| **Losses** | % per mile | 0.01% | All |

*Table M-3. Electricity Transmission Costs*

| | Salt Cavern | Pipe Farm | Liquefied $H_2$ |
|---|---|---|---|
| **Sizing Basis[1, 2, 3]** | | | |
| Capacity (MTH$_2$) | 5,000 | 500 | 700 |
| Maximum storage pressure (bar) | 150 | 100 | <10 |
| Maximum annual turnover (cycles/yr)[4] | 12 | 36 | 36 |
| **Capital Cost[5, 6, 7, 8, 9]** | | | |
| Storage ($/kgH$_2$ working capacity) | 15 | 750 | 35 |
| Processing ($/kgH$_2$/day nameplate capacity) | 200 | 200 | 2,880 |
| **Operating Cost** | | | |
| Fixed O&M | 2% | 2% | 2% |
| Compression/liquefaction power (kWh$_e$/kgH$_2$) | 2 | 1 | 10 |

Notes: (1) Salt cavern storage capacity typical for single cavern similar to recent U.S. storage sites (e.g., Moss Bluff, Spindletop). Pipe farm storage capacity based on Argonne National Laboratory study (Papadias & Ahluwalia, 2021: *Int. J. Hydrogen Energy*, 46, p. 23,527). Liquid storage based on 10,000 m$^3$ sphere, which is twice the current world scale installed at NASA Launch Complex 39B. Papadias, D.D., and R.K. Ahluwalia. 2021. "Bulk Storage of Hydrogen." *International Journal of Hydrogen Energy*, August. https://doi.org/10.1016/j.ijhydene.2021.08.028. (2) Papadias, D.D., and R.K. Ahluwalia. 2021. "Bulk Storage of Hydrogen." *International Journal of Hydrogen Energy*, August. https://doi.org/10.1016/j.ijhydene.2021.08.028. (3) Liquid storage based on 10,000 m$^3$ sphere, which is twice the current world scale installed at NASA Launch Complex 39B. (4) Maximum annual turnover represents the largest number of working capacity volumes that can be discharged from the storage facility per year, effectively setting the H$_2$ processing equipment size relative to a fixed storage quantity. Maximum filling rate is assumed to be 20% of maximum emptying rate. (5) Chen, F., Ma, Z., Nasrabadi, H., Chen, B., Saad Mehana, M.Z., and Van Wijk, J. 2022. "Capacity Assessment and Cost Analysis of Geologic Storage of Hydrogen: A Case Study in Intermountain-West Region USA." *International Journal of Hydrogen Energy*, December. https://doi.org/10.1016/j.ijhydene.2022.11.292. (6) Papadias, D.D., and R.K. Ahluwalia. 2021. "Bulk Storage of Hydrogen." *International Journal of Hydrogen Energy*, August. https://doi.org/10.1016/j.ijhydene.2021.08.028. A 1.3x contingency factor is applied to published values, considering lack of large-scale demonstrated pipe farm storage for H$_2$. (7) "Global Hydrogen Review 2021–Analysis." International Energy Agency. October 2021. https://www.iea.org/reports/global-hydrogen-review-2021. (8) "Current Status of Hydrogen Liquefaction Costs." Department of Energy, August 6, 2019. https://www.hydrogen.energy.gov/docs/hydrogenprogramlibraries/pdfs/19001_hydrogen_liquefaction_costs.pdf?Status=Master. (9) "DOE Technical Targets for Hydrogen Delivery." Department of Energy. n.d. https://www.energy.gov/eere/fuelcells/doe-technical-targets-hydrogen-delivery.

*Table M-4. Summary of Hydrogen Storage Modeling Parameters*

| T&S Cost Tier | $CO_2$ Transport ($/MTCO_2$-mile) | $CO_2$ Storage ($/MTCO_2$) | Region(s) |
|---|---|---|---|
| A1 | 0.10 | 8 | South, Gulf Coast |
| B1 | 0.15 | 8 | Great Lakes |
| C1 | 0.18 | 8 | Appalachian, West |
| D1 | 0.22 | 8 | Mid-Atlantic |
| E1 | 0.33 | 8 | New England |
| A2 | 0.10 | 12 | Central, Mountain |
| C2 | 0.18 | 12 | Northwest |
| D2 | 0.22 | 12 | Alaska & Hawai'i |

*Table M-5. Summary of Carbon Dioxide Transportation and Storage Modeling Parameters*

| Parameters | Units | Compressed Gas Hydrogen ($CGH_2$) Station | Liquefied Hydrogen ($LH_2$) Station |
|---|---|---|---|
| Capital Recovery Period | Years | 20 | 20 |
| Capex | M$/(MTH_2$/d) | 3.2 | 1.2 |
| Opex | | | |
| O&M | $/kgH_2$ | 0.35 | 0.25 |
| Electricity | $kWh_e/kgH_2$ | 1.5 | 0.5 |

*Table M-6. Technoeconomic Assumptions for Heavy Duty Refueling Stations*

# *Appendix N*

# ICF REPORT
# ON PIPELINE AND
# COMPRESSION COSTS

**T**his appendix contains updated pipeline and compressor construction costs prepared by ICF for use in the NPC *Harnessing Hydrogen* Report. Due to its size and to enhance its ease of use, Appendix N is only available digitally via the NPC report's website, https://harnessing hydrogen.npc.org, and is not included in the printed version of the report.

# Appendix O

# HYDROGEN POLICY AND INITIATIVES IN SELECT COUNTRIES

This appendix provides additional information on the various hydrogen policies and initiatives being developed in a number of countries assessed in Chapter 6: Policy. Specifically, additional information is provided for the following locations:

- Australia
- Canada
- China
- European Union
- France
- Germany
- India
- Japan
- Singapore
- South Korea
- United Kingdom
- Scotland

Note that the information summarized here was current as of June 2023.[1]

## I. AUSTRALIA

### A. Hydrogen Strategy

Building off its leading position as a liquefied natural gas (LNG) exporter, Australia seeks to position itself as a top three exporter of $H_2$ to Asia by 2030. Development of Australia's $H_2$ industry will provide energy security, contribute to its energy transition goals, create jobs and, like LNG, will position Australia as a global $H_2$ supplier. Australia is looking to build out both renewable electrolytic hydrogen (RE $H_2$) and natural gas with carbon capture and storage-based $H_2$ (NG+CCS $H_2$) production facilities. However, multiple state-led initiatives are focused more on the RE $H_2$-only approach.

In February 2023, the Australian government agreed to undertake a review of the National Hydrogen Strategy[2], which was released in 2019. This review was largely triggered as a response to the U.S. Inflation Reduction Act (IRA), which was passed in 2022. While there is no formal indication of the scope of the review, it is possible that subsidies may be considered.

Western Australia's goal is to achieve a market share in global $H_2$ exports by 2030, similar to the 12% share it has in LNG exports today. In parallel, Western Australia also aims to achieve a 10% RE $H_2$ blend in its gas pipelines and networks, and to see RE $H_2$ used in heavy haulage and as a fuel source for regional transportation in regional Western Australia. The Western Australian government is committed to providing available, industrial land in metropolitan and regional locations to support new $H_2$ projects. Announced in March 2021, the $50 million Industrial Land Development Fund will enable the state to consider reduced lease rates for projects deemed to be of strategic importance to Western Australia.

---

1 Excludes Belgium and Norway, as limited information was available at the time of report.

2 https://www.dcceew.gov.au/sites/default/files/documents/australias-national-hydrogen-strategy.pdf.

Pilbara Hydrogen Hub: The Pilbara region has been identified as a promising center for $H_2$ production. Estimates for $H_2$ production and exports in this Pilbara region range from 3 to over 10 million metric tons per annum (MMTpa) by 2050. In 2021, the state government committed $70 million in funding to support the Pilbara Hydrogen Hub, and in April 2022, the federal government committed matching funds.

Oakajee Hub: Western Australia is actively seeking opportunities for colocation of $H_2$ producers, users, and exporters to the Oakajee Hub, located in Mid West Australia. In late 2020, Western Australia launched a global expression of interest process for the development of the Oakajee Strategic Industrial Area, which attracted more than 65 national, international, and multinational submissions.

## B. Deployment Targets/Timing

Producing $H_2$ at under $2 (AUD) a kilogram ("$H_2$ under 2"), is a stretch goal of the federal government's Low Emissions Technology Investment Roadmap. Some Australian states are more specific. For example by 2030, Western Australia's goal is a market share of 12% (similar to its share in LNG today) in global $H_2$ exports. Overall, Australia is primarily focused on West Coast export opportunities. While domestic supply/use is also considered, it is a lower priority.

## C. Supply Policies

While Australia's national $H_2$ strategy is initially focused on building a domestic demand for use of $H_2$ for transport, Hume highway (major intercity national highways), and decarbonization of certain hard-to-abate industries, the country's longer-term goal is to become a leading global $H_2$ player.

In May 2023, Australia announced its "Hydrogen Headstart" program. As part of this program, the government will invest $2 billion AUD (~$1.3 billion USD) to provide revenue support for large-scale RE $H_2$ projects. Selected projects will be able to receive funding as a production tax credit.[3]

---

3   Hydrogen Headstart program - DCCEEW.

The government is investing $464 million in $H_2$ hubs as part of its $1.2 billion AUD commitment toward building a $H_2$ industry as well as research and development (R&D) funding from several different agencies. Australia has a proposed methodology for $H_2$ production and consumption to generate Australian Carbon Credit Units (Australian offsets), which could provide an additional revenue stream to producers or incentivize users to fuel switch.

Additionally, there have been some facilitating initiatives to help remove barriers to executing $H_2$ projects (e.g., regulatory framework reviews, special taskforces to help shepherd hydrogen projects through approvals, etc.), but nothing that currently competes against the U.S.'s IRA.

## D. Infrastructure Policies

A National Hydrogen Infrastructure Assessment (NHIA), commissioned by the Australian government, provides the first nationwide infrastructure assessment focused on development of the clean hydrogen industry. It highlights the importance of strategic and timely investment in Australia's $H_2$ supply chain infrastructure. This will be key to rapid scale-up of a competitive $H_2$ industry needed over the next decade to decarbonize domestic economy and secure a position as a major global $H_2$ player and future energy supplier. In NHIA, "clean hydrogen" is both electrolytic hydrogen (RE $H_2$) and fossil fuel-based $H_2$ with carbon capture (NG+CCS $H_2$).

## E. Demand Policies

At the state level, there are several $H_2$ demand-stimulation schemes at varying levels of development and implementation. Examples include New South Wales Renewable Fuels Scheme and Western Australia Renewable Hydrogen Target requiring certain power generators/industrials/others to use certain percent of hydrogen demonstrated through a certificate scheme. Additionally, state and federal emissions reduction policies have the potential to stimulate demand indirectly.

## F. Public Investments

**Australia's Clean Hydrogen Industrial Hubs** program was launched in September 2021. The

Department of Industry Science and Resources (DISER) identified seven prospective hydrogen hub locations across Australia, including: Bell Bay (TAS), Darwin (NT), Eyre Peninsula (SA), Gladstone (QLD), Latrobe Valley (VIC), Hunter Valley (NSW), and Pilbara (WA).

The government is committed to investing $464 million AUD in hydrogen hubs.[4] Researchers identified that hubs are critical to helping Australian industry produce hydrogen at under $2 AUD/ kilogram ("$H_2$ under 2"), a stretch goal of the Technology Investment Roadmap. There are two grant types for hubs at different stages of development:

- The Hub Development and Design Grants is a program that provides $500,000 to $3 million (AUD) grants to project consortia that support the initial development, feasibility, and design work needed to carry out Hydrogen Hub Proposals.[5]

- The Hub Implementation Round 1 Grants allocated $30 million to $70 million (AUD) for industry hydrogen hub projects that are closer to investment decisions and are ready for the next stage of implementation.

## G. Trade Agreements

As of June 2021, Australia and Germany will invest in a series of new initiatives to accelerate the development of hydrogen industry, creating new economic opportunities and jobs while reducing emissions. The New Hydrogen Accord included three major initiatives:

- Establishing a German-Australian Hydrogen Innovation and Technology Incubator (HyGATE) to support real-world pilot, trial, demonstration, and research projects

- Facilitating industry-to-industry cooperation on demonstration projects in Australian $H_2$ hubs

- Exploring options to facilitate the trade of hydrogen and its derivatives produced from

renewables (such as ammonia) from Australia to Germany, including through Germany's $H_2$ Global Initiative

In October 2020 and June 2021, Australia and Singapore signed a Memorandum of Understanding (MOU) to advance low-emissions technologies and solutions, with a priority focus on Hydrogen, Carbon Capture Utilization and Storage.

- Established a $30 million (AUD) partnership to accelerate the deployment of low-emissions fuels and technologies in maritime and port operations

In January 2022, Australia and Japan established the Australia-Japan Clean Hydrogen Trade Partnership that is looking to attract overseas investment in hydrogen supply chains originating in Australia. The $150 million (AUD) Australian Clean Hydrogen Trade Program (ACHTP) will support Australian-based $H_2$ supply chain projects. The first round of the program will focus on the export of clean hydrogen to Japan under the Japan-Australia Partnership on Decarbonization through Technology.

In October 2021, Australia partnered with the Republic of Korea to support research on $H_2$ supply chains between Korean and Australian companies.

## H. Other: Carbon Footprint/Life Cycle Assessment (LCA)

Since 2020, the Australian federal government has been working on the development of a proposed Guarantee of Origin (GO) Scheme, which will certify the carbon intensity of hydrogen products originating from Australia. The GO Scheme was expected to be implemented in 2024.

The scheme does not intend to define whether a product is "clean" or not, rather it aims to provide high-integrity data of the emissions associated with the manufacture/carbon intensity of the product such that markets can determine whether or not it meets their requirements. The scheme is aligned with the IPHE[6] accounting methodologies and is intended for other international certification

---

4   Future hydrogen industry to create jobs, lower emissions and boost regional Australia | Ministers for the Department of Industry, Science and Resources.

5   Activating a Regional Hydrogen Industry – Clean Hydrogen Industrial Hubs: Hub Development and Design Grants | business.gov.au.

---

6   IPHE = International Partnership for Hydrogen and Fuel Cells in the Economy.

schemes (e.g., CertifHy, GH$_2$, CFAA) to be able to apply their stamp showing the product met their green or clean definition using the data from the GO certificate.

## II. CANADA

### A. Hydrogen Strategy

The government of Canada published *The Hydrogen Strategy* for Canada in December 2020.[7] In addition, the provinces of Alberta, British Columbia, Ontario, and Québec have each developed hydrogen strategies.

### B. Deployment Targets/Timing

The federal hydrogen strategy describes three periods of national hydrogen development:

- Near Term: "Laying the Groundwork" (2020-2025); current production is 3 MMTpa (high carbon intensity, or CI)

- Mid Term: "Growth and Diversification" (2025-2030); target production is 4 MMTpa (low CI)

- Long Term: "Rapid Market Expansion" (2030-2050); target production is 20 MMTpa by 2050 (low CI)

### C. Supply

#### 1. Focus

The federal hydrogen strategy adopts a diverse, technology-neutral approach to hydrogen production. Production pathways include hydrogen production from fossil fuels with carbon capture and storage, production via electrolysis powered by renewable, hydro, and nuclear electricity, and hydrogen from biomass gasification and landfill/sewage/agricultural gas reformation.

#### 2. Policies

**Clean Hydrogen Investment Tax Credit (ITC):** In the 2022 Fall Economic Statement, the government of Canada proposed a tax credit for investments in clean hydrogen production. The government intends for the new ITC to be available across a range of LCI H$_2$ pathways. The proposed tax credit will be refundable, and available for eligible investments made as of the day of Budget 2023. The credit will be phased out after 2030. The lowest carbon intensity tier that meets all eligibility requirements is proposed to receive an ITC of at least 40%. Draft legislative language for the low carbon intensity (LCI) H$_2$ ITC had not been released as of October 2023.

**Carbon Capture, Utilization, and Storage (CCUS) ITC:** In August 2022, Canada's Department of Finance released draft legislative proposals to the Income Tax Act and the Income Tax Regulations related to the ITC for carbon capture, utilization, and storage (CCUS) for public comments. This legislative proposal was previously announced as a part of the 2021 federal budget and updated as a part of the 2022 federal budget. The 2023 federal budget reaffirmed support for the CCUS ITC and included new details such as labor provisions. On August 4, 2023, the Department of Finance of Canada released legislative proposals that include draft legislation for the CCUS ITC. The public comment period on the proposal ended September 8, 2023.

### D. Infrastructure

#### 1. Focus

The Canadian Hydrogen Strategy recognizes the value of developing a diverse set of hydrogen carriers and supporting distribution and delivery infrastructure, including gaseous and liquid hydrogen, natural gas/hydrogen blending, and chemical carriers such as ammonia or liquid organic hydrogen.

**Transport:** By 2050, the pressure limits in tube trailer trucks transport are projected to increase from 250 bar (today's levels) to 450+ bar; liquid hydrogen truck transport will expand from an East Coast focus to countrywide. Pipe transport will expand to include both blended and dedicated hydrogen infrastructure. Initially, existing hydrogen distribution and dispensing infrastructure can be leveraged, followed by the development of new hydrogen distribution infrastructure. This will help support early deployment

---

7    "The Hydrogen Strategy for Canada," https://www.nrcan.gc.ca/sites/nrcan/files/environment/hydrogen/NRCan_Hydrogen%20Strategy%20for%20Canada%20Dec%2015%20 2200%20clean_low_accessible.pdf.

hydrogen hubs in mature applications while supporting Canadian demonstrations in emerging applications.

**Blending:** The Canada Hydrogen Strategy 2050 vision aspires to convert more than 50% of energy currently supplied by natural gas to be supplied by hydrogen through blending in existing pipelines and new dedicated hydrogen pipelines. The strategy concludes that blending LCI $H_2$ into Canada's natural gas networks, for use in both industry and the built environment, provides the largest potential demand opportunity for hydrogen.

## 2. Policies

In 2022 the Canada Infrastructure Bank announced the launch of its $500 million CAD zero emission vehicle Charging and Hydrogen Refueling Infrastructure Initiative.

## E. Demand

### 1. Focus

The adoption of $H_2$ will be focused on energy-intensive applications where it offers advantages over alternative low-carbon options. This includes using $H_2$ as a fuel for long-range transportation and power generation, to provide heat for industry and buildings, and as a feedstock for heavy industrial processes, like steel and cement making. Domestic deployment of $H_2$ will be critical to supporting Canada's world-leading $H_2$ and fuel cell sector, as well as to meeting the national climate change objectives.

### 2. Policies

While there are no specific policies driving $H_2$ use, Canada has a number of federal and provincial policies in place that will drive demand for low carbon intensity energy, including (but not limited to):

- Canada Nationally Determined Contribution to the Paris Agreement: 40%–45% GHG reductions below 2005 levels by 2030

- Canadian Net Zero Emissions Accountability Act: codifies Canada's net zero target

- Greenhouse Gas Pollution Pricing Act: Carbon Fuel Tax, Facility Output-Based Pricing System, and provincial carbon pricing regulations

- Federal Clean Fuel Standard (CFS): The Federal CFS came into effect July 1, 2023, requiring liquid fossil fuel suppliers to reduce the CI of the fuels used in Canada from 2016 levels by 2.4 g $CO_2e$/MJ in 2022, increasing to a 12 g $CO_2e$/MJ reduction in 2030. LCI $H_2$ is a compliance option.

## F. Public Investment

**Net Zero Accelerator Initiative:** Up to $8 billion CAD to support large-scale investments in key Industrial sectors across the country for the development of clean technologies such as hydrogen.

**Low-Carbon and Zero-Emissions Fuels Fund:** $1.5 billion (CAD) fund to increase the production and use of low-carbon fuels, including hydrogen.

**The Zero Emission Vehicle Infrastructure Program (ZEVIP):** $680 million (CAD) initiative ending in 2027 and its objective is to address the lack of charging and refueling stations.

**Canada Growth Fund:** investments that catalyze substantial private sector investment in Canadian businesses and projects to help transform and grow Canada's economy at speed and scale on the path to net zero; eligible business opportunities include hydrogen.

## G. Trade Agreements

There are no trade agreements between the United States and Canada specific to hydrogen. In October 2021, the government of Canada and the government of the Netherlands signed a Memorandum of Understanding to cooperate in the field of hydrogen energy.[8] In August 2022, the government of Canada and the government of Germany signed a joint declaration of intent establishing a Canada-Germany Hydrogen Alliance.[9]

---

8  https://natural-resources.canada.ca/climate-change/ canadas-green-future/the-hydrogen-strategy/memorandum-understanding-between-the-government-canada-and-the-government-the-netherl/23907.

9  https://natural-resources.canada.ca/climate-change-adapting-impacts-and-reducing-emissions/canadas-green-future/ the-hydrogen-strategy/joint-declaration-intent-between-the-government-canada-and-the-government- the-federal/2460.

## H. Export Goals

The government of Canada is considering the potential to be a major exporter of LCI $H_2$ to complement fossil fuel exports. Five key markets have been identified as potential export markets for Canada: the United States (particularly California and the Eastern United States), Japan, South Korea, China, and the European Union.

### 1. Other: Carbon Footprint/LCA

The government of Canada's Fuel Life Cycle Assessment (LCA) Model is the tool used to calculate the life cycle CI of fuels and energy sources used and produced in Canada. Finance Canada is considering input from its 2022 public consultation on a Clean Hydrogen Investment Tax Credit related to the Fuel Life Cycle Assessment Model for calculating the life cycle CI of clean hydrogen production.

## III. CHINA

### A. Hydrogen Strategy

The central government mentioned $H_2$ in two important policies released during the past two years:

- 14th Five-Years Plan (2021–2025):[10] Addresses hydrogen as a "frontier" area, encourages R&D, and considers hydrogen as one of the six industries for the future

- Medium- and Long-Term Hydrogen Industry Development Plan (2021–2035):[11] Released in March 2022, this document sets the government strategy to boost low carbon hydrogen supply in the country and notably decarbonize high-energy-consuming and high-emissions industries. It explicitly favors renewable hydrogen over unabated hydrogen. By 2025, the plan envisions a solid policy environment for the development of the hydrogen energy industry, significant improvements in industrial innovation capability, a mastering of core technologies

and manufacturing processes, and a relatively complete supply chain and industrial system. It also sets directional goals to the 2030 and 2035 horizons.

Apart from the central government objectives, more than 500 hydrogen-related policies have been released by local and provincial governments. Ten provinces have already adopted specific hydrogen strategies. For example, Inner Mongolia province—which will undoubtedly become China's main green $H_2$ producer—suggested building a 500,000 MTpa renewable $H_2$ production capacity. Shanghai plans to become China's de facto center for clean hydrogen and unveiled policies that include the creation of a national hydrogen trading platform, and the construction of a "leading hydrogen energy port."[12]

In August 2023, China released standard guidelines covering the whole industrial chain of hydrogen energy production. The standards were issued jointly by the National Standards Commission and six departments, including the National Energy Administration. Alongside hydrogen energy production, storage, transmission, and use, the standards encompass five subsystems of foundation and safety, refueling, application, and technology, as well as 20 secondary subsystems and 69 third-level subsystems.[13]

### B. Deployment Targets/Timing

Under the Medium- and Long-Term Hydrogen Industry Development Plan, the central government set a target to produce between 100,000 and 200,000 MT of RE $H_2$ per year and to reach 50,000 $H_2$ fuel cell vehicles by 2025.

By 2030, China is seeking a reasonable and orderly industrial layout and wide use of hydrogen production from renewable energy to support China's peak carbon goal.

By 2035, the proportion of hydrogen produced from renewable energy in end-use energy consumption will increase significantly. According to the plan, this will play an important

---

10  https://en.ndrc.gov.cn/policies/202204/P0202204266 47700434555.pdf.

11  https://en.ndrc.gov.cn/news/pressreleases/202203/ t20220329_1321487.html (press release) or https://www.ndrc. gov.cn/xxgk/zcfb/ghwb/202203/P020220323314396580505. pdf (full text in Chinese).

12  https://en.lingang.gov.cn/2022-08/22/c_793640.htm.

13  https://www.h2-view.com/story/china-issues-standards-for-hydrogen-industry-construction/.

supporting role in the country's green energy transformation.

## C. Supply

### 1. Focus

The central government's hydrogen plan highlights the principle of building a low-carbon, low-cost, and multiapproach hydrogen production system, with a focus on hydrogen production from renewable energy sources and strict controls over hydrogen production from fossil energy sources.

In addition, the government promotes lower-carbon hydrogen production by solid oxide electrolytic cells or by photolysis of water, as well as hydrogen electrolysis production from seawater and nuclear energy.

### 2. Policies

See description of the Medium- and Long-Term Hydrogen Industry Development Plan (2021–2035).

## D. Infrastructure

### 1. Focus

The central government aims to coordinate the development of the national hydrogen energy industry, facilitate the progress of industrial development, promote the construction of hydrogen energy infrastructure in an orderly manner, strengthen the safety management of hydrogen energy infrastructure, and avoid disruptive competition.

This includes active promotion of innovative technical materials and processes, improved efficiency of high-pressure gaseous storage and transportation, and accelerated reduction of storage cost. In addition, the government and its state-owned enterprises (SOE) will coordinate the planning and construction of hydrogen refueling stations to power the new fleet of hydrogen fuel cell vehicles.

The Hydrogen Industry Development Plan expresses government interest in exploring the application of solid state, cryogenic high pressure, and organic liquid storage and transporta-

tion methods. Also, plans include pilot demonstrations of hydrogen blending into natural gas pipelines and pure hydrogen pipelines, and to gradually build a high-density, lightweight, low-cost, diversified hydrogen energy storage and transportation system.

### 2. Policies

See description of the Medium- and Long-Term Hydrogen Industry Development Plan (2021–2035).

## E. Demand

### 1. Focus

The China Hydrogen Alliance[14] estimates that China's hydrogen demand should reach 35 MMT in 2030 (at least 5% of the Chinese energy supply) and 130 MMT in 2060 (20% of the Chinese energy supply). This is similar to Standard & Poor's estimates of 37.15 MMT in 2030 and 130.30 MMT in 2060 (77.94 MMT in the Industrial sector, 40.51 MMT in Transportation, 6 MMT in Power, and 5.85 MMT in Residential/Commercial).[15]

The central government plans to improve the economics of hydrogen energy utilization and expand the use of low-carbon hydrogen energy in hard-to-abate industries. It has approved clusters of cities, led by Daxing district in Beijing, including Shanghai, Foshan in Guangdong, Zhengzhou in Henan, and Zhangjiakou in Hebei Province. Over four years of demonstration projects, these cities should deploy FCEVs and expand their hydrogen refueling station networks.

### 2. Policies

See description of the Medium- and Long-Term Hydrogen Industry Development Plan (2021–2035).

---

14  The China Hydrogen Alliance was jointly launched in February 2018 by China Energy Corporation and 18 other sponsors ranging from large companies in fields such as energy production, equipment manufacturing, transportation, and metallurgical materials and prestigious universities and research institutes. At present, the Alliance has 87 members globally. http://h2cn.org.cn/en/index.

15  https://www.spglobal.com/commodityinsights/en/market-insights/latest-news/energy-transition/033022-factbox-chinas-national-hydrogen-plan-starts-small-but-aims-for-economies-of-scale.

| Classification | Low-Carbon Hydrogen | Clean Hydrogen | Renewable Hydrogen |
|---|---|---|---|
| Carbon emissions per unit of hydrogen (kg $CO_2e$/kg $H_2$) | 14.51 | 4.9 | 4.9 |
| Requires renewable energy for hydrogen production | No | No | Yes |

Source: Australian National University, China's hydrogen plans (China Hydrogen Alliance, 2020) Policy brief - hydrogen, (anu.edu.au) Page 9.

*Table O-1. China Low Carbon Hydrogen, Clean Hydrogen and Renewable Hydrogen Standards*

## F. Public Investment

The Hydrogen Plan aims to develop the industry through central government funding, initially encouraging financial institutions to offer additional support for hydrogen. Also, state governments can raise funds through special bonds for developing hydrogen and other strategic projects.

The Chinese government has set up a number of funds to support hydrogen development, combining public and private investments, including National Oil Companies and SOE, research institutions, universities, local governments, and commercial institutions.

**Chengdu municipal government:** Issued about $30 million USD in bonds for a hydrogen industrial park.[16]

**Shanghai, Zhejiang, Sichuan, and Beijing:** In the first half of 2022, the financing scales were ~$89 million, ~$76 million, ~$33.5 million, and ~$13 million.

**Sinopec:** Announced four LCI $H_2$ projects, aiming to produce between 10,000 and 100,000 MTpa from different renewable sources. For example, Sinopec plans to build a RE $H_2$ plant in the Inner Mongolian city of Ordos, with a planned annual capacity of 30,000 MT. The company also aims to build 1,000 hydrogen refilling stations during the 14th five-year plan period (2021–25) with refilling capacity of 200,000 MTpa. Sinopec has announced plans to build a 400-km pipeline with an initial capacity of 100,000 MTpa to transfer $H_2$ from renewable energy projects in the northwestern Inner Mongolia region to cities in eastern China.

## G. Trade Agreements

There are no trade agreements in place specific to hydrogen. In 2022, the Chinese government signed an MOU with the Kingdom of Saudi Arabia covering $H_2$, among other fuels. In addition, several SOEs have signed MOUs with companies around Asia.

## H. Export Goals

China is exploring hydrogen export opportunities, as the main hydrogen producer worldwide. However, it is primarily focused on having enough production to cover its local necessities before prioritizing other markets.

## I. Other: Carbon Footprint/LCA

China's hydrogen strategy does not regulate or define the carbon footprint of various hydrogen production pathways. However, in December 2020, the China Hydrogen Alliance proposed the "Standard and evaluation of low-carbon hydrogen, clean hydrogen, and renewable hydrogen," the first formal low-carbon hydrogen standard worldwide. This standard uses the LCA method to establish the quantitative evaluation system of low-carbon hydrogen, "clean" hydrogen, and renewable hydrogen, and promotes the sustainable development of a hydrogen energy industry supply chain. Carbon intensities of production are captured in Table O-1. The standard has not yet been endorsed or used by the government.

## IV. EUROPEAN UNION

### A. Hydrogen Strategy

In July 2020, the European Commission published a hydrogen strategy for a climate-neutral Europe. It was updated in May 2022 with the

---

16  https://greenfdc.org/hydrogen-chinas-progress-and-opportunities-for-a-green-belt-and-road-initiative/.

REPowerEU plan after the start of the Russian invasion of Ukraine.

The European Union has already approved state aid of €5.2 billion of public support by 13 Member States for the Important Project of Common European Interest (IPCEI) to support research and innovation, first industrial deployment, and construction of relevant infrastructure in the hydrogen value chain, and €5.4 billion of public support by 15 member states to develop hydrogen technologies (fuel cell, electrolyzer, storage, etc.).

## B. Deployment Targets/Timing

The European strategy initially set a target of at least 6 GW of renewable hydrogen electrolyzers in the EU by 2024 and 40 GW of renewable hydrogen electrolyzers by 2030. In addition, 40 GW could be installed in Europe's neighborhood with export to the EU.

These targets were updated in 2022 with 10 MMT of domestic renewable hydrogen production and 10 MMT of renewable hydrogen imports by 2030.

## C. Supply

### 1. Focus

The focus for the EU is to develop renewable hydrogen by electrolysis powered by renewable electricity. In the short and medium term, the European Union considers that other forms of low-carbon hydrogen (e.g., NG+CCS $H_2$, or hydrogen produced from nuclear electricity) are needed to rapidly reduce emissions from existing hydrogen production and support the parallel and future uptake of renewable hydrogen.

### 2. Policies

In 2022, the European Commission announced a new EU Hydrogen bank to guarantee the supply of hydrogen, using money from the Innovation Fund and making €3 billion available to kickstart the market. A pilot phase started in 2023 with: 1) a Contract for Difference to support 100% of the cost gap in comparison to unabated hydrogen produced in the EU, and 2) potentially a component on $H_2$ imports.

In autumn 2023, a first auction of €800 million was organized for supporting the production of RE $H_2$ with a fixed premium for each kg of RE $H_2$ produced over a period of 10 years (premium would be based on the received bids). The first auction was for RE $H_2$ but future auctions may include LCI $H_2$.

## D. Infrastructure

### 1. Focus

In the short term, the European Union considers infrastructure needs to be likely limited, placing local hydrogen production hubs close to hydrogen consumption.

In the medium term, the planning of a European hydrogen backbone has started with the release of preliminary hydrogen infrastructure needs. Moreover, to allow the import of hydrogen, the European Union will support the development of three hydrogen corridors via the Mediterranean, the North Sea area, and Ukraine.

### 2. Policies

In 2021, the European Commission published a proposal[17] for a hydrogen and decarbonized gas market package to define the rules for natural gas infrastructure to be reused for hydrogen. The costs for cross-border tariffs between member states could be reduced for hydrogen. Additionally, the blending of natural gas with up to 5% hydrogen could be allowed.

This bill proposes rules to enable the development of dedicated hydrogen infrastructure and a market, and foster planning for electricity, gas, and hydrogen. The same natural gas unbundling rules—that is, no participation of network operators will be allowed in energy production or supply—should be applied for hydrogen networks.

## E. Demand

### 1. Focus

In the current strategy, the European Union focus the use of hydrogen as a fuel, an energy carrier, or as a feedstock for the hard-to-abate

---

17  https://ec.europa.eu/commission/presscorner/detail/en/ip_23_6085.

sectors, particularly in industry and transportation.

## 2. Policies

In the European Union, the Renewable Energy Directive promotes the use of renewable hydrogen with binding targets to decarbonize industry and heavy-duty and long-distance transportation. Fuel suppliers might have an obligation to supply the Transportation sector at least 2.6% of renewable fuels of nonbiological origin (RFNBO, e.g., renewable hydrogen or e-fuels) by 2030, with specific targets for the aviation and the maritime sectors.

By 2035, $CO_2$ emissions for new passenger cars and light commercial vehicles should be zero emissions (e.g., FCEV). Through the Alternative Fuel Infrastructure regulation, one refueling station for hydrogen should be available every 150 km along the European core network and in every urban node.

For industry, a carbon tax has been in effect since 2005 using the principle of cap and trade, with a cap reduced over time. In 2023, the EU Emissions Trading System (ETS) price was around €85/MT $CO_2$. In addition, industries consuming hydrogen might have to consume at least 50% of renewable hydrogen by 2030.

### F. Trade Agreements

There are no trade agreements between the United States and the European Union specific to hydrogen. In March 2022, a joint statement between the European Commission and the United States on European Energy Security was published in order to collaborate on the production and use of clean and renewable hydrogen to displace unabated fossil fuels and cut greenhouse gas emissions, including by investing in technology development and supporting infrastructure.

### G. Other: Carbon Footprint/LCA

In 2023, the European Commission released the criteria for renewable electricity supplying the electrolyzer:

- **Additionality:** Renewable power asset should be in operation no earlier than 36 months before

the electrolyzer and not connected to the grid. If it is connected, it must be equipped with a smart metering system. Power purchase agreement (PPA) with a renewable energy source that came into operation in the same 36 months as the electrolyzer or earlier and without any support excluding support received before a repowering or support fully repaid except:

  – Until 01/01/2028 with a grandfathering clause until 01/01/2038 or

  – If the CI of the bidding zone is <18g$CO_2$/MJ but still needs PPA

  – If the average proportion of renewable in the bidding zone is higher than 90%

- **Temporal correlation:** same month as the renewable electricity production before 01/01/2030 and same hour after or from a new storage asset behind the same connection point. Note that the Delegated Act calls for a study assessing the impact of the requirements to be submitted to the European Parliament and the Council by July 1, 2028. The study would look at the possible impacts of temporal matching and other requirements on hydrogen production costs, GHG emissions, and the broader energy system.

- **Geographical correlation:** same bidding zone or interconnected bidding zone if the day-ahead electricity price is higher or interconnected offshore bidding zone.

## V. FRANCE

### A. Hydrogen Strategy

France was a pioneer in the field of hydrogen. Their first strategy, published in 2018, aimed to create a carbon-free Industrial sector. The limited budget (€100 million) made it possible to launch the first calls for projects dedicated to the deployments of $H_2$ in industry, transport, and energy. Specific objectives for hydrogen in Industrial uses were introduced: 10% carbon-free hydrogen by 2023, and between 20% and 40% by 2028.

Following the publication of the German and European strategies, the French government also published a specific strategy in 2020[18] with

---

18  Présentation de la stratégie nationale pour le développement de l'hydrogène décarboné en France | economie.gouv.fr.

a financial envelope of €9 billion that will be updated periodically.

## B. Deployment Targets/Timing

The French strategy has an objective of installing 6.5 GW of carbon-free hydrogen production capacity by electrolyzers by 2030 to meet the challenges of decarbonizing the industry, to promote growth of use of $H_2$ in the Transportation sector, and support R&D. In 2023, 4.5-MW electrolysis projects for industry and 22-MW electrolysis projects for the Transportation sector have been installed. In addition, four projects of dual mode electric/$H_2$ trains have been launched.

Unlike the European Union, France has not developed a strategy for the import of hydrogen or its derivatives.

## C. Supply

### 1. Focus

Given its electricity mix and the absence of natural gas on its territory, the French strategy adopts an approach focused on the production of hydrogen by electrolysis powered by renewable electricity or nuclear electricity. The production of renewable hydrogen from biomass is not considered at this stage.

### 2. Policies

**Important Project of Common European Interest (IPCEI):** Through the IPCEI subsidy scheme, €3 billion has been allocated to build four gigafactories to produce electrolyzers in France (alkaline, PEM, SOEC), and to launch industrial decarbonization projects of refineries.

**Contract for Difference (CfD):** €4 billion has been allocated to subsidize the production of LCI $H_2$ and RE $H_2$ in France through a Contract for Difference approach that should compensate the cost of LCI $H_2$ compared to a fossil fuel scenario.

## D. Infrastructure

### 1. Focus

In the current national strategy, there is no focus on hydrogen infrastructure. However, a revised strategy could introduce the deployment of infrastructure to connect the production to the consumers.

### 2. Policies

There is currently no blending target of hydrogen for the natural gas grid.

## E. Demand

### 1. Focus

In the revised national strategy, the French government plans to focus on industry and less on mobility.

### 2. Policies

France set an obligation on fuel suppliers to ensure that the share of renewable energy in the Transportation sector is at least 14% by 2030, with a tax to pay (TIRUERT) if fuel suppliers do not achieve this target. Using renewable or LCI $H_2$ directly for mobility, or as an intermediate product in a refinery or a biorefinery, will generate tax credits.

In 2021, France introduced a regulatory framework that defined the different categories of hydrogen and created the basis of a complete system of physical and virtual traceability of renewable and LCI $H_2$, including when injected into natural gas networks.

## F. Trade Agreements

There are no trade agreements between the United States and France specific to hydrogen. In May 2021, Energy Ministries of the governments of France and the United States released a joint statement[19] where they committed to work together on new technologies and the ongoing energy transition to contribute significantly to zero-carbon generation solutions, including the production of hydrogen to decarbonize transportation and other energy sectors.

## G. Other: Carbon Footprint/LCA

France's LCA model has not been published yet, so it is unclear what threshold needs to be met

---

19  Joint Statement of the United States and France Energy Ministers on Energy Technology and Policy Resolve | Department of Energy.

to qualify its hydrogen production as renewable or low carbon (but potentially, levels could be up to 3.4 $kgCO_2/kgH_2$).

# VI. GERMANY

## A. Hydrogen Strategy

In June 2020, the German government published its national strategy for the development of hydrogen.[20] In terms of funding, Germany is planning €7 billion for local production and an additional €2 billion for the import of renewable hydrogen. The new energy coalition presented its climate roadmap in early 2022, which was transcribed into a revision of the federal strategy in 2023.

## B. Deployment Targets/Timing

The German strategy has defined targets for the deployment of renewable hydrogen (5 GW by 2030, an additional 5 GW for 2035 or even 2040) to decarbonize the Industrial and Transportation sectors.[21]

The government plans to finance imports of renewable hydrogen, with an initial budget of €2 billion, as well as the installation of combined cycle gas turbine $H_2$-ready power plants.

## C. Supply

### 1. Focus

The federal strategy adopts an approach focused on the production of hydrogen by electrolysis powered by renewable electricity. The German government is not in favor of subsidizing natural gas-based hydrogen and considers that CCS technology should be reserved for unavoidable residual emissions. However, Germany is not opposed to the use of LCI $H_2$ by Industry for their decarbonization, even if it is imported (e.g., from Norway).

### 2. Policies

**IPCEI:** Germany participates in and coordinates the IPCEI. Sixty-two projects have been selected for public funding of €8 billion (Federal State + Länder). The projects covered the production of renewable hydrogen (2 GW), transportation infrastructure, industrial projects, as well as mobility (manufacture of fuel cells). At this stage, one project has been awarded for hydrogen generation technology, three for fuel cell technologies, one for storage, transportation, and distribution technology, and one for end-user technology.

**Carbon Contract for Difference (CCfD):** Germany plans to introduce a carbon contract for difference (CCfD) policy/subsidy scheme to support hydrogen production. The budget envelope is not yet defined. This support could take the form of a 10-year contract concluded between the state and an industrialist and subsidizing the operating expenses (and possibly capital expenses) based on the differential between a $CO_2$ cost fixed by the contract and the EU ETS price. If the EU ETS price is higher than the cost fixed by the contract, the company should reimburse the state. The industries concerned would initially be those in the steel, cement, limestone, and ammonia sectors.

**$H_2$Global:** the European Commission has approved the $H_2$Global state aid mechanism, which will make it possible to offset the additional cost of imported renewable hydrogen derivatives for German Industrial consumers through a system of double auctions. A private intermediary—financed by public funds up to €900 million—will sign 10-year contracts with producers located in countries outside the EU and one-year contracts with German industrials. First tenders for $eNH_3$, eMeOH, and eSAF have been launched.

## D. Infrastructure

### 1. Focus

The German energy transition is limited by the congestion of the electricity network between the north and the south of the country. The government is therefore in favor of hydrogen transport infrastructure to allow a reliable supply and bring some flexibility to the energy system.

### 2. Policies

Germany is debating blending percentages, with a 10% upper limit $H_2$ concentration into existing natural gas networks.

---

20  Nationales Reformprogramm 2020 (bmwk.de).

21  In July 2023, Germany doubled its 2030 target to 10 GW.

## E. Demand

### 1. Focus

In the current strategy, the German government plans to focus on the decarbonization of the Industrial and Transportation sectors, and the promotion of sector coupling and $H_2$ as an energy storage.

### 2. Policies

Germany set an obligation on fuel suppliers to ensure that the share of renewable energy within the final consumption of Transportation sector energy is at least 14% by 2030. In case of non-achievement of the objective, a penalty has to be paid to the government.

## F. Trade Agreements

There are no trade agreements between the United States and Germany specific to hydrogen. In May 2022, the United States and Germany formally launched a Climate and Energy Partnership on hydrogen with the establishment of working groups.

## VII. INDIA

### A. Hydrogen Strategy

India has committed to reaching net zero by 2070 and becoming energy independent by 2047. Hydrogen is considered critical to enabling this transition, with the government of India publishing its hydrogen strategy—the National Green Hydrogen Mission—in January 2023.[22]

### B. Deployment Targets/Timing

The strategy sets a target of 5 MMTpa renewable hydrogen production, and 125 GW renewable energy capacity for hydrogen production by 2030. With a primary focus on RE $H_2$, India's hydrogen strategy has two phases:

- Phase I (2022–2026): Create demand in target sectors (refinery, fertilizer, and gas distribution), while enabling hydrogen production and domestic electrolyzer manufacturing

---

22  https://mnre.gov.in/national-green-hydrogen-mission/.

- Phase II (2026–2030): Drive hydrogen consumption in all sectors to further decarbonize the economy

### C. Supply

As part of the strategy, the government of India introduced two incentive mechanisms: 1) INR ₹130 billion/USD $1.58 billion for hydrogen production, and 2) INR ₹45 billion/USD $540 million for electrolyzer manufacturing.

In addition, the government is extending a series of waivers to incentivize hydrogen production. In key states, the electricity duty waiver will be initiated to reduce the cost of power (accounting for 60% LCI $H_2$ production cost), and the transmission fee waiver will be extended to hydrogen projects commissioned before 2031.

The government plans to introduce a customs duty waiver to initially enable imports without levy. However, the duty will be imposed from 2025–2026 to encourage domestic manufacturing. Land availability at competitive costs will be detailed in conjunction with states, and companies are encouraged to set up hydrogen facilities in industrial zones.

### D. Demand

Currently, around 5 MMT of unabated hydrogen is consumed annually in India. This is primarily used in petroleum refining and the production of ammonia for fertilizers. While there are no domestic consumption targets yet, the government of India will introduce sector targets to increase domestic demand.

India aims to export 10 MMT of renewable hydrogen and ammonia per year by 2030, capturing 10% of the global market. Given this ambition, the government is developing strategic international partnerships to enable the export of hydrogen and its derivatives. The U.S.–India Hydrogen Taskforce was launched in 2021. The taskforce aims to introduce the latest technology and financing mechanisms in developing and deploying hydrogen. In 2022, India signed the Germany-India Hydrogen Taskforce. The partnership will bolster collaboration in production, trade, utilization, storage, and distribution of renewable hydrogen.

## E. Infrastructure

India's strategy recognizes the importance of building infrastructure for the transport and storage of renewable hydrogen. The government plans to develop port and pipeline infrastructure to support exports of hydrogen and its derivatives. Producers of renewable hydrogen and its derivatives will be encouraged to develop projects in large-scale hydrogen hubs.

A regulatory framework to allow storage and dispensing of hydrogen at par with international norms will be established, and the government plans to blend hydrogen into the natural gas distribution system. While older networks will require retrofitting and upgrading, new networks are likely to be compatible with high blend ratios of hydrogen and natural gas.

The government is yet to publish a hydrogen standard; however, there are plans that this will be developed in line with global industry requirements for emerging technologies.

## VIII. JAPAN

### A. Hydrogen Strategy

Japan sees hydrogen as a major way to decarbonize its economy while sustaining its industrial competitiveness, as well as a response to scarce natural resources. Japan was the first country to adopt a national hydrogen framework in 2017. In 2019, it released its "3rd Strategic Roadmap for Hydrogen and Fuel Cells," which prioritized reducing hydrogen costs, achieving large-scale deployment, and building international partnerships and supply chains.[23] Hydrogen is also covered within Japan's Green Growth Strategy.[24]

### B. Deployment Targets/Timing

Japan has established a goal of expanding hydrogen deployment from 2 MMTpa to 3 MMTpa by 2030, 12 MMTpa by 2040, and 20 MMTpa by 2050.[25] A significant amount of this supply is expected to be imported from the Middle East, Australia, and the West Coast of North America.

It has also established certain end-use targets, including increasing fuel cell vehicles from 40,000 to 800,000 by 2030, fuel cell buses from 100 to 1,200 by 2030, and hydrogen-powered forklifts from 500 to 10,000 by 2030.[26]

In the Power sector, Japan aims to use 0.3 MMTpa in electricity generation by 2030 (corresponding to 1 GW of power capacity), rising to 5–10 MMTpa (15–30 GW) in the longer term.[27]

### C. Supply

#### 1. Focus

Japan is highly focused on securing access to hydrogen feedstocks. A large renewable hydrogen research and production facility opened in Fukushima Prefecture in March 2020, with 10 MW of production capacity (the largest in the world). Meanwhile, the Japanese government and industry are involved in several bilateral supply chain projects with partner countries.[28]

#### 2. Policies

Japan provides significant funding for hydrogen research development and demonstration, including more than $600 million USD in 2020. Hydrogen projects are also eligible for the Green Innovation Fund, dedicated to developing carbon-neutral projects and large-scale supply chains.[29]

Overall, the Japanese government has committed to invest more than $100 billion USD over the

---

23  https://www.csis.org/analysis/japans-hydrogen-industrial-strategy.

24  https://www.meti.go.jp/english/press/2020/pdf/1225_001b.pdf.

25  https://www.csis.org/analysis/japans-hydrogen-industrial-strategy.

26  https://cms.law/en/int/expert-guides/cms-expert-guide-to-hydrogen/japan.

27  IEA Global Energy Review 2021. https://iea.blob.core.windows.net/assets/5bd46d7b-906a-4429-abda-e9c507a62341/GlobalHydrogenReview2021.pdf.

28  Jane Nakano, 2021. "Japan's Hydrogen Industrial Strategy." CSIS. https://www.csis.org/analysis/japans-hydrogen-industrial-strategy.

29  https://www.csis.org/analysis/japans-hydrogen-industrial-strategy.

next 15 years to promote hydrogen production and use.[30]

Japan plans to enact new legislation to financially support industries involved in LCI $H_2$ and ammonia production and distribution. This will likely include a subsidy of the difference in price between hydrogen (or ammonia) and existing fossil fuels (LNG or coal) for 15 years. In total, more than $50 billion USD of subsidies are expected over the next 10 years to help establish a hydrogen and ammonia supply network,[31] with a goal of reducing the production costs of clean hydrogen by two-thirds.[32]

## D. Infrastructure

### 1. Focus

Japan's public and private sectors are investing heavily in the development of maritime transport. R&D is focused on several different hydrogen carriers, including liquefied hydrogen, methylcyclohexane, ammonia, and methanation.

### 2. Policies

The Japanese government also provides financial support for the construction and operation of hydrogen refueling stations. At more than 130 stations nationwide, it currently has the largest fleet of hydrogen refueling stations in the world.[33]

## E. Demand

### 1. Focus

Japan has adopted a broad end-use approach, including the Power, Transportation, heavy Industry, and refining sectors, along with Residential. Japan is particularly interested in leveraging a first-mover advantage in fuel cell technology and is keen on exporting FCEV technology to the rest of the world.

Japan sees the Power sector as a means to increase hydrogen demand in the future (after 2030). In 2017, Japan's Chugoku Electric Power Corporation successfully demonstrated cofiring a 1% share of ammonia in a commercial coal power plant. Japan's largest utility (JERA) plans to transition to 20% ammonia cofiring by 2024, and smaller projects are under development with up to 100% ammonia.[34]

### 2. Policies

Some hydrogen uptake in the Power sector is being driven by a new efficiency standard for coal power, which requires generators at coal plants to meet a fleetwide energy efficiency of 43% by 2030. Existing plants can meet that standard by cofiring existing coal plants with ammonia.[35]

In the Transportation sector, Japan aims to make FCEVs price competitive with hybrid electric vehicles by reducing the cost of fuel cells, hydrogen storage systems, and hydrogen refueling stations. Japan is also exploring hydrogen- and ammonia-fueled ships to meet IMO standards on GHG emissions for global shipping.[36]

## F. Trade Agreements

Some recent international agreements include:

- In 2022, Japan received the world's first international shipment of liquefied hydrogen from Australia[37]

- Clean Hydrogen Partnership with the Quad to develop a supply chain in the Indo-Pacific[38]

- MOU with California on low-carbon energy[39]

30 https://www.reuters.com/business/energy/japan-invest-107-bln-hydrogen-supply-over-15-years-2023-06-06/.

31 Daisuke Akimoto, 2023. "Japan looks to promote a hydrogen society." The Diplomat.

32 https://www.economist.com/business/2021/07/24/japan-inc-wants-to-become-a-hydrogen-superpower.

33 https://www.csis.org/analysis/japans-hydrogen-industrial-strategy.

34 IEA Global Hydrogen Review. 2022. https://iea.blob.core.windows.net/assets/c5bc75b1-9e4d-460d-9056-6e8e626a11c4/GlobalHydrogenReview2022.pdf.

35 https://asia.nikkei.com/Spotlight/Environment/Climate-Change/Bucking-trend-Japan-to-keep-coal-power-plants-under-tougher-rules.

36 IEA Global Hydrogen Review. 2021. https://iea.blob.core.windows.net/assets/5bd46d7b-906a-4429-abda-e9c507a62341/GlobalHydrogenReview2021.pdf.

37 https://www.dfat.gov.au/about-us/publications/trade-investment/business-envoy/business-envoy-february-2022/clean-hydrogen-collaboration-japan.

38 https://www.whitehouse.gov/briefing-room/statements-releases/2021/09/24/fact-sheet-quad-leaders-summit/.

39 https://www.gov.ca.gov/2022/03/21/california-and-japan-partner-to-bolster-economic-relations-and-trade-tackle-climate-change/.

- Agreement with United Arab Emirates to cooperate on technology development, regulatory frameworks, and standards to create an international hydrogen supply chain[40]

- Agreement with Argentina to strengthen collaboration on the use of clean fuels and promote investments to deploy large-scale hydrogen production from renewable energy[41]

### G. Other: Carbon Footprint/LCA

Japan's revised Hydrogen Strategy includes an emissions intensity standard to define LCI $H_2$ as 3.4 $kgCO_2/kgH_2$ on a well-to-gate basis, as well as target less than 0.84 $kgCO_2/kgNH_3$ for ammonia on a gate-to-gate basis.[42]

## IX. SINGAPORE

### A. Hydrogen Strategy

Singapore released its National Hydrogen Strategy in late 2022 as part of Singapore International Energy Week.[43] This comprehensive document outlines Singapore's journey toward net zero in its key industries and the importance of investment in technology advancement, international collaboration, and infrastructure planning. Hydrogen is expected to play an important role in energy security and resilience as well as a pathway to lowering carbon emissions to support Singapore's transition toward net zero by 2050.

Singapore sees hydrogen as a pathway to domestic emissions reductions, playing a role to lower carbon emissions in the Power and Industrial sectors, as well as a solution for lowering the carbon emissions in the maritime and aviation sectors, both of which Singapore is a global hub for.

Singapore has focused on five key areas as part of its strategy:

1. Advancing hydrogen technologies on the verge of commercial readiness

2. Investing in R&D

3. Pursuing international collaborations to enable supply chains

4. Undertaking long-term land and infrastructure planning

5. Supporting workforce training and development

### B. Deployment Targets/Timing

Singapore's hydrogen ambitions are all tied to its goal to have net zero emissions by 2050. As a small and densely populated city-state, Singapore has limited in-country abilities to help support these goals.

The Power sector in Singapore currently accounts for about 40% of its primary greenhouse gas emissions; therefore, lowering the carbon emissions of this sector is a key focus for the government. In March 2022, the Energy 2050 Committee commissioned by the Energy Market Authority made recommendations on how Singapore can lower the CI of the Power sector, noting that hydrogen could be a major component of Singapore's 2050 fuel mix, depending on technological developments and the extent of international cooperation in the low-carbon energy trade. Further, the 2022 National Hydrogen Strategy assessed that hydrogen has the potential to supply up to 50% of Singapore's projected electricity demand by 2050, given recent developments in the global energy market and further acceleration in momentum behind hydrogen. That said, the eventual fuel mix is not expected to be fixed and will depend on the development of technologies over time.

Singapore's Industrial sector base is immensely important, accounting for nearly 21% of the GDP—but it also accounted for 44% of its total emissions in 2020. Therefore, lowering the CI of the Industrial sector will be important to keep the sector competitive and to achieve Singapore's net zero targets. Singapore sees hydrogen as a pathway to lower the carbon emissions of this sector

---

40 https://www.iea.org/policies/13316-memorandum-of-cooperation-moc-on-hydrogen-between-japan-and-uae.

41 http://www.ngvjournal.com/s1-news/c7-lng-h2-blends/argentina-and-japan-join-forces-to-promote-the-use-of-hydrogen-as-clean-fuel/#:~:text=Espa%C3%B1ol-Argentina%20and%20Japan%20join%20forces%20to%20promote,of%20hydrogen%20as%20clean%20fuel&text=Within%20the%20framework%20of%20the,a%20non%2Dpolluting%20fuel%20source.

42 https://www.spglobal.com/commodityinsights/en/market-insights/latest-news/energy-transition/072123-interview-japans-eneos-shifts-into-high-gear-for-hydrogen-as-new-landscape-emerges#:~:text=Japan%20will%20aim%20to%20achieve,intensity%20for%20ammonia%20by%202030.

43 https://www.mti.gov.sg/Industries/Hydrogen.

as both a feedstock for industrial processes as well as a fuel for heat, power, and steam generation. Hydrogen has been identified as a key enabler in Singapore's Sustainable Jurong Island plan to lower the carbon emissions of the energy and chemical sector.[44]

Singapore and the Port of Singapore play a critical role in the international shipment of goods, but also as the largest bunkering port in the world. Therefore, Singapore can play a leading role in lowering the CI of this sector, including the use of low-carbon fuels. Singapore captures its strategy, including the use of hydrogen and hydrogen derivatives, in its Maritime Singapore Decarbonization Blueprint: Working Toward 2050 released in 2022. The transition is projected to include the use of biofuels, methanol, and ammonia, with liquid hydrogen playing a role in the longer term. Beyond shipping, port operations is another target sector identified in the National Hydrogen Strategy. Focus areas include container handling operations and local harbor craft being fueled by net zero fuels.

Singapore is also home to a global aviation hub at Singapore Changi International Airport (SIN). Singapore envisions SIN as being a leader in the development of SAFs, including opening the world's largest production plan for SAFs in 2023. LCI $H_2$ will be an important part of supporting the production of SAFs in the near term. Other areas for potential hydrogen use include on the airport operations side, with SIN looking at opportunities to lower the carbon emissions of all airside vehicles.

Land transportation is mentioned in the National Hydrogen Strategy, but more so as a watch-and-see sector as technology develops. Currently, Singapore seems to be more focused on the electrification of vehicles.

## C. Supply

### 1. Focus

Singapore is primarily focused on the importation of hydrogen and hydrogen derivatives at this point with no stated goals of hydrogen production. In the near term, Singapore plans to build capabilities in importing, handling, and utilizing low carbon intensity ammonia as a hydrogen carrier or directly as a fuel in power generation as well as support for marine bunkering needs. In December 2022, Singapore launched an Expression of Interest (EOI) to solicit proposals from industry players to develop an end-to-end ammonia value chain for power generation and marine bunkering.

### 2. Policies

Through pathfinder projects, such as the ammonia EOI, Singapore plans to work with industry to facilitate the cocreation of solutions to regulatory- and infrastructure-related challenges.

## D. Infrastructure

### 1. Focus

As part of its National Hydrogen Strategy, Singapore is currently assessing what a storage and distribution network may look like. In the nation's strategy, Singapore contemplates blending up to 10% $H_2$ into existing natural gas pipelines, but also highlights the potential need to build a dedicated hydrogen distribution network.

### 2. Policies

Similar to the supply side, there is an expectation as part of the recent EOIs that industry and the Singapore government will work together to develop a plan for infrastructure.

## E. Demand

### 1. Focus

As outlined above, Singapore has prioritized the Power sector, Industrial sector, maritime fuels, aviation, and land transportation.

### 2. Policies

Not applicable currently.

## F. Public Investment

Singapore introduced the Low-Carbon Energy Research (LCER) Funding Initiative in 2020. The

---

44 https://www.edb.gov.sg/en/about-edb/media-releases-publications/sustainable-jurong-island-edb-outlines-plans-to-transform-jurong-island-into-a-sustainability-showcase-for-energy-and-chemicals.html.

first phase of the program awarded S $55 million to projects aiming to improve the technoeconomic viability of low-carbon technologies such as CCUS and hydrogen. The LCER funded projects in areas such as the development of catalysts for ammonia cracking and methane pyrolysis.

Given the rapid developments in the global hydrogen economy, more resources will be committed to support hydrogen R&D and innovation. An additional S $129 million of research funding under LCER Phase 2 was recently announced to support the development of low-carbon technologies with an initial focus on $H_2$.

## G. Trade Agreements

- Singapore is part of the Indo-Pacific Economic Framework for Prosperity (IPEF), which aims to advance cooperation on clean energy and climate-friendly technologies, as well as mobilize investment and promote usage of low- and zero-emissions goods and services.

- Singapore and the United States signed the Singapore Partnership for Growth and Innovation in 2021. Clean energy and technologies are one of four focus areas.

- Singapore and New Zealand signed an Arrangement of Cooperation on LCI $H_2$ in 2021.

- Australia and Singapore (October 2020 and June 2021) created an MOU to advance low-emissions technologies and solutions, with a priority focus on Hydrogen, Carbon Capture Utilization and Storage. They also established a $30 million AUD partnership to accelerate the deployment of low-emissions fuels and technologies in maritime and port operations.

## H. Export Goals

Singapore does not intend to be a large-scale exporter of hydrogen.

## I. Other: Carbon Footprint/LCA

The tentative threshold for fossil fuel-based hydrogen with carbon capture being considered is 5 kgCO$_2$e/kgH$_2$ (accounting for approximately a 60% reduction in CI from the fossil fuel baseline), with future tightening possible. The calculation would be on a well-to-gate basis for domestic production and a well-to-import for imports.[45]

## X. SOUTH KOREA

### A. Hydrogen Strategy

South Korea adopted its Hydrogen Economy Roadmap in 2019 and Basic Plan for Implementing the Hydrogen Economy of Korea in 2021. Together, these documents outline a goal of becoming the world's leading hydrogen economy—including achieving the world's largest market share in hydrogen fuel cells and fuel cell vehicles and becoming a hydrogen producer. South Korea sees hydrogen as an engine of economic growth and job creation, as well as a key decarbonization tool.

### B. Deployment Targets/Timing

South Korea aims to deploy 3.9 MMTpa by 2030 (including 50% overseas production) and 28 MMTpa by 2050 (with 82% overseas production).[46]

Within the Power sector, Korea aims to progressively replace coal power plants with 20% ammonia cofiring by 2027 and 50% hydrogen cofiring by 2030—and 100% ammonia and hydrogen firing by 2050.[47] Overall, ammonia is expected to account for 3.6% of power generation by 2030,[48] while hydrogen-based fuels will account for up to 21.5% of power generation by 2050.[49]

South Korea has also set strong targets for hydrogen usage. By 2040, it aims to domestically produce 2.9 million FCEVs, 30,000 fuel cell trucks, and 40,000 fuel cell buses. It also seeks to expand the fleet of hydrogen refueling stations

---

45 Hinicio SA & Ludwig-Bolkow-Systemtechnik GmbH. 2022. "A roadmap for robust certification for hydrogen." Slides from 8th Task Team 3 meeting, Hydrogen Council. September 21, 2022.

46 https://www.spglobal.com/commodityinsights/en/market-insights/latest-news/energy-transition/112621-s-korea-to-provide-279-mil-mtyear-of-clean-hydrogen-by-2050.

47 https://www.ammoniaenergy.org/articles/south-korea-sets-targets-for-hydrogen-ammonia-power-generation/.

48 https://iea.blob.core.windows.net/assets/a57dae0b-4b80-429b-bf37-eaa33041c4b7/StrategiesforCoalTransitioninKorea.pdf.

49 https://www.ammoniaenergy.org/articles/south-korea-sets-targets-for-hydrogen-ammonia-power-generation/.

from two dozen such stations in 2019 to 1,200 by 2040, while deploying 15 GW of utility-scale fuel cells.[50]

## C. Supply

### 1. Focus

South Korea's hydrogen strategy includes a near-term focus on natural gas with CCS hydrogen (leveraging the country's extensive LNG networks) and a shift to renewable hydrogen as demand rises. By 2050, the country aims to produce 3 MMTpa of renewable hydrogen and 2 MMTpa of natural gas with CCS hydrogen. Imports will account for the remaining 23 MMTpa of supply.[51]

Ammonia is currently promoted as the main carrier of hydrogen, although a large degree of interest in liquid hydrogen has arisen as well. For example, a public-private renewable ammonia alliance was launched in 2021 by 13 energy and industrial firms, with ammonia produced at domestic firms' overseas sites.[52]

### 2. Policies

The South Korean government promotes hydrogen through a variety of R&D subsidies, loans, and tax exemptions, with its annual budget for the hydrogen economy reaching $700 million USD in 2021.[53] South Korea has outlined a goal of nurturing 1,000 hydrogen-based companies by 2040, including providing incentives for companies converting into a hydrogen business, supporting tech sharing between companies, and offering public loans for hydrogen-related projects of up to $8.4 million.[54]

South Korea has also implemented a series of "hydrogen city" projects, starting with three pilot projects in Ulsan, Ansan, and Jeonji. These pilots, designed to test hydrogen's application in transportation, industry, and space heating, are now being followed up with another six hydrogen cities in Pyeongtaek, Namyangju, Dangjin, Boryeong, Gwangyang, and Pohang. Each city will receive $30 million (USD) per year of public funds and will demonstrate a different aspect of the hydrogen economy. For example, Pyeongtaek will construct a new hydrogen port and "blue hydrogen production special complex" for residential and commercial buildings, while Namyangju will demonstrate a self-sufficient hydrogen network with fuel cells in public buildings along with new waste-to-hydrogen and biogas-based production facilities.[55]

In addition to the public support provided for hydrogen development, the private sector is investing heavily. A privately led hydrogen fund was launched in July 2022, with a goal of raising $381 million by the end of the year.[56]

## D. Infrastructure

### 1. Focus

South Korea's hydrogen roadmap lays out a long-term goal of building a specialized hydrogen pipeline network throughout the country. Much of this will come from converting natural gas supply pipelines to hydrogen blends (20% by 2025) and eventually unblended hydrogen.[57]

South Korea has also dedicated resources to R&D on liquefied hydrogen storage technology, as well as the development of hydrogen-receiving infrastructure to enable imports.[58]

50 Nakano, Jane. 2021. "South Korea's Hydrogen Industrial Strategy." CSIS. https://www.csis.org/analysis/south-koreas-hydrogen-industrial-strategy.

51 https://www.spglobal.com/commodityinsights/en/market-insights/latest-news/energy-transition/112621-s-korea-to-provide-279-mil-mtyear-of-clean-hydrogen-by-2050#.

52 https://www.ammoniaenergy.org/articles/the-korean-green-ammonia-alliance/.

53 https://www.csis.org/analysis/south-koreas-hydrogen-industrial-strategy.

54 https://cms.law/en/int/expert-guides/cms-expert-guide-to-hydrogen/south-korea.

55 Collins, Leigh. 2023. "South Korea to create six 'hydrogen cities' that would use $H_2$ in buildings and transport as part of daily life." Hydrogen Insight. https://www.hydrogeninsight.com/policy/south-korea-to-create-six-hydrogen-cities-that-would-use-h2-in-buildings-and-transport-as-part-of-daily-life/2-1-1385821.

56 Argus Media. 2022. "S Korea looks to roll out $H_2$ certification system." https://www.argusmedia.com/en/news/2353013-s-korea-looks-to-roll-out-h2-certification-system.

57 https://www.iea.org/policies/6566-korea-hydrogen-economy-roadmap-2040.

58 Nakano, Jane. 2021. "South Korea's Hydrogen Industrial Strategy." CSIS. https://www.csis.org/analysis/south-koreas-hydrogen-industrial-strategy.

## 2. Policies

To address the short-term profitability challenges of hydrogen infrastructure investments, the government is considering a "Build-Transfer-Lease" model of development. Under this model, the private sector would construct hydrogen infrastructure, transfer ownership to the government, and lease it back over a 30- or 50-year period.[59]

### E. Demand

#### 1. Focus

South Korea has prioritized Transportation, Power, and Industry as primary end uses for hydrogen.

#### 2. Policies

In the Transportation sector, the government has committed more than $2 billion to build a public-private hydrogen vehicle industry. It subsidizes nearly half the cost of installing hydrogen refueling stations and offers subsidies of $27,300 to $30,300 for FCEVs and up to $250,000 for fuel cell buses.[60, 61]

Hydrogen uptake in the Power sector is being driven by South Korea's renewable portfolio standard (RPS), which requires power companies with more than 500 MW of installed capacity to increase generation from new and renewable technologies, including fuel cells.

Within the RPS system, fuel cells receive a higher level of renewable electricity certificate "credit," which has ensured revenues of at least $0.15/kWh and contributed to significant utility-scale fuel cell capacity being built (370 MW by 2021).[62] The government will introduce plans for a more comprehensive "clean hydrogen power system" for $H_2$ power plants in 2023.[63]

The government has also introduced subsidies for fuel cells in residential and commercial buildings, covering up to 80% of equipment installation costs and offering 6.5% price savings on grid natural gas used in fuel cells. However, the total installed stationary fuel cell capacity was still relatively low by 2021, at 15.7 MWe.[64]

### F. Trade Agreements

- South Korea is part of the Indo-Pacific Economic Framework for Prosperity (IPEF), which aims to advance cooperation on clean energy and climate-friendly technologies, as well as mobilize investment and promote usage of low- and zero-emissions goods and services.[65]

- Korea has signed a MOU with the Australian government to expand hydrogen cooperation—including imports of hydrogen, exports of FCEVs, and cooperation on R&D for liquefaction technology.[66]

- South Korea has also signed MOUs with Norway (for cooperation around hydrogen and shipping),[67] Saudi Arabia (provision of LNG for South Korea to produce hydrogen),[68] and Israel.[69]

- It has signed a letter of intent to investigate the development of a liquid hydrogen supply chain between New Zealand and South Korea.[70]

59  CMS. 2021. "Hydrogen Law, Regulations & Strategy in South Korea." https://cms.law/en/int/expert-guides/cms-expert-guide-to-hydrogen/south-korea.

60  Nakano, Jane. 2021. "South Korea's Hydrogen Industrial Strategy." CSIS. https://www.csis.org/analysis/south-koreas-hydrogen-industrial-strategy.

61  IEA Global Hydrogen Review. 2021. https://iea.blob.core.windows.net/assets/3a2ed84c-9ea0-458c-9421-d166a9510bc0/GlobalHydrogenReview2021.pdf.

62  Intralink. 2021. "The Hydrogen Economy South Korea – Market Intelligence Report." https://www.intralinkgroup.com/getmedia/daeb142b-c1c2-420c-b3bc-93e2e36f4c94/Korean-Market-Intelligence-Report-Hydrogen-Economy-April-2021pdf.

63  Argus Media. 2022. "S Korea looks to roll out $H_2$ certification system." https://www.argusmedia.com/en/news/2353013-s-korea-looks-to-roll-out-h2-certification-system.

64  IEA Global Hydrogen Review 2021. https://iea.blob.core.windows.net/assets/3a2ed84c-9ea0-458c-9421-d166a9510bc0/GlobalHydrogenReview2021.pdf.

65  https://www.ifri.org/sites/default/files/atoms/files/av133_south-korea-ipef_choo_fev-2023.pdf.

66  https://www.argusmedia.com/en/news/2270023-australia-south-korea-partner-on-hydrogen-technology.

67  https://www.koreaherald.com/view.php?ud=20190613000650.

68  https://www.arabnews.com/node/2006701/business-economy.

69  https://www.koreatimes.co.kr/www/nation/2023/06/113_272303.html.

70  https://koreatimes.co.kr/www/nation/2020/08/176_280362.html.

## G. Other

In 2020, the Hydrogen Economy Promotion and Hydrogen Safety Management Act ("Hydrogen Act") was passed, regulating the hydrogen industry. This includes certain safety requirements, including technical review and periodic inspections by the Korea Gas Safety Corporation and the issuance of manufacturing licenses to domestic producers.[71]

## H. Carbon Footprint/LCA

Korea's industry and trade ministry is in the process of developing a Clean Hydrogen Certification System, which was planned to go into effect in 2024. The system will require energy companies to use LCI $H_2$, while taking into account hydrogen production methods, international trends, and domestic industrial status. It will include definitions for carbon-free hydrogen, low-carbon hydrogen, and low-carbon hydrogen compounds.[72] Initial news stories suggest Korea is considering certifications for renewable hydrogen (renewable electricity through a direct connection or grid with PPA), natural gas with CCS hydrogen, hydrogen derivatives, biomass or waste-based hydrogen, and nuclear-based hydrogen.[73]

# XI. UNITED KINGDOM & SCOTLAND

## A. Hydrogen Strategy

The United Kingdom first released a hydrogen strategy in 2021 and decided to update it in 2022.[74] In parallel, the hydrogen Scottish plan was released in 2022.[75]

## B. Deployment Targets/Timing

In the United Kingdom, hydrogen use is currently concentrated in chemicals and refineries

and is produced from natural gas. The government estimates that 250–460 TWh of hydrogen could be needed in 2050, making up 20%–35% of the final energy consumption.

### 1. Focus

In its strategy, the United Kingdom is considering installing 10GW of production capacity by 2030 with at least 50% from electrolytic hydrogen. By 2025, 1GW of electrolytic hydrogen and up to 1GW of CCUS-enabled methane reformation should be operational or in construction. In Scotland, the supply capacity is defined at 5GW by 2030 and 25GW by 2045.

Unlike Continental Europe, the United Kingdom and Scotland have an agnostic approach on hydrogen production pathways—they support renewable and low-carbon hydrogen as long as the hydrogen meets the U.K.'s Low Carbon Hydrogen Standard.

### 2. Policies

The United Kingdom has already committed public subsidies to support the production of hydrogen with the Net Zero Hydrogen Fund (£240 million). The United Kingdom has also consulted the stakeholders on a business model for LCI $H_2$ that could lead to a Contract for Difference to address the market price risk in the early stages of the creation of the LCI $H_2$ economy. Scotland has £100m funding for renewable $H_2$ projects in the next five years.

## C. Infrastructure

### 1. Focus

In the United Kingdom, the infrastructure is expected to go from direct pipelines and vehicular transport in the early to mid-2020s, to a large cluster-wide network in the late 2020s as the number of consumers in the clusters increases. From the mid-2030s, a regional or even a national network could be needed as new consumers become more geographically dispersed.

### 2. Policies

A business model for hydrogen transport infrastructure specifically is not currently available to

71 Byung-wook, Kim. 2021. "World's first 'hydrogen law' takes effect. What's in it?" *Korea Herald.* http://www.koreaherald.com/view.php?ud=20210208000926.

72 Shin & Kim, 2022. "Promoting the Korean Hydrogen Economy." https://www.shinkim.com/eng/media/newsletter/1818.

73 https://www.argusmedia.com/en/news-and-insights/latest-market-news/2440217-s-korea-outlines-clean-hydrogen-certification-system.

74 https://www.gov.uk/government/publications/uk-hydrogen-strategy.

75 https://www.gov.scot/publications/hydrogen-action-plan/.

allow for the development of pipelines. The U.K. government has recently consulted stakeholders on different business model designs for the regulations of these infrastructures.

Moreover, a policy decision was made in 2023 to allow up to 20% hydrogen blending (by volume) in the gas networks.

## D. Demand

### 1. Focus

For the U.K. government, the main focus for hydrogen demand will be the following sectors: Industry, Power, Transport, and potentially heat. Scotland has a similar approach with hard-to-electrify sectors, including transport for large and heavy vehicles, energy-intensive industries, domestic heating via the gas grid, and flexibility, balancing, and resilience energy services.

### 2. Policies

The United Kingdom introduced several demand-side support policies: Zero Emission Road Freight Demonstration (£200 million), $H_2$ Village trials, Industrial Energy Transition Fund Phase 2 (£70 million), Industrial $H_2$ Accelerator Programme (£26 million), Hydrogen Bioenergy with CCS Innovation Programme (£5 million), Clean Steel Fund (£250 million), Industrial Fuel Switching Competition (£55 million), Clean Maritime Demonstration Competition Round 2 (£12 million), and Zero Emission Bus Regional Areas (£270 million).

In addition, the United Kingdom introduced a carbon price for the Industrial sector (U.K. ETS) as well as a Renewable Transport Fuel Obligation to promote biofuels and renewable fuels, including LCI $H_2$, into the Transportation sector.

## E. Trade Agreements

In December 2022, the United Kingdom and United States formed an Energy Security and Affordability Partnership to reduce global reliance on Russian energy by driving efforts to increase energy efficiency, supporting the transition to clean energy, expediting the development of clean hydrogen globally, and promoting civil nuclear as a secure use of energy.[76]

## F. Other: Carbon Footprint/LCA

A hydrogen certification system for exports and imports is targeted to be established by 2025. The threshold used to qualify as LCI $H_2$ is 2.4kg$CO_2$/kg$H_2$ in the United Kingdom.

---

76  https://www.state.gov/civil-nuclear-and-clean-energy-initiatives/.

# *Appendix P*

# INTERSTATE HYDROGEN PIPELINE REGIME COMPARISON

This appendix provides a summary of federal interstate pipeline regimes as further background to the discussions in Chapter 6: Policy.

Three federal regimes currently regulate the rates, terms, and conditions of service of interstate pipelines, none of which have been applied to dedicated (i.e., unblended) hydrogen pipelines: 1) the Interstate Commerce Commission Termination Act (ICCTA) administered by the Surface Transportation Board (STB); 2) the Interstate Commerce Act administered by the Federal Energy Regulatory Commission (FERC); and 3) the Natural Gas Act (NGA) administered by FERC.

The analysis below summarizes these regimes to evaluate their relative strengths and weaknesses, and to assess whether one of these existing regimes is preferable for the regulation of unblended $H_2$ pipelines. Additionally, this section evaluates the merits of exempting unblended $H_2$ interstate pipelines from regulation or enacting a new regulatory regime specifically for unblended $H_2$ transportation that draws upon aspects of the various regimes already in effect. This analysis does not address state regulation or noneconomic federal regulations such as those involving safety, international trade, or federal lands.

## I. CURRENT STATE OF HYDROGEN PIPELINES

There are more than 1,600 miles of unblended $H_2$ pipelines in the United States primarily serving the petrochemical (i.e., petroleum refining)

sector. These pipelines have existed for decades without federal regulation applied to their economic practices. These pipelines are owned and operated by a small group of industrial gas companies. There is little interest or ability on the part of third parties to use this existing infrastructure that operates as functionally deregulated.

## II. INTERSTATE COMMERCE COMMISSION TERMINATION ACT (ICCTA)

### A. Background

The STB regulates interstate pipelines carrying "commodit[ies] other than water, gas, or oil."[1] This authority originates in 1906 with the Hepburn Act, which gave the Interstate Commerce Commission (ICC, the STB's predecessor) authority over the interstate "transportation of oil or other commodity, except water and except natural or artificial gas, by means of pipelines."[2] In 1977, the Department of Energy Organizational Act (DOE Act) split jurisdiction over Hepburn Act pipelines, transferring the regulation of those carrying oil to the newly created FERC, while leaving those carrying everything else to the oversight of the ICC.[3] In 1995, ICCTA dissolved the ICC and replaced it with the STB, which retained the same

---

1  "49 U.S. Code § 15301: General Pipeline Jurisdiction." Cornell Law School, Legal Information Institute. December 29, 1995. https://www.law.cornell.edu/uscode/text/49/15301.

2  "34 Stat.584 (Public Law 59-337)." USLawLink. 1906. https://uslaw.link/citation/stat/34/584.

3  "Public Law 95-91." U.S. Government Publishing Office. 1977. https://www.govinfo.gov/content/pkg/STATUTE-91/pdf/STATUTE-91-Pg565.pdf.

jurisdictional delineations put in place in 1906 and 1977.[4]

In general, there is much less ICC and STB precedent applicable to Hepburn Act pipelines than there is FERC precedent. To date, analyses included in government publications have all indicated a belief that $H_2$ pipelines fall within the scope of STB's ICCTA jurisdiction.[5,6,7] However, the STB has not yet had cause to address whether it has jurisdiction over interstate $H_2$ pipelines under ICCTA.

## B. Reach of Regulation

ICCTA applies to transportation between states or between a state and a foreign country.[8] However, it does not cover other aspects of the value chain, such as storage or commodity purchases and sales. When a shipment through a pipeline occurs entirely within one state, it may not be clear whether that transportation is considered an interstate movement, especially when the pipeline transports both interstate and intrastate traffic. There is no recent STB precedent regarding this aspect of the agency's jurisdiction, but decisions of the ICC and Supreme Court focus on the essential character of the commerce from the perspective of the shipper to determine whether the transporta-

tion is part of a larger interstate, or international, movement.[9]

Even if a pipeline movement crosses state or international boundaries, there is a narrow exemption under ICCTA called the Uncle Sam rule. This exemption states that contained pipeline systems are not jurisdictional—like when a pipeline crosses state lines but only transports oil from the owner's well to the owner's refinery.[10] The movement is therefore contained to only transporting the product of a single shipper for a single purpose. This exemption rarely applies.

ICCTA does not permit the STB to investigate a pipeline unless acting according to a complaint.[11] Further, any complaint that is not resolved by the STB with a final order within three years is automatically dismissed.[12]

## C. Regulation of Infrastructure

The STB has no authority over the siting of pipelines. No federal certificates are required to construct or expand an STB-regulated pipeline, to commence or abandon service, or to convert a pipeline to another service. Relatedly, the ICCTA does not grant federal eminent domain power or preempt state regulation. As such, interstate pipelines subject to the ICCTA must obtain any applicable state and local permits for construction and siting from each jurisdiction in which their facilities are to be located.

## D. Economic Regulation

ICCTA is a common carrier regime. Under ICCTA, a pipeline must "provide the transportation or service on reasonable

4  "Interstate Commerce Commission Termination Act of 1995." Federal Trade Commission. July 19, 2013. https://www.ftc.gov/legal-library/browse/statutes/interstate-commerce-commission-termination-act-1995.

5  "Pipeline Transportation of Hydrogen: Regulation, Research, and Policy." Congressional Research Service. March 2, 2021. https://crsreports.congress.gov/product/pdf/R/R46700.

6  Department of Transportation, Research, and Innovative Technology Administration. "72 FR 609: Statement Regarding a Coordinated Framework for Regulation of a Hydrogen Economy." *Federal Register*, Vol. 72, No. 3, January 5, 2007: 609-624. https://www.federalregister.gov/documents/2007/01/05/E6-22554/statement-regarding-a-coordinated-framework-for-regulation-of-a-hydrogen-economy.

7  "Surface Transportation: Issues Associated with Pipeline Regulation by the Surface Transportation Board." U.S. Government Accountability Office. April 21, 1998. https://www.gao.gov/products/rced-98-99. https://www.gao.gov/products/rced-98-99.

8  "49 U.S. Code § 15301: General Pipeline Jurisdiction." Cornell Law School, Legal Information Institute. December 29, 1995. https://www.law.cornell.edu/uscode/text/49/15301.

9  "Aircraft Serv. Int'l, Inc. V. Fed. Energy Regulatory Comm'n, 985 F.3d 1013." Casetext. January 22, 2021. https://casetext.com/case/aircraft-serv-intl-inc-v-fed-energy-regulatory-commn.

10  "U.S. Reports: The Pipe Line Cases, 234 U.S. 548 (1914)." Library of Congress. 1914. https://www.loc.gov/item/usrep234548/.

11  "49 U.S. Code § 15901-General Authority." Cornell Law School, Legal Information Institute. December 29, 1995. https://www.law.cornell.edu/uscode/text/49/15901#b.

12  "49 U.S. Code § 15901-General Authority." Cornell Law School, Legal Information Institute. December 29, 1995. https://www.law.cornell.edu/uscode/text/49/15901#b.

request."[13] STB regulations also require pipelines to "promptly establish and provide to the requester a rate and applicable service terms" upon request where the pipeline does not yet have an existing tariff.[14]

Unlike the Interstate Commerce Act (ICA) and NGA, ICCTA does not require pipelines to publicly file their tariffs. However, ICCTA still requires pipelines to establish a tariff, setting forth rates and terms of service, and to promptly provide that tariff to any person upon reasonable request.[15, 16, 17] ICCTA pipelines must adhere to their tariffs and provide notice to shippers before changing them.[18, 19]

ICCTA pipelines must charge reasonable rates.[20] Based on its experience regulating railroads, the STB employs what it calls "constrained market pricing principles" that are aimed at determining the rate a carrier would need to charge to stay in business without cross-subsidies of traffic.[21] Rates meeting this standard are considered reasonable. ICCTA pipelines whose rates are challenged can claim as an affirmative defense that they lack market power to defend their existing rate levels in response to a complaint without seeking prior authorization to charge market-based rates.[22]

ICCTA prohibits pipelines from engaging in unreasonable discrimination.[23] This requirement creates uncertainty regarding how the agency would treat contracts for committed service because committed service contracts are facially discriminatory, in that they treat contract shippers differently than shippers who transport under the pipeline's tariff. The STB does not have a contract rate policy or body of precedent allowing such contracts under certain circumstances like FERC developed under its similar statute, the ICA.

## E. Other Regulation

Because ICCTA is limited to regulating interstate transportation, other parts of the value chain (such as storage and transactions) are subject to generally applicable state and federal law.

# III. INTERSTATE COMMERCE ACT (ICA)

## A. Background

FERC regulates interstate pipelines carrying oil under the ICA.[24] This authority originates in 1906 with the Hepburn Act, which gave the ICC authority over the interstate "transportation of oil or other commodity, except water and except natural or artificial gas, by means of pipelines."[25] In 1977, FERC assumed jurisdiction of pipelines carrying oil, which included "crude and refined petroleum and petroleum byproducts,

13 "49 U.S. Code § 15701-Providing Transportation and Service." Cornell Law School, Legal Information Institute. https://www.law.cornell.edu/uscode/text/49/15701.

14 "49 CFR § 1305.3: Response to Request for Establishment of a New Rate." Cornell Law School, Legal Information Institute. October 1, 2022. https://www.law.cornell.edu/cfr/text/49/1305.3.

15 "2011 U.S. Code: Title 49-Section 15502: Authority for Pipeline Carriers to Establish Rates, Classifications, Rules, and Practices." Justia Law. 2011. https://law.justia.com/codes/us/2011/title-49/subtitle-iv/part-c/chapter-155/section-15502.

16 "49 U.S. Code § 15701-Providing Transportation and Service." Cornell Law School, Legal Information Institute. https://www.law.cornell.edu/uscode/text/49/15701.

17 "49 CFR § 1305.2: Disclosure Requirement for Existing Rates." Cornell Law School, Legal Information Institute. 2014. https://www.law.cornell.edu/cfr/text/49/1305.2.

18 "49 U.S. Code § 15701-Providing Transportation and Service." Cornell Law School, Legal Information Institute. https://www.law.cornell.edu/uscode/text/49/15701.

19 "49 CFR § 1305.4: Notice Requirement." Cornell Law School, Legal Information Institute. October 1, 2023. https://www.law.cornell.edu/cfr/text/49/1305.4.

20 "49 U.S. Code § 15501: Standards for Pipeline Rates, Classifications, through Routes, Rules, and Practices." Cornell Law School, Legal Information Institute. https://www.law.cornell.edu/uscode/text/49/15501.

21 CF Indus., Inc. v. Koch Pipeline Co., L.P., 4 S.T.B. 637, 642-43 (2000) (citing Coal Rate Guidelines, Nationwide, 1 I.C.C. 2d 520 (1985)).

22 CF Industries v. Koch Pipeline, 4 S.T.B. at 655.

23 "49 U.S.C. § 15505: Prohibition against discrimination by pipeline carriers." Casetext. 1996. https://casetext.com/statute/united-states-code/title-49-transportation/subtitle-iv-interstate-transportation/part-b-motor-carriers-water-carriers-brokers-and-freight-forwarders/chapter-149-civil-and-criminal-penalties/part-c-pipeline-carriers/chapter-155-rates/section-15505-prohibition-against-discrimination-by-pipeline-carriers.

24 "49 U.S.C. app. §§ 1, et seq.: Interstate Commerce Act." Federal Energy Regulatory Commission. 1988. https://www.ferc.gov/sites/default/files/2020-06/Interstate-Commerce-Act.pdf.

25 "34 Stat. 584: An Act to Regulate Commerce." USLaw Link. 1906. https://uslaw.link/citation/stat/34/584.

derivatives or petrochemicals."[26] The Energy Policy Act of 1992 (EPAct 1992) directed FERC to develop simplified ratemaking procedures for ICA pipelines.[27]

Today, FERC's ICA pipelines include those carrying crude oil, refined petroleum products, and natural gas liquids.[28] The ICA's key statutory provisions are closely related to ICCTA, but FERC has a more robust set of policies and body of precedents applicable to ICA pipelines.

## B. Reach of Regulation

Under the ICA, transportation is regulated if it crosses a state or national boundary or, in cases in which the pipeline is located within a single state, the essential character of that transportation involves continuous movements across the facilities of multiple transporters with the intent of shipping a commodity through multiple states or internationally.[29] Many of FERC's ICA pipelines provide both FERC-regulated interstate and state-regulated or unregulated intrastate service on the same facilities.

Even when pipelines technically fall within the ICA's jurisdiction, FERC regularly grants indefinite waivers of the ICA's tariff filing and reporting requirements. These waivers are granted when: 1) the pipeline owns all the product shipped, 2) no third parties have requested access, 3) there is no likely interest from third parties in shipping, and 4) the request is unopposed.[30]

## C. Regulation of Infrastructure

FERC, like the STB, has no authority over the siting of pipelines subject to its jurisdiction under the ICA. The ICA does not require a certificate to construct or expand a pipeline, to commence or abandon service, or to convert a pipeline to another service. Relatedly, the ICA does not grant federal eminent domain power or preemption of state regulation. As such, interstate pipelines subject to the ICA must obtain any applicable state and local permits for construction and siting from each jurisdiction in which their facilities are to be located.

## D. Economic Regulation

The ICA is a common carrier regime with a robust body of precedent and regulations. ICA pipelines must provide transportation upon reasonable request.[31] ICA pipelines must publish their rates and terms of service in tariffs filed at FERC, must charge only those rates on file, and must apply to change their rates or terms of service.[32, 33] ICA pipelines also must maintain their books and records following FERC's Uniform System of Accounts and file an annual Form 6 disclosing the pipeline's cost and revenue data.[34, 35]

The ICA prohibits undue discrimination on the part of pipelines[36] and requires rates to be just and reasonable.[37] Under FERC's ICA

---

26  DOE Act § 306, 91 Stat. at 581; S. Rep. No. 95-367, at 69 (1st Sess. 1977) (Conf. Rep.); H.R. Rep. No. 95-539, at 69 (1st Sess. 1977) (Conf. Rep.)

27  "Public Law 102-486: To Provide for Improved Energy Efficiency." U.S. Government Publishing Office. October 24, 1992. https://www.govinfo.gov/content/pkg/STATUTE-106/pdf/STATUTE-106-Pg2776.pdf.

28  "925 F.2d 476: CF Industries v Federal Energy Regulatory Commission." FERC. 1991. https://www.ferc.gov/sites/default/files/2020-06/15.pdf.

29  "169 FERC ¶ 61,119: Aircraft Serv. Int'l Grp. v. Cent. Fl. Pipeline LLC." FERC. November 21, 2019. https://www.ferc.gov/sites/default/files/2020-07/11-2019-G-6.pdf.

30  "85 FR 77460: Roaring Fork Midstream, LLC; Notice of Request for Temporary Waiver." FERC. *Federal Register*, Vol. 85, No. 232, December 2, 2020: 77460. https://www.federalregister.gov/documents/2020/12/02/2020-26565/roaring-fork-midstream-llc-notice-of-request-for-temporary-waiver.

31  "49 U.S.C. app. §§ 1, et seq.: Interstate Commerce Act." FERC. 1988. https://www.ferc.gov/sites/default/files/2020-06/Interstate-Commerce-Act.pdf.

32  "ICA §§ 6(1) & 6(7): Interstate Commerce Act." FERC. 1988. https://www.ferc.gov/sites/default/files/2020-06/ica.pdf.

33  "18 CFR § 341.8: Terminal and Other Services." Cornell Law School, Legal Information Institute. 1993. https://www.law.cornell.edu/cfr/text/18/341.8.

34  "18 CFR Part 357-PART 357: Annual Special or Periodic: Carries Subject to Part 1 of the Interstate Commerce Act." Cornell Law School, Legal Information Institute. 1988. https://www.law.cornell.edu/cfr/text/18/part-357.

35  "49 U.S.C. app. §§ 1, et seq.: Interstate Commerce Act." FERC. 1988. https://www.ferc.gov/sites/default/files/2020-06/Interstate-Commerce-Act.pdf.

36  "49 U.S.C. app. §§ 1, et seq.: Interstate Commerce Act." FERC. 1988. https://www.ferc.gov/sites/default/files/2020-06/Interstate-Commerce-Act.pdf.

37  "49 U.S.C. app. §§ 1, et seq.: Interstate Commerce Act." FERC. 1988. https://www.ferc.gov/sites/default/files/2020-06/Interstate-Commerce-Act.pdf.

regime, there are several ways that a pipeline can choose to set or change these rates.[38] An ICA pipeline can set its rates by agreement with one or more unaffiliated shippers that intend to use the service, so long as no other interested party objects.[39] ICA pipelines also have the option to set rates on a traditional cost-of-service basis.[40,41] ICA pipelines can also increase their rates by implementing simplified procedures using an index designed to keep pace with inflation while accounting for cost changes unique to the pipeline industry.[42, 43] Most ICA pipeline rate changes occur by way of index adjustment. ICA pipelines can also set market-based rates if they can demonstrate to FERC through an application proceeding that they lack market power.[44, 45, 46] Finally, FERC has developed a body of precedent allowing ICA pipelines to contract firm-committed service on new or expanded infrastructure, if the pipeline first offers the ability to sign contracts to all interested shippers through a fair and transparent open season.[47, 48, 49] Pipelines utilizing contract rates must reserve some capacity for non-committed shippers.[50]

## E. Other Regulation

Because the ICA is limited to regulating interstate transportation, other parts of the value chain such as storage and transactions are subject to generally applicable state and federal law. Storage might be regulated, however, if it is an integral part of jurisdictional transportation.[51]

# IV. NATURAL GAS ACT

## A. Background

The Natural Gas Act (NGA) was passed in 1938.[52] Passage of the NGA was motivated by the need to regulate interstate transportation of natural gas that was beyond the reach of state authority. There have been many changes to the NGA since 1938, the most prominent being the Natural Gas Policy Act of 1978 (NPGA). That act began the gradual shift away from comprehensive regulation of the entirety of the natural gas industry toward more focused regulation on pipeline transportation.[53]

38 "18 CFR Part 342: Oil Pipeline Rate Methodologies and Procedures." Cornell Law School, Legal Information Institute. 1993. https://www.law.cornell.edu/cfr/text/18/part-342.

39 "18 CFR Part 342: Oil Pipeline Rate Methodologies and Procedures." Cornell Law School, Legal Information Institute. 1993. https://www.law.cornell.edu/cfr/text/18/part-342.

40 "18 CFR Part 342: Oil Pipeline Rate Methodologies and Procedures." Cornell Law School, Legal Information Institute. 1993. https://www.law.cornell.edu/cfr/text/18/part-342.

41 "31 FERC ¶ 61,377: Williams Pipe Line Company, Opinion No. 154-B." FERC. 1985. https://www.ferc.gov/sites/default/files/2020-04/opinion-154b_0.pdf.

42 "18 CFR Part 342: Oil Pipeline Rate Methodologies and Procedures." Cornell Law School, Legal Information Institute. 1993. https://www.law.cornell.edu/cfr/text/18/part-342.

43 "Ass'n of Oil Pipe Lines v. Fed. Energy Regulatory Commission." VLex. 2017. https://case-law.vlex.com/vid/ass-n-of-oil-890430820.

44 "18 CFR Part 342: Oil Pipeline Rate Methodologies and Procedures." Cornell Law School, Legal Information Institute. 1993. https://www.law.cornell.edu/cfr/text/18/part-342.

45 "572 FERC ¶ 31,007: Market Base Ratemaking for Oil Pipelines." FERC. 1994. https://www.ferc.gov/sites/default/files/2020-06/Order-No-572-Market-Based-Ratemaking-for-Oil-Pipelines.pdf.

46 "Association of Oil Pipe Lines v Federal Energy Regulatory Commission, 83 F.3d 1424." Casetext. May 10, 1996. https://casetext.com/case/association-of-oil-pipe-lines-v-ferc.

47 "86 FR 54964: Tesoro Logistics Northwest Pipeline LLC; Notice of Petition for Declaratory Order." FERC. Federal Register, Vol. 86, No. 190, October 5, 2021: 54964. https://www.federalregister.gov/documents/2021/10/05/2021-21700/tesoro-logistics-northwest-pipeline-llc-notice-of-petition-for-declaratory-order.

48 "87 FR 78670: Oil Pipeline Affiliate Committed Service." FERC. Federal Register, Vol. 87, No. 245, December 22, 2022: 78670-78679. https://www.federalregister.gov/documents/2022/12/22/2022-27850/oil-pipeline-affiliate-committed-service.

49 "146 FERC ¶ 61,206: Order on Petition for Declaratory Order." FERC. 2014. https://www.ferc.gov/sites/default/files/2020-06/Colonial%20Pipeline%20Company%2C.pdf.

50 "85 FR 66972: Oil Pipeline Affiliate Contracts." FERC. Federal Register, Vol. 85, No. 204, October 21, 2020: 66972-66981. https://www.federalregister.gov/documents/2020/10/21/2020-23289/oil-pipeline-affiliate-contracts.

51 See N.D. Pipeline Co., LLC, 153 FERC ¶ 61,250, at P 19. 2015.

52 "15 U.S. Code § 717-Regulation of Natural Gas Companies." Cornell Law School, Legal Information Institute. 2005. https://www.law.cornell.edu/uscode/text/15/717.

53 "TOPN: Natural Gas Policy Act of 1978." Cornell Law School, Legal Information Institute. 1978. https://www.law.cornell.edu/topn/natural_gas_policy_act_of_1978.

## B. Reach of Regulation

The NGA covers transportation, storage, and nonexempt sales of natural gas in interstate commerce, as well as the companies engaged in those activities.[54] Activities of natural gas pipelines are considered in interstate commerce whenever the pipeline crosses a state line or if the gas transported is commingled with gas that has crossed state lines.[55] NGA jurisdiction covers facilities that store interstate natural gas and nonexempt transactions involving interstate natural gas as well. Notably, international natural gas transportation is not subject to the NGA unless that international movement is part of an interstate movement of natural gas.[56, 57]

The NGA contains some exemptions to its jurisdictional scope. Pipelines engaged in gathering or local distribution are exempt from NGA regulation.[58] Under the Hinshaw Amendment,[59] natural gas pipelines are also exempt from NGA regulation if: 1) the pipeline receives the natural gas within or at the boundary of a state, 2) all the natural gas received is ultimately consumed in that state, and 3) pipeline is subject to the regulation of its rates and services by a state commission.[60] Under, NPGA Section 311, FERC can allow intrastate or local distribution pipelines to provide service on behalf of an interstate pipeline, and vice versa, without jeopardizing their exemptions.[61, 62]

## C. Regulation of Infrastructure

Since 1942, NGA pipelines have been required to obtain certificates of public convenience and necessity.[63] Since 1947, these certificates also preempt requirements of state or local agencies that conflict with the terms of the certificates,[64] and provide the certificated entity with federal eminent domain authority.[65] Congress granted this authority to ensure that in the absence of state eminent domain rights, holders of certificates would have more than "an illusory right to build."[66] Certificated pipelines must "comply with all other federal, state, and local regulations not preempted by the NGA."[67] Other federal requirements still apply, including those administered by states.[68] FERC acts as the "lead agency for the purposes of coordinating all applicable [f]ederal authorizations and for the purposes of

54  "15 U.S. Code § 717b-Exportation or Importation of Natural Gas; LNG Terminals." Cornell Law School. Legal Information Institute. https://www.law.cornell.edu/uscode/text/15/717b.

55  "Oklahoma Natural Gas Co. v FERC, 28 F.3d 1281." Casetext July 22, 1994. https://casetext.com/case/oklahoma-natural-gas-co-v-ferc-2.

56  See, e.g., Nexus Gas Transmission, LLC, 172 FERC ¶ 61,199, at P 15 n.32 (2020) (citing Border Pipe Line Co. v. FPC, 171 F.2d 149, 151 (D.C. Cir. 1948).

57  "81 FR 925: Trans-Pecos Pipeline, LLC; Notice of Availability of the Environmental Assessment for the Proposed Presidio Border Crossing Project." FERC. Federal Register, Vol. 81, No. 5, January 8, 2016: 925-926. https://www.federalregister.gov/documents/2016/01/08/2016-00119/trans-pecos-pipeline-llc-notice-of-availability-of-the-environmental-assessment-for-the-proposed.

58  "15 U.S. Code § 717b-Exportation or Importation of Natural Gas; LNG Terminals." Cornell Law School. Legal Information Institute. https://www.law.cornell.edu/uscode/text/15/717b.

59  "Public Law 323: To Amend Section 1 of the Natural Gas Act." U.S. Congress. 1954. https://www.congress.gov/83/statute/STATUTE-68/STATUTE-68-Pg36-2.pdf.

60  "15 U.S. Code § 717c-Rates and Charges." Cornell Law School, Legal Information Institute. 2005. https://www.law.cornell.edu/uscode/text/15/717c.

61  "15 U.S. Code § 717f-Construction, Extension, or Abandonment of Facilities." Cornell Law School, Legal Information Institute. 2019. https://www.law.cornell.edu/uscode/text/15/717f.

62  "86 FR 38073: CenterPoint Energy Resources Corp.; Summit Utilities Arkansas, Inc.; Notice of Application and Establishing Intervention Deadline." FERC. Federal Register, Vol. 86, No. 135, July 19, 2021: 38073-38074. https://www.federal-register.gov/documents/2021/07/19/2021-15179/centerpoint-energy-resources-corp-summit-utilities-arkansas-inc-notice-of-application-and.

63  "15 U.S. Code § 717f-Construction, Extension, or Abandonment of Facilities." Cornell Law School, Legal Information Institute. 2019. https://www.law.cornell.edu/uscode/text/15/717f.

64  See, e.g., Algonquin Gas Transmission, 154 FERC ¶ 61,048, at P 33 (2016) (citing Schneidewind v. ANR Pipeline Co., 485 U.S. 293 (1988)) ("[FERC'] regulations implementing [the NGA] generally preempt state and local law that conflict with federal regulation, or would unreasonably delay the construction and operation of facilities approved by the Commission'."), aff'd, City of Bos. Delegation v. FERC, 897 F.3d 241 (D.C. Cir. 2018).

65  "61 Stat. 459: AN ACT To Enable the Osage Tribal Council to Determine the Bonus Value of Tracts Offered for Lease for Oil, Gas, and Other Mining Purposes." USLaw Link. 1938. https://uslaw.link/citation/stat/61/459.

66  "Penneast Pipeline Company v New Jersey." Cornell Law School, Legal Information Institute. 2021. https://www.law.cornell.edu/supremecourt/text/19-1039.

67  "Dominion Transmission, Inc. v Summers, 723 F.3d 238." Casetext 2013. https://casetext.com/case/dominion-transmission-inc-v-summers.

68  "Sierra Club v West Virginia DEP, No. 22-1008 (4th Cir. 2023)." Justia Law. April 2023. https://law.justia.com/cases/federal/appellate-courts/ca4/22-1008/22-1008-2023-04-03.html.

complying with the National Environmental Policy Act" (NEPA).[69]

Pipelines regulated under the NGA must obtain a certificate before they can construct, expand, operate, sell, or abandon a pipeline, storage facility, or route.[70] The environmental aspect of this review, whereby pipelines must undergo an evaluation of their environmental impact, has generated the most controversy.[71] However, the primary purpose of FERC's analysis in granting a certificate is to determine whether a proposed project is "required by the public convenience and necessity."[72]

FERC has an established framework for determining when NGA infrastructure is "required by the public convenience and necessity."[73, 74, 75, 76, 77] This evaluation includes an assessment of need, and impacts on: existing customers of the applicant, other pipelines and their customers, the environment, landowners, and communities.[78] FERC does not employ bright-line rules for when a certificate applicant has met this standard, but in general the greater the adverse economic impacts on other industry participants or environmental impacts under NEPA, the greater the need must be shown to justify the project.[79]

## D. Economic Regulation

The NGA is a contract carrier, as opposed to a common carrier, regime. Despite having the ability to contract out all the capacity on a certificated natural gas pipeline, NGA pipelines are prohibited from unduly discriminating in their services.[80] Pursuant to the NGA's anti-discrimination authority,[81] FERC developed regulations requiring natural gas pipelines to provide open access.[82, 83] FERC's natural gas open-access regime unbundled transportation and sales of natural gas such that pipelines can no longer act as merchants of natural gas. Instead, NGA pipelines now serve as transporters of natural gas, providing transportation service upon reasonable request, under firm contracts.[84] NGA pipelines must offer contract transportation, but if capacity is available, natural gas pipelines must also allow interested shippers

69    "15 U.S. Code § 717n: Process Coordination; Hearings; Rules of Procedure." Cornell Law School, Legal Information Institute. 2005. https://www.law.cornell.edu/uscode/text/15/717n.

70    "15 U.S. Code § 717f-Construction, Extension, or Abandonment of Facilities." Cornell Law School, Legal Information Institute. 2019. https://www.law.cornell.edu/uscode/text/15/717f.

71    "87 FR 14104: Consideration of Greenhouse Gas Emissions in Natural Gas Infrastructure Project Reviews." FERC. *Federal Register*, Vol. 87, No. 48, March 11, 2022: 14104-14142. https://www.federalregister.gov/documents/2022/03/11/2022-04536/consideration-of-greenhouse-gas-emissions-in-natural-gas-infrastructure-project-reviews.

72    "15 U.S. Code § 717f-Construction, Extension, or Abandonment of Facilities." Cornell Law School, Legal Information Institute. 2019. https://www.law.cornell.edu/uscode/text/15/717f.

73    "88 FERC ¶ 61,227: Certification of New Interstate Natural Gas Pipeline Facilities." FERC. 1999. https://www.ferc.gov/sites/default/files/2020-04/PL99-3-000.pdf.

74    "90 FERC ¶ 61,128: Certification of New Interstate Natural Gas Pipeline Facilities (clarification)." FERC. 2000. https://www.ferc.gov/sites/default/files/2020-04/PL99-3-001.pdf.

75    "92 FERC ¶ 61,094: Certification of New Interstate Natural Gas Pipeline Facilities (further clarification)." FERC. 2000. https://www.ferc.gov/sites/default/files/2020-04/PL99-3-002.pdf.

76    "178 FERC ¶ 61,107: FERC issues an Updated Policy Statement on the Certification of Interstate Natural Gas Pipeline Facilities." Westlaw. February 22, 2023. https://content.next.westlaw.com/practical-law/document/Ib4012eel933c11ec9f24ec7b211d8087/Legal-Updates-FERC-Issues-Updated-Policy-Statement-on-Certification-of-Interstate-Natural-Gas-Pipeline-Applications?viewType=FullText&originationContext=document&transitionType=DocumentItem&ppcid=4c1950ee9e274a1292ba1760d56e9d0e&contextData=(sc.DocLink).

77    "179 FERC ¶ 61,012: Certification of New Interstate Natural Gas Pipeline Facilities (rehearing)." Politico Pro. 2022. https://subscriber.politicopro.com/eenews/f/eenews/?id=00000180-2052-dc58-a78d-27fa1c190000.

78    "88 FERC ¶ 61,227: Certification of New Interstate Natural Gas Pipeline Facilities." FERC. 1999. https://www.ferc.gov/sites/default/files/2020-04/PL99-3-000.pdf.

79    "88 FERC ¶ 61,227: Certification of New Interstate Natural Gas Pipeline Facilities." FERC. 1999. https://www.ferc.gov/sites/default/files/2020-04/PL99-3-000.pdf.

80    "15 U.S. Code § 717c-Rates and Charges." Cornell Law School, Legal Information Institute. 2005. https://www.law.cornell.edu/uscode/text/15/717c.

81    "18 CFR § 284.1-Definitions." Cornell Law School, Legal Information Institute. 2010. https://www.law.cornell.edu/cfr/text/18/284.1.

82    "18 CFR 284: Pipeline Service Obligations and Revisions to Regulations Governing Self-Implementing Transportation Under Part 284 and Regulation of Natural Gas Pipelines After Partial Wellhead Decontrol." FERC. *Federal Register*, Vol. 62, No. 44, March 6, 1997: 10204-10219. https://www.federalregister.gov/documents/1997/03/06/97-5363/pipeline-service-obligations-and-revisions-to-regulations-governing-self-implementing-transportation.

83    "18 CFR 284: Regulation of Short-Term Natural Gas Transportation Services, and Regulation of Interstate Natural Gas Transportation Services." FERC. *Federal Register*, Vol. 67, No. 104, May 30, 2002: 37669-37770. https://www.govinfo.gov/content/pkg/FR-2002-05-30/pdf/02-12940.pdf.

84    "18 CFR 284: Regulation of Short-Term Natural Gas Transportation Services, and Regulation of Interstate Natural Gas Transportation Services." FERC. *Federal Register*, Vol. 67, No. 104, May 30, 2002: 37669-37770. https://www.govinfo.gov/content/pkg/FR-2002-05-30/pdf/02-12940.pdf.

to utilize that capacity.[85] NGA-regulated pipelines also must offer a capacity release program under which shippers can transfer some or all of their transportation capacity to another creditworthy shipper that either commits to pay the pipeline's maximum rate or successfully bids for the capacity in an open auction process.[86] FERC also regulates other aspects of NGA pipelines such as the quality specifications of gas they transport.[87]

NGA pipelines must publish their tariffs providing their cost-based recourse rates.[88] NGA pipelines also can grant discounts from their recourse rates, and, with FERC's approval, can charge negotiated rates that are higher or lower than their recourse rates.[89, 90, 91] These rates must be just and reasonable.[92] NGA pipelines must file at FERC to change their rates.[93, 94]

## E. Other Regulation

The NGA applies more broadly than other pipeline regulatory regimes, including to natural gas storage and jurisdictional transactions. The NGA applies to interstate gas storage facilities.[95, 96] Any project that stores NGA-jurisdictional gas must acquire FERC permission in the form of securing a certificate of public convenience and necessity to be built, operated, or abandoned.[97] The provision of such storage service is also generally subject to the same economic regulations regarding natural gas pipeline rates. However, unlike natural gas pipeline rates, natural gas storage services may be offered at market-based rates upon showing that the storage facility lacks market power.[98, 99] The NGA also separately regulates the siting of export and import terminals for the import and export of liquefied natural gas (LNG), whether or not they are connected to interstate pipelines.[100, 101, 102]

The NGA regulation also applies to certain NGA-jurisdictional transactions. Most notably, while many categories of sales have been exempted from natural gas regulation, the NGA still regulates nonexempt sales.[103] Nonpipeline buyers

85  "18 CFR § 284.7-Firm Transportation Service." Cornell Law School, Legal Information Institute. 1985. https://www.law.cornell.edu/cfr/text/18/284.7.

86  "18 CFR § 284.8-Release of Firm Capacity on Interstate Pipelines." Cornell Law School, Legal Information Institute. December 30, 2008. https://www.law.cornell.edu/cfr/text/18/284.8.

87  "71 FR 35893: Before Commissioners: Joseph T. Kelliher, Chairman; Nora Mead Brownell, and Suedeen G. Kelly; Natural Gas Interchangeability; Policy Statement on Provisions Governing Natural Gas Quality and Interchangeability in Interstate Natural Gas Pipeline Company Tariffs." FERC. *Federal Register*, Vol. 71, No. 120, June 22, 2006: 35893-35904; https://www.federalregister.gov/documents/2006/06/22/06-5582/before-commissioners-joseph-t-kelliher-chairman-nora-mead-brownell-and-suedeen-g-kelly-natural-gas.

88  "15 U.S. Code § 717c-Rates and Charges." Cornell Law School, Legal Information Institute. 2005. https://www.law.cornell.edu/uscode/text/15/717c.

89  "61 FR 4633: Alternatives to Traditional Cost-of Service Rate-making for Natural Gas Pipelines and Regulation of Negotiated Transportation Services of Natural Gas Pipelines; Statement of Policy and Request for Comments." FERC. *Federal Register*, Vol. 61, No. 26, February 7, 1996: 4633-4646. https://www.federalregister.gov/documents/1996/02/07/96-2547/alternatives-to-traditional-cost-of-service-ratemaking-for-natural-gas-pipelines-and-regulation-of.

90  "87 FR 39934: Improvements to Generator Interconnection Procedures and Agreements." FERC. *Federal Register*, Vol. 87, No. 127, July 5, 2022: 39934-40032. https://www.federalregister.gov/documents/2022/07/05/2022-13470/improvements-to-generator-interconnection-procedures-and-agreements.

91  75 FERC ¶61,024 (1996).

92  "15 U.S. Code § 717c-Rates and Charges." Cornell Law School, Legal Information Institute. 2005. https://www.law.cornell.edu/uscode/text/15/717c.

93  "15 U.S. Code § 717c-Rates and Charges." Cornell Law School, Legal Information Institute. 2005. https://www.law.cornell.edu/uscode/text/15/717c.

94  "18 CFR Part 154-Rate Schedules and Tariffs." Law School, Legal Information Institute. 1995. https://www.law.cornell.edu/cfr/text/18/part-154.

95  "15 U.S. Code § 717b-Exportation or Importation of Natural Gas; LNG Terminals." Cornell Law School. Legal Information Institute. https://www.law.cornell.edu/uscode/text/15/717b.

96  "Border Pipe Line Co. v Federal Power Commission, 171 F.2d 149 (D.C. Cir. 1948)." Justia Law. November 22, 1948. https://law.justia.com/cases/federal/appellate-courts/F2/171/149/1487586/.

97  "15 U.S. Code § 717f-Construction, Extension, or Abandonment of Facilities." Cornell Law School, Legal Information Institute. 2019. https://www.law.cornell.edu/uscode/text/15/717f.

98  "15 U.S. Code § 717c-Rates and Charges." Cornell Law School, Legal Information Institute. 2005. https://www.law.cornell.edu/uscode/text/15/717c.

99  "18 CFR § 284.501-Applicability." Cornell Law School, Legal Information Institute. 2024. https://www.law.cornell.edu/cfr/text/18/284.501.

100 "15 U.S. Code § 717-Regulation of Natural Gas Companies." Cornell Law School, Legal Information Institute. 2005. https://www.law.cornell.edu/uscode/text/15/717.

101 "86 FR 54966: NFEnergia LLC Notice of Application and Establishing Intervention Deadline." FERC. *Federal Register*, Vol. 86, No. 190, October 5, 2021: 54966-54968. https://www.federalregister.gov/documents/2021/10/05/2021-21704/nfenerga-llc-notice-of-application-and-establishing-intervention-deadline.

102 "176 FERC ¶ 61,031: Interstate and Intrastate Natural Gas Pipelines; Rate Changes Relating to Federal Income Tax Rate." FERC. July 18, 2018. https://www.ferc.gov/sites/default/files/2020-04/final-rule-order-849.pdf.

103 "15 U.S. Code § 717c-Rates and Charges." Cornell Law School, Legal Information Institute. 2005. https://www.law.cornell.edu/uscode/text/15/717c.

and sellers of natural gas are automatically given blanket certificates to conduct such sales,[104] but must make informational filings disclosing these transactions[105] and abide by a code of conduct.[106] FERC's regulations also restrict bundled sales of gas made by pipelines and require that all natural gas pipelines retain title to that natural gas during transportation.[107]

According to the NGA's prohibition on discrimination, FERC also imposes affiliate standards of conduct governing communications and other activities between NGA pipeline (and storage) owners and their marketing affiliates.[108] The purpose of these regulations is to prevent collusion between pipelines and their marketing affiliates that would lead to discrimination against unaffiliated shippers or manipulation of energy markets. FERC also administers a market manipulation regime that covers any action made in connection with activities subject to FERC's NGA jurisdiction.[109, 110]

## V. EXEMPTION FROM REGULATION

Another legislative option would involve exempting those $H_2$ pipelines from federal regulation of their economic practices. Evaluation of complete deregulation does not require the same statutory and regulatory analysis conducted for existing pipeline regulatory regimes. However, in evaluating deregulation of hydrogen pipelines, there is an existing model. Since 1906, interstate water pipelines have been exempted from regulation. This exemption was meant to protect large irrigation projects from regulation.[111, 112] Since then, numerous water pipeline projects have been built without concern for interstate regulation of the economic aspects of this transportation service.

Even if exempt from federal regulation, there are common law/common carrier obligations applying to businesses, including pipelines, that choose to transport another person's products. These common law obligations may still be applied to $H_2$ pipeline transportation since no statute would exist preempting them.

## VI. ALTERNATIVE HYDROGEN-SPECIFIC STATUTE

Hydrogen pipelines could also be regulated at the federal level by an entirely new statute and regulatory framework. Because the possibilities are limitless it is not possible to briefly summarize this option or weigh its pros and cons.

A new statute tailored to the $H_2$ pipeline industry could draw from any of the aspects of the other existing regulatory regimes, picking and choosing among various characteristics to create a new regulatory paradigm specific to $H_2$ pipelines. In developing such a statute, lawmakers would need to determine whether it was based on common carrier or contract carrier principles, as those regimes are mutually exclusive. The act would also need to designate a regulator, be it the FERC, STB, or an entirely new agency.

The new regime could choose to employ some or all of the common traits of existing pipeline regulatory regimes. Some aspects common to all existing pipeline regulatory regimes include:

104 "18 CFR § 284.402-Blanket Marketing Certificates." Cornell Law School, Legal Information Institute. 2003. https://www.law.cornell.edu/cfr/text/18/284.402.

105 "18 CFR § 260.401-FERC Form No. 552, Annual Report of Natural Gas Transactions." Cornell Law School, Legal Information Institute. 2010. https://www.law.cornell.edu/cfr/text/18/260.401.

106 "18 CFR § 284.403-Code of Conduct for Persons Holding Blanket Marketing Certificates." Cornell Law School, Legal Information Institute. September 26, 2008. https://www.law.cornell.edu/cfr/text/18/284.403.

107 "18 CFR Part 284—Certain Sales and Transportation of Natural Gas Under the Natural Gas Policy Act of 1978 and Related Authorities." Cornell Law School, Legal Information Institute. 1978. https://www.law.cornell.edu/cfr/text/18/part-284#:~:text=AND%20RELATED%20AUTHORITIES-.

108 "18 CFR Part 358—Standards of Conduct." Cornell Law School, Legal Information Institute. 2008. https://www.law.cornell.edu/cfr/text/18/part-358.

109 "15 U.S. Code § 717c-Rates and Charges." Cornell Law School, Legal Information Institute. 2005. https://www.law.cornell.edu/uscode/text/15/717c.

110 "18 CFR § 1c.1-Prohibition of Natural Gas Market Manipulation." Cornell Law School, Legal Information Institute. 2006. https://www.law.cornell.edu/cfr/text/18/1c.1.

111 "Congressional Record: May 4, 1906." U.S. Congress. 1906. https://www.congress.gov/59/crecb/1906/05/04/GPO-CRECB-1906-pt7-v40-7.pdf.

112 "Congressional Record: May 17, 1906." U.S. Congress. 1906. https://www.congress.gov/bound-congressional-record/1906/05/17/senate-section.

1) tariff filing requirements, 2) the requirement that rates be just and reasonable, 3) prohibitions against undue discrimination and preference, and 4) reporting requirements concerning a pipeline's cost of service, as well as regulations concerning regulatory accounting and information retention. Finally, lawmakers would need to decide whether $H_2$ pipelines would be subject to a certification requirement, like that applied to NGA-jurisdictional pipelines. If so, drafters would then need to determine what kind of review certification would entail, whether certification would include siting authority, and what powers certification would grant, including the use of federal eminent domain authority.

Alternatively, interstate $H_2$ pipelines could be made subject to one of the three existing stat-utes, but with specific limitations tailoring the regulation to only those aspects of the $H_2$ industry that require regulation. For instance, in section 311(e) of the Energy Policy Act of 2005, Congress amended the NGA to temporarily prohibit FERC from conditioning approval of an LNG terminal on a requirement that service be offered on an open-access basis, or any regulation of rates, charges, or terms or conditions of service, or on the filing of a tariff.[113, 114] Similarly, exemptions for existing $H_2$ pipelines would need to be affected through $H_2$-specific legislation.

113 "Energy Policy Act of 2005." U.S. Congress. 2005. https://www.congress.gov/109/plaws/publ58/PLAW-109publ58.pdf.

114 "15 U.S. Code § 717b-Exportation or Importation of Natural Gas; LNG Terminals." Cornell Law School. Legal Information Institute. https://www.law.cornell.edu/uscode/text/15/717b.

# Appendix Q

# MENU OF POLICY OPTIONS

Appendix Q provides a high-level summary of hydrogen policy mechanisms and options. The goal is to present policies focused primarily on clean/low-carbon energy options. These policies are grouped by the following general topics: 1) explicit carbon pricing, 2) implicit carbon pricing, 3) clean or "green" power markets, 4) command and control (mandates), 5) market making and market design, 6) public engagement and information policies, and 7) energy strategies. This summary is not intended to recommend any policy over another but is intended to highlight a range of policy options. Note that the range of options includes both existing policies that are being implemented, along with concepts yet to be tested.

## I. EXPLICIT CARBON PRICING POLICIES

Explicit market carbon pricing refers to initiatives that put a direct price on greenhouse gas (GHG) emissions. It is expressed as a value per metric ton of carbon dioxide equivalent ($MTCO_2e$). Some examples of such policies include "Measuring and Comparing Carbon Pricing and the Pricing of Embodied and Transport Emissions" (a publication of the World Bank and World Trade Organization) (https://www.wto.org/english/tratop_e/tessd_e/world_bank_17may22.pdf) and "IEA Levels of Explicit Carbon Pricing in Selected Economies" (https://www.iea.org/data-and-statistics/charts/levels-of-explicity-carbon-pricing-in-selected-economies).

### 1. Sources

- https://www.rff.org/publications/explainers/carbon-pricing-101/

- https://carbonpricingdashboard.worldbank.org/

- https://d306pr3pise04h.cloudfront.net/docs/issues_doc%2FEnvironment%2Fclimate%2FCarbonPricingExecutiveGuide.pdf

- https://www.carbonpricingleadership.org/

- https://www.oecd.org/tax/tax-policy/tax-policy-and-climate-change-imf-oecd-g20-report-september-2021.pdf

- https://www.api.org/climate#carbon-price

## A. Carbon Tax

### 1. Description

A carbon tax directly sets a price on carbon. It does so by defining an explicit tax rate on GHG emissions or, more commonly, on the carbon content of fossil fuels, i.e., a price per $MTCO_2e$. It is different from an emissions trading system (ETS) in that the emissions reduction outcome of a carbon tax is not predefined, but the carbon price is.

### 2. Critical Elements/Notes

- Point of regulation options include producer or emitter

- Price setting

- Stringency/phase-in prices

- Coverage (for example, which sectors)

- Revenue use

- Oversight and compliance

### 3. Examples/Schemes

- British Columbia Carbon Tax

- Hawai'i Carbon Tax
- South Africa Carbon Tax
- Argentina Carbon Tax

### 4. Sources

- https://openknowledge.worldbank.org/server/api/core/bitstreams/3f3c5326-7c41-513a-a598-6e8e535e7lb9/content
- https://www.imf.org/-/media/Files/Publications/Staff-Climate-Notes/2022/English/CLNEA2022006.ashx

## B. Emissions Trading System (ETS) (Compliance Carbon Offset Credits)

### 1. Description

An ETS is a system where emitters can trade emissions allowances—typically allocated through regulatory guidance—to meet their emissions targets. To comply with their emissions targets at the lowest cost, regulated entities can either implement internal abatement measures or acquire emissions allowances in the market, depending on the relative costs of these options. By creating supply and demand for emissions allowances, an ETS establishes a market price for GHG emissions. The two main types of ETS markets are cap and trade and baseline and credit. Cap and trade applies a cap, or absolute limit, on the emissions within the ETS. Emissions allowances are distributed, usually for free or through auctions, for emissions equivalent to the cap. Baseline and credit defines a baseline emissions level for individual regulated entities and credits are issued to entities that have reduced their emissions below this level.

Two ETS types:
- Cap and trade ETS
- Baseline and credit ETS

### 2. Critical Elements/Notes

- Government sponsored/managed
- Price setting, e.g., Social Cost of Carbon (SCC)
- Revenue use
- Emissions allowances

- Banking/borrowing of allowances
- Stringency/phase-in
- Coverage (which sectors)

### 3. Examples/Schemes

- California Cap and Trade
- Washington Cap and Invest
- European Union ETS

### 4. Sources

- https://openknowledge.worldbank.org/server/api/core/bitstreams/3f3c5326-7c41-513a-a598-6e8e535e7lb9/content
- https://www.imf.org/-/media/Files/Publications/Staff-Climate-Notes/2022/English/CLNEA2022006.ashx

## C. Hybrid ETS/Carbon Tax

### 1. Description

ETS credits can be sold to other entities exceeding their baseline emissions levels. With a tax, the price is known in advance (but not the quantity of emissions per year). Alternatively, with a cap, the emissions are known in advance (but not the price). Hybrid systems combine elements of both.

### 2. Critical Elements/Notes

Hybrid types:
- Self-adjusting tax provides emissions reduction certainty of a cap
- Adopt a cap with a tax as a backstop
- Start with tax and transition to a cap
- Implement a tax with a cap as a backstop

### 3. Examples/Schemes

- Oregon ETS
- Washington ETS

### 4. Sources

- https://www.sightline.org/2014/10/24/four-carbon-cap-tax-hybrids/
- https://www.journals.uchicago.edu/doi/full/10.1093/reep/rez022

- https://institute.smartprosperity.ca/sites/default/files/publications/files/Hybrid Carbon Pricing.pdf

### D. Carbon Border Adjustment or Border Tax Adjustment

#### 1. Description

A carbon border adjustment (CBA) is a trade policy instrument. It consists of charges on imports and sometimes rebates on exports. CBAs can have several different goals, including to: prevent emissions leakage (whereby more emissions-intensive imported products displace lower-emissions-intensity domestic production, increasing overall global emissions); establish a competitive playing field so that regulatory costs or investment costs to produce lower-emissions-intensity products are not competitively undermined by foreign producers that are not burdened by those costs; reduce incentives for offshoring of production; and create incentives for global decarbonization. In most cases, a CBA is meant to level the playing field regarding differences in GHG-focused environmental policies or performance. Depending on its purpose and design, it may also be called a Border Tax Adjustment, carbon intensity import fee, border-adjusted tax, or destination tax.

The European Union has developed (and the United Kingdom is planning to develop) a carbon border adjustment mechanism (CBAM) that explicitly seeks to level the playing field between regulatory costs imposed through the European Union and United Kingdom ETS on domestic producers, with a comparable cost imposed as a border tax.

#### 2. Critical Elements/Notes

- Establish products covered
- Establish scope of emissions
- Account for the cost of carbon emissions
- Implement import fees and export rebates

#### 3. Examples/Schemes

- EU CBAM
- Clean Competition Act (U.S. legislative proposal)
- Foreign Pollution Fee (U.S. legislative proposal)

#### 4. Sources

- https://media.rff.org/documents/Policy_Guidance_Upate.pdf
- https://www.resources.org/common-resources/implementing-framework-border-tax-adjustments-us-greenhouse-gas-tax-legislation-and-regulations/
- https://www.weforum.org/agenda/2021/10/what-is-a-carbon-border-tax-what-does-it-mean-for-trade/
- https://www.rff.org/publications/explainers/border-carbon-adjustments-101/
- https://crsreports.congress.gov/product/pdf/R/R47167
- https://clcouncil.org/report/principles/
- https://clcouncil.org/reports/Carbon_Import_Fees_and_the_WTO.pdf

## II. IMPLICIT CARBON PRICING POLICIES

Implicit carbon pricing refers to initiatives that put an indirect price on GHG emissions. It is expressed as a value per metric ton of carbon dioxide equivalent ($MTCO_2e$).

#### 1. Sources:

- https://institute.smartprosperity.ca/sites/default/files/hidden-factor-climate-policy.pdf

### A. Voluntary Carbon Offset Credits

#### 1. Description

Offset credits designate the GHG emissions reductions from project- or program-based activities, which can be sold either domestically or internationally. Crediting mechanisms issue carbon credits according to an accounting protocol and have their own registry. These credits can be used to meet compliance under an international agreement, domestic policies, or corporate citizenship objectives related to GHG emissions mitigation. Certificates offset the buyer's $CO_2$ emissions with an equal amount of $CO_2$ reductions somewhere else.

## 2. Critical Elements/Notes

Sponsored/managed by NGOs

### a. Offset Project Types:

- Methane destruction (landfill, livestock, coal)
- Industrial gases (ozone, nitrous oxide)
- Forestry (avoided conversion, improvements)
- Carbon dioxide removal (CDR), e.g., direct air capture (DAC), ocean-based, agriculture/soils
- Renewables (biomass/gas, solar, wind)
- Energy efficiency (cookstove improvements)
- Community improvements ($H_2O$, sanitation)

## 3. Examples/Schemes

- Clean Development Mechanism
- American Carbon Registry – Mostly United States
- Climate Action Reserve – United States/Mexico
- The Gold Standard –
- Plan Vivo – International
- The Verified Carbon Standard – International

## 4. Sources

- https://www.offsetguide.org/understanding-carbon-offsets/carbon-offset-projects/
- https://carbonpricingdashboard.worldbank.org/

## B. Production Tax Credits (PTC)

## 1. Description

A PTC is a tax incentive that provides direct financial support for the actual production (or manufacturing) of low GHG goods. These subsidies are structured to reduce the organization's tax liability, thereby creating a bankable income stream that can offset and incentivize clean production investments.

## 2. Critical Elements/Notes

Federal or state PTC are typically paid directly to the producer and are calculated per unit produced prior to tax filing periods as a refundable credit. The PTC may be paid directly (direct pay) to the producer with variations on years received via direct pay or as a refundable credit. These credits are typically time limited and subject to eligibility requirements.

## 3. Examples/Schemes

- Clean Hydrogen – 45V (per kg)
- Renewable power – 45Y (per kW)
- CCUS – 45Q (per ton of $CO_2$ captured and utilized or sequestered)

## 4. Sources

- https://www.carboncollective.co/sustainable-investing/production-tax-credit-ptc
- https://bidenwhitehouse.archives.gov/wp-content/uploads/2022/12/Inflation-Reduction-Act-Guidebook.pdf

## C. Investment Tax Credits (ITC)

## 1. Description

An ITC is a tax incentive that provides a percentage of direct financial support for the capital costs of low GHG production facilities. As with a PTC, these subsidies are structured to reduce the organization's tax liability and incentivize capital investments in cleaner production technologies and methods.

## 2. Critical Elements/Notes

Federal or state ITCs are typically paid directly to the producer and are calculated per unit produced prior to tax filing periods. Additional requirements could be added (e.g., domestic production) to enhance the value of the baseline ITC. These credits are subject to eligibility requirements.

## 3. Examples/Schemes

- Renewable power construction – 48 ITC
- Carbon dioxide transportation Infrastructure Finance and Innovation Act (CIFIA)
- Clean Hydrogen

## 4. Sources

- https://www.carboncollective.co/sustainable-investing/investment-tax-credit-itc

- https://bidenwhitehouse.archives.gov/wp-content/uploads/2022/12/Inflation-Reduction-Act-Guidebook.pdf

## D. Demand Sector Tax Incentives (Credits)

### 1. Description

Clean goods or energy demand sector tax incentives are usually reimbursed as a percentage of cost, a flat amount, or a percentage (with a capped credit) for certain qualified expenditures made by a taxpayer related to specified IRS tax code demand sectors.

### 2. Critical Elements/Notes

Clean product or energy demand tax incentives are typically given in the form of credits intended to stimulate change or growth in a market. There are usually greater incentives for early adopters as the incentives typically expire or phase out over time.

### 3. Examples/Schemes

- Home efficiency tax credits (residential/commercial)
- EV/FCEV tax credit (transport)

### 4. Sources

- https://www.irs.gov/pub/taxpros/fs-2022-40.pdf
- https://afdc.energy.gov/laws/409

## E. Tax Deductions

### 1. Description

Clean product or energy-related tax deductions (if enacted) reduce consumer or producer taxable income. Deductions reduce the amount of income before taxes are calculated (while credits reduce the amount of tax owed).

### 2. Critical Elements/Notes

Similar to clean product or energy tax credits, except these involve a reduction in itemized taxable income.

### 3. Examples/Schemes

- Charitable donations
- Education expenses

### 4. Sources

- https://www.energystar.gov/about/federal-tax-credits

## F. Tax/Fee Exemptions

### 1. Description

Federal or state sales or income tax exemptions related to clean production or demand.

### 2. Critical Elements/Notes

Exemptions can be demand/customer focused or can be production focused on certain types of low carbon intensity production methods.

### 3. Examples/Schemes

- Texas has energy sales tax exemptions for specific types of manufacturing facilities

### 4. Sources

- https://www.iea.org/policies/3634-tax-exemption-for-renewable-energy-use
- https://comptroller.texas.gov/taxes/property-tax/docs/96-1569.pdf

## G. Contracts for Difference (CfD)

### 1. Description

CfDs are financial contracts involving two parties, with one usually being the government/state and the other a market actor. The contract concerns the difference between two prices: a market-based reference price and a contractual strike price. The owner of the contract, e.g., a producer, will sell its product and receive both the market price and the remaining difference between the market price and strike price (from the government/state under the contract). As a result, the producer will effectively receive the contractual strike price for each unit sold. Over time, the size of the payouts under the contract will vary with changes in the market price. If the contracts are designed as a two-way CfD, then if the market price exceeds the strike price, the producer must pay back the difference to the state.

CfDs secure a specific price (the predefined strike price) for each unit sold or purchased, thus transferring price risk between the parties in the contract. If the strike price is high enough, it can increase the effective price and be used as a support mechanism. A CfD is a flexible way to implement a de facto price guarantee to support investment in assets that are favored by the state without establishing a fixed price in the market. The resulting price certainty lends financial support that can help trigger private investment, which may be a useful tool to help kickstart the development of a hydrogen market.

## 2. Critical Elements/Notes

- An example is in the power markets, whereby a CfD is a long-term contractual agreement between a low-carbon electricity generator and a low-carbon contracts company. Those CfDs are designed to provide the generator with price certainty over the lifetime of the contract. The contract is awarded through a competitive allocation process, which determines the preagreed price (the strike price). As a private law contract, the CfD cannot be unilaterally changed once it has been signed.

- The CfD generator then has a number of milestones to meet within the first few years of the contract in order to preserve the term for payments, which is typically 15 years. This includes proving commitment to the project within 12 months of contract signing, and commissioning 80% of the initial capacity estimate within the target commissioning window.

- CfDs can be structured to support demand and/or production.

## 3. Examples/Schemes

- Renewable CfDs
- U.K. $H_2$ CfDs

## 4. Sources

- https://www.lowcarboncontracts.uk/contracts-for-difference
- https://thema.no/en/nyheter/how-can-contracts-for-difference-kick-start-a-norwegian-hydrogen-market/
- https://www.whitecase.com/insight-alert/carbon-contracts-difference-new-funding-program-companies

- https://www.gov.uk/government/publications/contracts-for-difference/contract-for-difference
- https://www.catf.us/2022/08/why-carbon-contracts-difference-could-policy-measure-europe-needs-decarbonise-industry/
- https://repository.ubn.ru.nl/bitstream/handle/2066/167551/167551.pdf
- https://fsr.eui.eu/contracts-for-difference/
- https://www.iea.org/policies/5731-contract-for-difference-cfd

## H. Energy Grants, Subsidies, or Direct Expenditures

### 1. Description

Direct financial support that can be given to both producers and consumers of an energy product or service that is meant to stimulate expanded activity in the targeted product or service. The grants, subsidies, or other financial assistance awards are made directly to recipients.

### 2. Examples/Schemes

- DOE H2Hub program

### 3. Sources

- https://www.eia.gov/analysis/requests/subsidy/

## I. Results-Based Climate Finance (RBCF)

### 1. Description

RBCF is a funding approach where payments are made after predefined outputs or outcomes related to managing climate change—such as emissions reductions—are delivered and verified. Many RBCF programs aim to purchase verified reductions in GHG emissions while at the same time to reduce poverty, improve access to clean energy, and offer health and community benefits.

### 2. Critical Elements/Notes

- RBCF is a new approach and could present opportunities for key sectors, including energy, transportation, water and sanitation, waste management, and tourism. These sectors are particularly important to a post-COVID-19 economic recovery and will require trillions of dollars of investment over the coming decades.

- RBCF approaches can increase the economic efficiency of public procurement and leverage private finance, which will help limited public funds stretch further. However, this new approach also faces important challenges to implementation. It is likely that support will be needed through the project design and development phase. Up-front funding is also likely to be needed in projects where results will take a significant amount of time to materialize. Once the concept is proven in specific sectors, support can be phased out.

### 3. Examples/Schemes

- None yet – This is an idea to consider

### 4. Sources

- https://www.worldbank.org/en/news/feature/2022/08/17/what-you-need-to-know-about-results-based-climate-finance

- https://www.tcafwb.org/sites/default/files/2023-05/WB_RBCF_Report_FINAL.pdf

- https://www.climatepolicyinitiative.org/publication/results-based-financing/

## III. CLEAN OR "GREEN" POWER MARKETS

The U.S. renewable electricity market consists of two buyer types: those who are required to purchase renewable electricity and those who voluntarily purchase it. Regardless of whether buyers are required to purchase renewable electricity, they generally want to make a claim or publicly state or disclose that they are purchasing or using renewable energy.

The mandatory market can be thought of as a natural floor to the market, representing the basic minimum percentage of renewable energy provided to users. The voluntary market theoretically represents an unlimited opportunity above this market floor that is only constrained by voluntary demand and capped by total demand for electricity.

An energy attribute certificate (EAC) provides information about the environmental attributes of one megawatt hour (MWh) of electricity. Wind, solar, and biomass generators produce electricity that has not emitted any carbon during its creation. EACs label that electricity as renewable, enabling companies to report lower Scope 2 emissions while demonstrating demand for renewable energy generation. Generators can sell EACs together with the electricity (bundled) or separate from the electricity (unbundled). Both methods are valid, robust ways to track and claim renewable electricity sourcing. Companies can also use EACs to report lower Scope 1 emissions by purchasing renewable gas guarantees of origin, which each represent one kilowatt hour (KWh) of biomethane or "green gas."

EACs, as a generic term, are sometimes also called electricity attribute certificates and can be traded in renewable energy certificates. EACs include, according to the GHG Protocol, "a variety of instruments with different names, including certificates, tags, credits, or generator declarations."

### 1. Sources:

- https://www.epa.gov/green-power-markets/us-renewable-electricity-market

- https://www.climateimpact.com/media/filer_public/83/d7/83d7161a-644f-45d6-ae66-7b3ed437fddb/climate_impact_partners_energy_attribute_certificate_factsheet.pdf

- https://www.epa.gov/green-power-markets/learn-about-green-power-market

- https://www.epa.gov/green-power-markets/renewable-energy-certificates-recs

- https://energy-attribute-certificates.com/

- https://www.epa.gov/green-power-markets/market-instruments

- https://www.enviromarkets.org/resources--what-are-environmental-markets

- https://www.trackingstandard.org/

- https://www.energy.gov/sites/default/files/2023-12/Assessing_Lifecycle_Greenhouse_Gas_Emissions_Associated_with_Electricity_Use_for_the_Section_45V_Clean_Hydrogen_Production_Tax_Credit.pdf

## A. Mandatory/Compliance Clean Power Markets

### 1. Description

Mandatory/compliance markets exist because of policy decisions, such as state renewable portfolio standards (RPSs). RPSs require electric service providers to have a minimum amount of renewable energy in their electricity supply. These policy decisions often specify eligible energy resources or technologies and describe how electricity service providers must comply. In these markets, policymakers may often consider criteria other than environmental attributes (e.g., economic or jobs growth) in setting mandatory market resource and technology eligibility criteria. Electricity service providers use renewable energy certificates (RECs) to demonstrate compliance with mandated renewable energy requirements.

### 2. Critical Elements/Notes

- Many U.S. states have standards that require electricity providers to get some of their electricity from renewable, alternative, or other clean energy sources. Common names for these types of standards include: RPSs, clean energy standards, renewable energy standards (RESs), or alternative energy standards. Whether or not designed explicitly as a climate policy, these standards have been effective at encouraging cleaner domestic electricity production.

- In addition to RESs, some states have clean energy targets or goals. These states have defined terms such as carbon free, carbon neutral, or clean energy in different ways. For example, some states may allow technologies such as nuclear energy or natural gas with carbon capture and storage to count toward clean energy policy targets. Other states have left implementation to regulatory processes and do not yet have formal guidelines on what qualifies to meet the targets.

### 3. Examples/Schemes

- RGGI – Regional Greenhouse Gas Initiative

- RPSs

### 4. Sources

- https://www.eia.gov/energyexplained/renewable-sources/portfolio-standards.php
- https://www.epa.gov/green-power-markets/renewable-energy-market-principles
- https://www.c2es.org/content/renewable-portfolio-standards/
- https://www.iea.org/policies/3514-state-level-renewable-portfolio-standards-rps
- https://emp.lbl.gov/publications/us-state-renewables-portfolio-clean
- https://cleanpower.org/policy/renewable-portfolio-standards/
- https://en.wikipedia.org/wiki/Renewable_portfolio_standard

## B. Voluntary Clean Power Markets

### 1. Description

Voluntary clean power markets (or green power markets) are driven by consumer demand for certain types of renewable energy—often corporate voluntary trading that supports organizational net zero commitments. Voluntary markets allow a consumer to procure renewable electricity at levels above and beyond what mandatory policy decisions require and to reduce the environmental impact of their electricity use. Voluntary green power products must offer a significant benefit and value to buyers to be successful.

To ensure that both compliance and voluntary markets work together to increase supply, it is important that the voluntary market is separate from and incremental to the mandatory market. A purchase made by an individual or organization in the voluntary market must be incremental to any renewable generation claimed under the mandatory market. This concept is often referred to as regulatory surplus and helps ensure that double claims are avoided on the same MWh of renewable energy generation.

### 2. Critical Elements/Notes

To capture clean power benefits, many states have designed their programs to encourage in-state development even though most also allow the environmental benefits to be quantified and traded in a market-based approach. An REC is a common type of EAC used in these programs. Credit trading sends a price signal that the environmental benefits from these clean energy sources have value.

Customers can purchase renewable energy (embodied in RECs) through several market mechanisms:

- Utility green pricing
- Utility green partnerships
- Unbundled EACs/RECs
- Competitive suppliers
- Community choice aggregation (CCA)
- Power purchase agreements (PPAs)
- Community solar

## 3. Sources

- http://resource-solutions.org/images/events/rem/presentations/2017/OShaughnessy-101.pdf
- https://www.mrets.org/about/tracking/
- https://www.mrets.org/wp-content/uploads/2021/02/A-Path-to-Supporting-Data-Driven-Renewable-Energy-Markets-March-2021.pdf
- https://www.nrel.gov/analysis/green-power.html
- http://pdf.wri.org/gpmdg_corporate_6.pdf

## IV. COMMAND AND CONTROL/MANDATES

Command and control (C&C) regulations and/or mandates have their origin in environmental laws and regulations that have had a significant impact on energy policy. C&C laws and regulations set specific limits for energy production, use, or emissions, and/or mandates that specific emissions-control technologies that must be used. As climate and energy policy are a growing societal need, there is growing interest in a heavier-handed or wartime powers approach to using mandates. Historically, C&C regulations have helped to protect the environment. However, they have a number of shortcomings, including: providing no incentive for

going beyond the limits they set, offering limited flexibility on where and how to reduce pollution, and often having politically motivated loopholes.

## 1. Sources:

- https://www.khanacademy.org/economics-finance-domain/microeconomics/market-failure-and-the-role-of-government/environmental-regulation/a/command-and-control-regulation-cnx

### A. Supply Mandates

## 1. Description

Supply mandates are federal, regional, or state minimum production quotas for lower carbon intensity (cleaner) energy.

## 2. Critical Elements/Notes

Supply mandates are requirements to meet certain quotas specified by sector and/or energy source.

## 3. Examples/Schemes

- Renewable fuel standard
- Renewable portfolio standard

## 4. Sources

- https://www.epa.gov/renewable-fuel-standard-program/overview-renewable-fuel-standard
- https://www.eia.gov/energyexplained/renewable-sources/portfolio-standards.php

### B. Energy Safety Laws and Regulations

## 1. Description

Energy safety regulations set safety requirements for production, handling, transport, distribution, and use.

## 2. Critical Elements/Notes

Energy safety regulations vary by industry and energy type. Some statutes specifically designate requirements, while others are only specified in regulations set by agencies. Agencies often incorporate industry standards, e.g., ASME, by reference in regulations.

### 3. Examples/Schemes

- Design standards
- OSHA worker standards

### 4. Sources

- https://www.energy.gov/ehss/health-and-safety

## C. Emissions Limit Mandates

### 1. Description

A policy that requires certain energy emissions to meet an energy-related GHG emissions target (e.g., a specific carbon intensity) within a specified jurisdiction and timeframe.

### 2. Critical Elements/Notes

Key energy emissions limit mandates include emissions or performance-related targets, e.g., miles per gallon limits. These targets are typically phased in over time.

### 3. Examples/Schemes

- Low Carbon Fuel Standard
- CAFE

### 4. Sources

- https://crsreports.congress.gov/product/pdf/R/R46835
- https://www.nhtsa.gov/laws-regulations/corporate-average-fuel-economy

## D. Emissions Monitoring, Reporting, and Verification (MRV) Requirements

### 1. Description

A GHG monitoring, reporting, and verification program requires emitters to measure, track, and verify their GHG emissions and then report to the relevant agency to compile GHG emissions summaries and provide emissions transparency.

### 2. Critical Elements/Notes

MRV is a policy intended to provide GHG emissions transparency. Accurately measuring emissions is an essential element to reducing GHG emissions.

### 3. Examples/Schemes

- EPA GHG Reporting Protocol (GHGRP)

### 4. Sources

- https://www.epa.gov/ghgreporting

## E. Technology Switching Requirements

### 1. Description

Phasing out older, higher-emitting technologies and phasing in newer, cleaner technologies is a fundamental component of innovation and change in the energy industry. Switching requirements are intended to accelerate this change beyond what would occur normally within the market.

### 2. Critical Elements/Notes

- Mandates to switch from higher-emitting energy sources to lower-emitting energy sources include targets and timelines.
- This policy approach bypasses market forces by picking winners and losers in the market and thus is not considered an efficient policy approach.

### 3. Examples/Schemes

- Switch from incandescent to LED bulbs
- Coal to gas policies
- Coal to renewable energy policies
- EPA Power Rule

### 4. Sources

- https://cleantechnica.com/2022/09/06/switching-the-world-to-renewable-energy-will-cost-62-trillion-but-the-payback-would-take-just-6-years/

## F. Environmental Laws and Regulations

### 1. Description

Environmental regulations seek to foster the responsible use of our energy resources, while protecting the environment. The definition of environmental laws and regulations have expanded to include GHG emissions.

## 2. Critical Elements/Notes

Energy laws and regulations are the most debated mandates related to energy. Environmental mandates are typically linked to permitting and siting requirements or emissions limitations and monitoring.

## 3. Examples/Schemes

- National Environmental Protection Act
- Endangered Species Act
- Clean Air Act
- Clean Water Act
- Safe Drinking Water Act

## 4. Sources

- https://www.energy.gov/lpo/environmental-compliance

## G. Carbon Intensity Life Cycle Assessment (LCA) Requirements

### 1. Description

LCA is a methodology for assessing environmental impacts associated with all the stages of the life cycle of a commercial product, process, or service. For instance, in the case of a manufactured product, environmental impacts are assessed from raw material extraction and processing (cradle), through the product's manufacture, distribution, and use, to the recycling or final disposal of the materials composing it (grave). LCA calculations are critical to determining what qualifies as low carbon/"clean" energy.

### 2. Critical Elements/Notes

Different energy sources and demand sectors can have different methods for determining LCA emissions. Some are cradle to grave, while others are cradle to gate.

### 3. Examples/Schemes

- Greenhouse gases, Regulated Emissions, and Energy use in Technologies (GREET) model

### 4. Sources

- https://en.wikipedia.org/wiki/Life-cycle_assessment

- https://www.energy.gov/eere/bioenergy/articles/greet-greenhouse-gases-regulated-emissions-and-energy-use-transportation

## V. MARKET MAKING AND MARKET DESIGN POLICIES

Ideally, market making and design is proactively developed and included as part of a well-developed national and/or regional strategy, instead of reactive legislative and/or regulatory responses to market failures or gaps.

Market making is: (1) the act of creating demand pull to stimulate production and supply chain development for a particular commodity/activity; (2) the act of establishing a support mechanism for new production of a commodity with an established market so that a new entrant can successfully compete (a classic example is the infant industry subsidy programs used to support startup domestic enterprise); (3) a greenfield endeavor aimed at establishing a new commodity market to meet a new/emergent demand (nature-based carbon markets fall into this realm).

## A. Demand Creation (Market Making)

### 1. Description

Demand creation policies stimulate demand and can vary widely and may include education campaigns, increasing/improving access to investment capital, government/industry demand commitments, etc.

### 2. Critical Elements/Notes

- Government manufacturing capacity support (e.g., Defense Production Act)
- Advanced market commitments
- Hydrogen banks
- Climate change case for action/Nationally Determined Contributions (NDC) sector pledges

### 3. Examples/Schemes

- Postal Service EV fleet purchase
- EU Hydrogen Bank
- First Movers Coalition
- Defense Production Act for heat pumps

## 4. Sources

- https://en.wikipedia.org/wiki/Advance_market_commitments
- https://energy.ec.europa.eu/news/commission-outlines-european-hydrogen-bank-boost-renewable-hydrogen-2023-03-16_en
- https://www.weforum.org/agenda/2021/11/first-movers-coalition-john-kerry-net-zero-decarbonization-green-tech/

## B.  Risk or Liability Reduction

### 1.  Description

There are five categories of risk to consider: 1) financial risk; 2) technology risk, e.g., risk of new technology failures; 3) policy risk, e.g., policy implementation uncertainty (will policy function as intended?); 4) liability risks, e.g., liability for climate impacts; and 5) physical risks, e.g., damage caused by climate change.

This is a hybrid of market making. Risk reduction is a policy endeavor aimed at stimulating investment for production activity and supply chain development.

### 2. Critical Elements/Notes

- Guaranteed loan programs (risk guarantees)
- Government managed/backed insurance
- Liability limits
- Climate risk disclosures and climate credit ratings
- Metrics to track policy effectiveness
- Technology diversification

### 3. Examples/Schemes

- Offshore oil spill pollution fund

### 4. Sources

- https://www.uscg.mil/Mariners/National-Pollution-Funds-Center/about_npfc/osltf/

## C.  Energy Technology or Capacity Development

### 1.  Description

Most energy research, development, and demonstration (RD&D) takes place in industrialized countries where both the public and private sectors are involved in the development of energy technologies. Given that the majority of energy technologies are deployed through the marketplace, the predominant locus of RD&D is within firms. Governments have historically played an important role in the RD&D of new energy technologies through direct financial support (e.g., gas turbines) as well as through policies that promote RD&D within firms. The rationale for government involvement in RD&D is multifaceted, including economic development, energy security, national security, etc.

Technology readiness: Although not purely a market making policy option, it does help and is grouped here. Consider how 1970s wind and solar RD&D efforts established the capability for the market that exists today.

### 2. Critical Elements/Notes

- Active government technology support for RD&D, e.g., Manhattan Project
- Passive government technology support for RD&D

### 3. Examples/Schemes

- Manhattan Project (Active)
- Defense Advanced Research Projects Agency (DARPA)-E (Active)
- DOE-funded RD&D labs
- Other government-funded RD&D (DOD, EPA, NOAA, NSF, etc.)

### 4. Sources

- https://www.energy.gov/eere/ssl/research-development
- https://www.iea.org/reports/world-energy-investment-2019/rd-and-d-and-new-technologies
- DOE Technology Readiness Assessment Guide: https://www.directives.doe.gov/directives-documents/400-series/0413.3-EGuide-04a/@@images/file
- https://www.energy.gov/sites/prod/files/em/Volume_I/O_SRP.pdf

## D. Market Barrier Removal (Market Design)

### 1. Description

Removal of perverse laws and regulations that have an unintended and undesirable result and are contrary to the intentions of their designers.

Deregulation is an attempt to remove regulations that may have had negative unintended consequences or to increase competition and consumer choice in the marketplace.

### 2. Critical Elements/Notes

Removal of or changing laws and regulations that may have been deemed inefficient or ineffective.

### 3. Examples/Schemes

- Texas power market deregulation

### 4. Sources

- https://en.wikipedia.org/wiki/Perverse_incentive
- https://en.wikipedia.org/wiki/Deregulation_of_the_Texas_electricity_market

## E. Market Structure and Regulation (Market Design)

### 1. Description

Energy market structure is often limited by access to transport of energy via infrastructure; therefore, energy transport infrastructure development and rates and tariffs may be regulated/approved by government bodies, e.g., the Federal Energy Regulatory Commission (FERC) and public utility commissions.

### 2. Critical Elements/Notes

Wholesale market structure and regulation via:

- Infrastructure permitting and siting
- Rates and tariffs

### 3. Examples/Schemes

- FERC natural gas rate regulation
- Public Utility Commission for power

### 4. Sources

- https://www.ferc.gov/natural-gas
- https://en.wikipedia.org/wiki/Public_utilities_commission

## F. "Clean Energy" Definitions

### 1. Description

Defining what is acceptable for GHG emissions is critical for determining clean energy sources. (This is an interpretation used to enforce laws/regulations, and thus considered a market design policy).

### 2. Critical Elements/Notes

"Clean energy" definitions vary by country and even by some states. Some define as zero emissions, while others accept low carbon intensity definitions.

### 3. Examples/Schemes

- Definition of clean hydrogen

### 4. Sources

- https://www.hydrogen.energy.gov/library/policies-acts/clean-hydrogen-production-standard

## G. Feed-in Tariff (FIT)

### 1. Description

A FIT is a policy designed to support the development of clean energy sources by providing a guaranteed, above-market price for producers. FITs usually involve long-term contracts, from 15 to 20 years. A FIT is a performance-based incentive rather than an investment-based incentive. In that respect, a FIT is more similar to production tax credits and the renewable energy credits of an RPS market than to investment tax credits or other investment subsidies. In the United States, FITs are typically used in combination with one or more of these other incentives.

This is an incentive mechanism that stimulates activity. There are commercial arrangements that underlie execution. This is more of a market making policy.

## 2. Critical Elements/Notes

FITs typically specify:

- Eligible technologies
- Rate and contract terms
- System size and sector restrictions
- Program size limitations

## 3. Examples/Schemes

- U.S. FITs
- Germany FITs
- Japan FITs

## 4. Sources

- https://www.eia.gov/todayinenergy/detail.php?id=11471
- https://en.wikipedia.org/wiki/Feed-in_tariff

## H. Tariffs (Import Restrictions)

## 1. Description

A tariff is a tax imposed by one country on some goods imported from another country for a variety of purposes. This is a market design policy by definition, because it shapes trade flows at the margin.

## 2. Critical Elements/Notes

- Governments impose tariffs to raise revenue, protect domestic industries for national security or environmental reasons, or countervail against uneven global policy and regulatory differences that may result in unfair competitive advantages (e.g., subsidies, protected home markets).

- Tariffs have been put in place by most countries in the world and efforts to lower or eliminate tariffs continue through trade agreement negotiations.

## 3. Examples/Schemes

- Tariffs to protect new industries

- Tariffs to counteract unfair trade imports (anti-dumping duties) and government subsidies (countervailing duties) that result in injury to producers in the import markets, e.g., export taxes and export subsidies; certain types of government support

- Tariffs imposed for natural security, environmental, or other reasons

## 4. Sources

- www.wto.org/english/tratop_e/tariffs_e/tariffs_e.htm
- https://trade-remedies.wto.org/en

## I. Export Restrictions

## 1. Description

The U.S. government restricts the export of a number of items it deems potentially threatening to national security or its vital economic interests, including weapons, technology, technical data, and even technical assistance and training. Most restrictions apply to specific items that have actual or potential military applications or that the U.S. government considers could harm the economic interests of the country.

In addition to restricting the export of specific items or know-how, the rules also restrict exports to specific countries, organizations, and even individuals. U.S. exporters must first apply for a license before exporting products, technology, or know-how subject to restrictions, or to a restricted country, organization, or individual. Some countries also limit the export of natural resources for other reasons (be it metal scrap, food, chemicals, or other goods).

This is a market design policy by definition, because it shapes trade flows at the margin.

## 2. Critical Elements/Notes

- The U.S. government imposes numerous restrictions on the export of a wide range of items it deems could threaten national security or vital economic interests.

- Most restricted items are weapons and advanced technology, but the rules also apply to technical data and even providing assistance or training to non-U.S. citizens.

- U.S. export restrictions also target specific countries, organizations, and even individuals.

- The complex set of rules is administered by a variety of different agencies, each with its own lists and often its own policies and procedures. Exporters must check both the item and the destination and reconcile information from at least two different agencies.

### 3. Examples/Schemes

- U.S. restrictions on high-tech drilling equipment export restrictions
- Advanced weapons technology export restrictions
- Nuclear energy technology

### 4. Sources

- https://www.investopedia.com/u-s-export-restrictions-6753407
- https://www.trade.gov/us-export-controls

## J. Trade Agreements

### 1. Description

A trade agreement (also known as trade pact) may include narrow, sector-specific agreements or more wide-ranging agreements that set rules for tariffs, market access, standards, customs and related measures, intellectual property, investment protections, and other issues. Trade agreements may be bilateral, regional, plurilateral, or global, such as the agreements creating the World Trade Organization. Trade treaties often include investment guarantees. They exist when two or more countries agree on terms that help them trade with each other.

The most common trade agreements are of the preferential and free trade types, which aim to reduce (or eliminate) tariffs, quotas, and other trade restrictions on items traded between the signatories.

This is a market design policy by definition, because it shapes trade flows at the margin.

### 2. Critical Elements/Notes

The logic of formal trade agreements is that they outline what is agreed upon and the punishments for deviation from the rules set in the agreement. Trade agreements therefore decrease the likelihood of misunderstandings and create confidence on both sides that cheating will be punished, thereby increasing the likelihood of long-term cooperation. An international organization, such as the International Monetary Fund (IMF), can further incentivize cooperation by monitoring compliance with agreements and reporting violations. Monitoring by international agencies may be needed to detect nontariff barriers, which are disguised attempts at creating trade barriers.

### 3. Examples/Schemes

- Geographic (North America)
- Bilateral vs. multilateral
- Scope or level of integration, e.g., EU, NAFTA
- Special agreements, e.g., energy only, food only

### 4. Sources

- www.wto.org/english/tratop_e/region_e/region_e.htm
- https://ustr.gov/trade-agreements
- https://www.energycharter.org/process/energy-charter-treaty-1994/energy-charter-treaty/
- https://www.api.org/news-policy-and-issues/trade

## K. Government Managed Supply

### 1. Description

The U.S. Strategic Petroleum Reserve (SPR) was created to provide a large stockpile for U.S. energy security and military fuel reserves. Government managed supply is contrary to market economics and should only be used for very specific needs.

This is a market intervention tool that can be used to mitigate price movements or volatility, i.e., it is like government-held storage. It is often motivated by national security objectives.

### 2. Critical Elements/Notes

- Direct government supply management

### 3. Examples/Schemes

- Direct government supply management

## 4. Sources

- https://www.energy.gov/ceser/strategic-petro leum-reserve

## L. Government Supply Oversight (Indirect Government Management)

### 1. Description

Typically reserved for use of U.S. resources on federal lands or offshore, this process allows for more equitable and efficient leasing of U.S. energy resources that are owned by the public.

It is best described as a market design policy, as it refers to the use of government-owned resources. This is a regulatory apparatus in a functioning market.

### 2. Critical Elements/Notes

- Government leasing planning cycles, e.g., energy industry supply mandates or quotas

### 3. Examples/Schemes

- BOEM 5-year plan for offshore leasing

### 4. Sources

- https://www.boem.gov/oil-gas-energy/ national-program/national-ocs-oil-and-gas-leasing-program

## M. Supply Chain Resiliency and Security

### 1. Description

Supply chain resiliency and security are typically improved through a variety of different policies, e.g., trade agreements, but may also require specific security monitoring and enforcement policies and workforce development/training programs.

This is an outcome of policy interventions. It is not really a market design or market making policy.

### 2. Critical Elements/Notes

- Workforce training and development programs
- Supply chain physical security
- Supply chain cyber security

### 3. Examples/Schemes

- Critical supply management agreements, e.g., critical minerals
- Security/trade agreements
- Arabian Gulf maritime security patrols
- U.S. nuclear fuels and training programs managed by DOE

### 4. Sources

- https://www.energy.gov/articles/doe-releases-first-ever-comprehensive-strategy-secure-americas-clean-energy-supply-chain

## VI. PUBLIC ENGAGEMENT & INFORMATION POLICIES

## A. Public Information Programs

### 1. Description

Programs to enhance public understanding and acceptance of initiatives intended to improve or change existing programs.

### 2. Critical Elements/Notes

- Government sponsored programs
- Industry sponsored programs

### 3. Examples/Schemes

- The Alliance to Save Energy
- U.S. public service advertisements to save energy or provide energy education

### 4. Sources

- https://pueblo.gpo.gov/Publications/Pueblo Pubs.php
- https://www.iea.org/commentaries/ empowering-people-to-act-how-awareness-and-behaviour-campaigns-can-enable-citizens-to-save-energy-during-and-beyond-today-s-energy-crisis
- https://sustainabledevelopment.un.org/ content/documents/1477background2.pdf
- https://www.adcouncil.org/

## B. Public Awareness Programs

### 1. Description

Programs intended to inform the public of existing or planned activities, structures, or safety hazards.

### 2. Critical Elements/Notes

- Establish programs
- Develop opportunities to interface with public
- Establish hotlines, websites, and other programs for the public to seek information when needed

### 3. Examples/Schemes

- U.S. pipeline hazard awareness – Call before you dig programs

### 4. Sources

- API RP 1162
- https://pipelineawareness.org/

## C. Community Engagement (CE)

### 1. Description

CE is the process of collaborating with stakeholders and community members to identify and evaluate investments and operations, e.g., clean energy solutions. Effective community engagement requires in-depth training, along with an understanding of facilitation methods, community groups, and their histories.

### 2. Critical Elements/Notes

CE program implementation options:

- Voluntary
- Industry recommended practices
- Government requirements/mandates
- Independent evaluation/monitoring
- Government policies w/incentives

### 3. Examples/Schemes

- Industry practices, e.g., API RP 1185 – pipelines
- IPIECA
- Federal Permitting Council

### 4. Sources

- https://www.nrel.gov/docs/fy22osti/82937.pdf (NREL Best Practices)
- IPIECA - https://www.ipieca.org/work/people/working-with-local-communities

## D. Environmental Justice and Other Justice Programs

### 1. Description

Environmental justice is the fair treatment and meaningful involvement of all people, regardless of race, color, national origin, or income, with respect to the development, implementation, and enforcement of environmental laws, regulations, and policies.

### 2. Sources

- https://www.epa.gov/environmentaljustice (inactive)
- https://iejusa.org/resources/
- https://mitsloan.mit.edu/ideas-made-to-matter/why-energy-justice-a-rising-priority-policymakers
- https://bidenwhitehouse.archives.gov/environmentaljustice/

## VII. ENERGY STRATEGIES

## A. National Energy Strategy

### 1. Description

A national energy policy is a set of measures covering that country's laws, treaties, and agency directives. These can be comprehensive for all energy sources and sectors or specific to a supply or demand sector. As the name implies, these are strategic in nature and thus are projected plans for years in advance, e.g., 10 to 30 years into the future.

### 2. Critical Elements/Notes

The energy policy of a sovereign nation may include one or more of the following:

a. Market design/formation or reformation focused on:

- Overcoming technical barriers and RD&D support

- Market structure, e.g., exchanges, indexes
- Raw material supply and policies
- Geographic barriers and policies
- Environmental issues and policies
- Economic policies (taxes, subsidies, etc.)
- Regulatory oversight
- Fairness, e.g., EJ, communities, health
- Economic impact and jobs

b. Supply (expansion)
- Goals/targets
- Competition and barriers to entry

c. Demand
- Acceptance and safety
- Growth vs. suppression (efficiency)

d. Infrastructure (transport and storage)

e. Energy Security
- Reliability
- Resilience
- Affordability

## 3. Examples/Schemes
- U.S. Clean $H_2$ Strategy & Roadmap (2023)
- British Energy Security Strategy

## 4. Sources
- https://en.wikipedia.org/wiki/Energy_policy
- https://iea.blob.core.windows.net/assets/c5bc75b1-9e4d-460d-9056-6e8e626a11c4/GlobalHydrogenReview2022.pdf
- https://www.hydrogen.energy.gov/docs/hydrogenprogramlibraries/pdfs/us-national-clean-hydrogen-strategy-roadmap.pdf?Status=Master

## B. Other Government Energy/Climate Strategies

## 1. Description

Strategies can be executed at the federal, state, regional, or local level. Additionally, govern-ment strategies can be organized by agency, e.g., DOD's climate strategy. Ideally, all federal, state, regional, and local energy strategies are aligned with the national strategy.

## 2. Examples/Schemes
- State climate strategies
- City climate strategies
- County climate strategies
- Agency climate strategies

## 3. Sources
- https://sustainable.dc.gov/climateready
- https://www.houstontx.gov/mayor/Resilient-Houston-Two-Year-Report.pdf
- https://www.codot.gov/programs/environmental/Sustainability/assets/colorado-climate-plan-2015
- https://ww2.arb.ca.gov/news/california-releases-final-2022-climate-scoping-plan-proposal
- https://www.defense.gov/News/News-Stories/Article/Article/2787056/dod-announces-plan-to-tackle-climate-crisis/

## C. Industry/Trade Energy Strategies (Nongovernment)

## 1. Description

Industry strategies are typically coordinated through relevant trade organizations

## 2. Critical Elements/Notes

Industry/companies may develop strategies to address risks to their industry/business inter-ests related to climate change. Some actions may include:

- Climate Action Plans
- GHG reporting
- Climate risks goals and targets
- GHG emissions goals and targets
- Internal carbon pricing
- Energy efficiency

- Climate financing
- Vision for climate adaptation

## 3. Examples/Schemes

- API Climate Action Framework
- API Climate Action Framework
- Global Steel Climate Council Climate Standard

## 4. Sources

- https://www.c2es.org/content/business-strategies-to-address-climate-change/
- https://www.api.org/climate
- https://globalsteelclimatecouncil.org/newsroom/gscc-publishes-label-for-certified-science-based-emissions-target/

# Appendix R

# CONSIDERATIONS FOR USING GRID-CONNECTED POWER FOR RENEWABLE HYDROGEN

The Section 45V Clean Hydrogen Production Credit discussed in Chapter 6: Policy is the primary policy mechanism for accelerating low carbon intensity hydrogen (LCI $H_2$) growth in the United States. In terms of renewable hydrogen (RE $H_2$), the policy introduces three key topics: 1) temporal matching, 2) geographic matching, and 3) additionality.[1] These requirements are inherently satisfied if the electrolyzers are directly connected to bespoke wind and/or solar electricity generation plants, as assumed for the Modeling in this study. However, many RE $H_2$ facilities may choose instead to connect to the electricity grid to accommodate the variability of wind and solar generation. Summarized in this appendix are considerations for the use of grid-connected power for RE $H_2$ production.[2]

The value of the 45V credit ranges from \$0.60 to \$3.00 per kilogram of $H_2$, depending on the carbon intensity (CI) of the production process. For grid-connected RE $H_2$ production, the CI of the grid influences the CI of the resulting RE $H_2$. In light of this, renewable electricity accounting frameworks, such as those underlying energy attribute certificates (like renewable energy certificates, which have been in existence for more than two decades), will need to be used.

The 45V provisions address the concern that the increased load from $H_2$ projects could divert energy from existing renewable capacity on the grid, which could lead to $H_2$ projects increasing overall grid emissions. One approach is for project developers to prove their energy consumption is being offset by renewable power that is new ("additional"), delivered within the same geographic area ("deliverability"), and occurs within times when the electrolyzer is consuming power for operation ("temporal matching").[3, 4, 5] Additional renewable power refers to using electricity only from power sources that would otherwise not exist on the grid, meaning that LCI $H_2$ projects would not divert existing zero-emitting power from regular grid needs. Temporal matching

---

1   These tenets are intended to prevent RE $H_2$ facilities from negatively impacting the use of renewable electricity for other purposes. "Temporal matching" requires the renewable electricity to be generated within a specified time period of its consumption by the electrolyzer: e.g., hourly, daily, or monthly. "Geographic matching" (or "deliverability") requires the renewable electricity to be generated within the same electricity distribution region as the electrolyzer. "Additionality" (or "incrementality") requires the renewable electricity to be generated by new generation capacity. The specific rules for meeting these requirements are provided in the associated regulations and tax code.

2   Department of the Treasury, Internal Revenue Service. "88 FR 89220: Section 45V Credit for Production of Clean Hydrogen; Section 48(a)(15) Election to Treat Clean Hydrogen Production Facilities as Energy Property." *Federal Register*, Vol. 88, No. 246, December 26, 2023: 89220-89255. https://www.federalregister.gov/documents/2023/12/26/2023-28359/section-45v-credit-for-production-of-clean-hydrogen-section-48a15-election-to-treat-clean-hydrogen.

3   EUR-Lex. "European Parliament on the Promotion of the Use of Energy from Renewable Sources." December 11, 2018. https://eur-lex.europa.eu/eli/dir/2018/2001/oj.

4   Baker McKenzie. "Hydrogen Developments." February 2024. https://resourcehub.bakermckenzie.com/en/resources/hydrogen-heat-map/emea/european-union/topics/hydrogen-developments.

5   Cybulsky, A., Giovanniello, M., Schittekatte, T., and Mallapragada, D. "Producing Hydrogen Producing Hydrogen from Electricity: From Electricity: An MIT Energy Initiative Working Paper How Modeling Additionality Drives the Emissions Impact of Time-Matching Requirements." Massachusetts Institute of Technology. April 2023. https://energy.mit.edu/wp-content/uploads/2023/04/MITEI-WP-2023-02.pdf.

would require the operator to track the power sources of $H_2$ plants over a specific duration (e.g., annually, quarterly, monthly, hourly) to account for the degree of alignment between electrolyzer operation and consumption of zero-emitting power. Lastly, deliverability is intended to ensure that the zero-emitting power used by the $H_2$ plants is in the same geographic area and is capable of supplying the plant without encountering congestion or transmission line losses.[6, 7]

The 45V requirements introduce several project-level uncertainties for grid-connected RE $H_2$ production. One is the impact on project costs. Another is the viability of tracking emissions at different temporal granularities, since reliable monitoring and verification methods for tracking hourly grid emissions are still in development.[8]

While such accounting measures are intended to ensure that LCI $H_2$ production is lowering emissions,[9] monitoring grid and RE $H_2$ CI comes with trade-offs. These include increased costs, reduced production, project delays, and capital risk.[10] Looser restrictions on time/regional matching and additionality, or excluding these requirements altogether, would likely expedite the deployment of electrolyzers. This may increase emissions in the near term, by allowing electrolyzers to run from higher-emissions grid power when dedicated renewable resources are not available or when they are unable to contract for zero-emitting power. However, the projected continual lower CI of supplying the grid as more renewables are brought online may mitigate this concern. Since GREET's CI for grid-connected projects is about 20 kg $CO_2$/kg $H_2$, any exclusive grid-powered $H_2$ production project would be excluded from 45V eligibility (at least at the higher-tier values).

As a compromise, a phase-in approach balances these trade-offs and provides strong market signals that incentivize LCI $H_2$ and encourage more renewables to come online. In February 2023, the European Union enacted a phased-in $H_2$ framework approach that would require additionality beginning in 2028 (with a grandfathering exemption clause), and hourly matching in 2030 (with no grandfathering or legacies allowed).[11] Clarity and consistency in rules and regulations are key so that both investors and industry favor lower emissions methods of production and can quickly make investment determinations.

6   Ruhnau, Oliver, and Johanna Schiele. 2023. "Flexible Green Hydrogen: The Effect of Relaxing Simultaneity Requirements for Project Design, Economics, and Power Sector Emissions." *Energy Policy* 182 (November): 113763. https://doi.org/10.1 Department of the Treasury, Internal Revenue Service. 016/j.enpol.2023.113763.

7   Note that the importance of these three elements for ensuring that grid emissions are not adversely affected by new hydrogen production load is a point of active debate. Early academic studies based on modeling argued that these elements were essential, but more recently, studies examining the underlying modeling assumptions or using historical data and taking a project-level (versus system-level) perspective have questioned the necessity of requiring all three elements at the same time. Given the lack of a clear corollary in how the nascent electrolytic hydrogen industry will actually affect grid emissions, this debate is likely to persist through at least the Activation phase, if not also the Expansion phase.

8   PJM interconnection has experience with hourly matching and discussions with M-RETS (https://www.mrets.org) and EnergyTag ("Carbon Accounting and Tracking for 24/7 Clean Grids," 2024; https://energytag.org/) that show the feasibility of hourly tracking. However, PJM's experience also underscores how regional differences can influence the viability of such tracking, given its heavy reliance on civilian nuclear—it makes up approximately one-third of generation of one-fifth of installed capacity—versus more intermittent sources of energy.

9   Ricks, W., Xu, O., and Jenkins, J.D. 2023. "Minimizing Emissions from Grid-Based Hydrogen Production in the United States." *Environmental Research Letters* 18 (1): 014025–25. https://doi.org/10.1088/1748-9326/acacb5.

10  Forcing intermittent operation could also impact equipment. For example, existing hydrogen users such as refineries and ammonia plants operate on a 24-7 basis, only shutting down every few years for significant maintenance or unanticipated events. Stopping and starting these facilities is detrimental to the equipment and it also entails greater energy usage in the start-up operations.

11  It is important to note that the EU Rules include a review clause in 2028 on these criteria. This is to review whether they are still relevant in view of the development of the market.

# Appendix S

# HISTORY AND EVOLUTION OF TODAY'S COMMUNITY AND ENVIRONMENTAL JUSTICE ISSUES

Note: This section has been jointly developed by the Societal Considerations and Impacts (SCI) Task Group 5 for the National Petroleum Council's (NPC) *Charting the Course* greenhouse gas emissions study and *Harnessing Hydrogen* hydrogen energy study.

## A. Introduction

From the outset, environmental justice (EJ) advocates have sought remedies for the disproportionate impact borne by marginalized communities due to social policies (i.e., redlining, blockbusting, predatory loans, restrictive covenants)[1, 2] or land use planning (i.e., racial zoning ordinances, urban redevelopment or gentrification, unequal enforcement of zoning, and environmental laws).[3, 4] These concepts were described as environmental racism, a form of institutional discrimination that involves a complex system of institutionalized policies, practices, and directives that differentially impact or disadvantage (intentionally or unintentionally), individuals, groups, or communities based on race.[5] In many cases, this environmental racism manifests as industrial facilities and their associated impacts being positioned disproportionately in minoritized neighborhoods.[6] Dr. Robert Bullard, often called the father of environmental justice, described it succinctly:

"Whether by conscious design or institutional neglect, communities of color in urban ghettos, in rural poverty pockets, or on economically impoverished Native American reservations face some of the worst environmental devastation in the nation."[7]

The mainstream environmental movement of the 1960s and 1970s heavily focused environmentalists' efforts on the natural world.[8] It was not until intersectional environmentalism and EJ came into the picture in the 1980s that built environments were fully integrated into advocacy

1   Rothstein, Richard. 2015. "The Making of Ferguson." *Journal of Affordable Housing & Community Development Law* 24 (2): 165–204. https://www.jstor.org/stable/26408162.

2   Holland, Joshua. "How a Century of Racist Policies Made Ferguson into a Pocket of Concentrated Despair." October 27, 2014. https://billmoyers.com/2014/10/27/century-racist-policies-created-ferguson/.

3   EPA. "Addressing Community Concerns: How Environmental Justice Relates to Land Use Planning and Zoning." 2003. https://www.epa.gov/sites/default/files/2015-02/documents/napa-land-use-zoning-63003.pdf.

4   EPA. "Equitable Development and Environmental Justice." https://www.epa.gov/environmentaljustice/equitable-development-and-environmental-justice.

5   Holland, Joshua. "How a Century of Racist Policies Made Ferguson into a Pocket of Concentrated Despair." October 27, 2014. https://billmoyers.com/2014/10/27/century-racist-policies-created-ferguson/.

6   Peña-Parr, Victoria. "The Complicated History of Environmental Racism." University of New Mexico. August 4, 2020. https://news.unm.edu/news/the-complicated-history-of-environmental-racism.

7   EPA. 2019. "Environmental Justice Timeline." https://www.epa.gov/environmentaljustice/environmental-justice-timeline.

8   University of Minnesota, Duluth. "Environmentalism vs. Environmental Justice." 2020. https://sustainability.d.umn.edu/environmentalism-vs-environmental-justice.

for environmental protections.[9, 10, 11] EJ advocates expanded the concept of the environment in the 1980s to include the places where people "live, work, play, go to school, as well as the physical and natural world,"[12] as a means of uniting the physical and cultural environments—and their respective justice movements—under integrated and collaborative banners.[13]

The EJ movement's birthplace is considered by many to be the Warren County, N.C., polychlorinated biphenyl (PCB) landfill battle in 1982. Civil rights organizers in North Carolina protested a proposed landfill in a county comprised of predominately Black American communities. The project posed environmental risks because a shallow water table at the landfill site created the opportunity for potential groundwater-soil-waste interactions. Because issues of racial, economic, and social justice had nexus with issues of environmental risks, the Warren County collective actions highlighted a previously unconsidered aspect of mainstream environmentalism: whether minorities and poor communities were facing environmental harms and risks at a greater rate than other groups in society.[14] The project proceeded and ultimately more than 120 million pounds of PCB-contaminated soil was placed in the landfill. Subsequently, scholars and community organizers shifted their focus from individual protest actions to documenting instances of perceived environmental racism and the correlation between pollution, race, and poverty.[15, 16, 17]

Several landmark studies starting in the 1980s[18] and continuing today[19, 20, 21] seek to establish correlations, and, where possible, hypothesize causation[22] for the economic, environmental,

9   University of Minnesota, Duluth. "Environmentalism vs. Environmental Justice." 2020. https://sustainability.d.umn.edu/environmentalism-vs-environmental-justice.

10  University of Washington, College of the Environment. "Climate Justice and Sustainability." https://environment.uw.edu/about/diversity-equity-inclusion/climate-justice-sustainability/.

11  Sandler, R. and Phaedra C. Pezzullo, ed. *Environmental Justice and Environmentalism: The Social Justice Challenge to the Environmental Movement.* 2007. The MIT Press. https://direct.mit.edu/books/edited-volume/4413/Environmental-Justice-and-Environmentalism.

12  Schweizer, Errol. "Environmental Justice: An Interview with Robert Bullard." *Earth First! Journal.* July 1999. http://www.ejnet.org/ej/bullard.html.

13  Schweizer, Errol. "Environmental Justice: An Interview with Robert Bullard." *Earth First! Journal.* July 1999. http://www.ejnet.org/ej/bullard.html.

14  Mohai, P., Pellow, D., and Roberts, J.T. 2009. "Environmental Justice." *Annual Review of Environment and Resources* 34 (1): 405–30. https://doi.org/10.1146/annurev-environ-082508-094348.

15  Bullard, Robert. 1994. "Journal of Civil Rights and Economic Development." *The Legacy of American Apartheid and Environmental Racism.* https://scholarship.law.stjohns.edu/cgi/viewcontent.cgi?article=1460&context=jcred.

16  Bullard, Robert D. 2003. "Confronting Environmental Racism in the 21st Century." *Race, Poverty & the Environment* 10 (1): 49–52. http://www.jstor.org/stable/41554377.

17  Bullard, Robert D. 2001. "Environmental Justice in the 21st Century: Race Still Matters." *Phylon (1960-)* 49 (3/4): 151. https://doi.org/10.2307/3132626.

18  Commission for Racial Justice, United Church of Christ. 1987. "Toxic Wastes and Race in the United States: A National Report on the Racial and Socio-Economic Characteristics of Communities with Hazardous Waste Sites." https://new.uccfiles.com/pdf/ToxicWastes&Race.pdf.

19  U.S. Government Accountability Office. "GAO-19-543, Environmental Justice: Federal Efforts Need Better Planning, Coordination, and Methods to Assess Progress." *GAO Highlights.* September 2019. https://www.liebertpub.com/doi/10.1089/env.2020.0054.

20  Kojola, Erik, and David N. Pellow. 2021. "New Directions in Environmental Justice Studies: Examining the State and Violence." *Environmental Politics* 30 (1-2): 100-118. https://doi.org/10.1080/09644016.2020.1836898.

21  Hendricks, Marccus D., and Shannon Van Zandt. 2021. "Unequal Protection Revisited: Planning for Environmental Justice, Hazard Vulnerability, and Critical Infrastructure in Communities of Color." *Environmental Justice* 14 (2). https://doi.org/10.1089/env.2020.0054.

22  Wolverton, Ann. 2009. "Effects of Socio-Economic and Input-Related Factors on Polluting Plants' Location Decisions." *The B.E. Journal of Economic Analysis & Policy* 9 (1). https://doi.org/10.2202/1935-1682.2083. https://ideas.repec.org/a/bpj/bejeap/v9y2009i1n14.html.

and social factors contributing to environmental racism.[23, 24, 25, 26] Early studies found that decisions on industrial development were often rationalized when it came to socioeconomic factors. However, this can cause timing and cause-and-effect problems, leading to erroneous conclusions about unfair treatment of residents in areas with industrial development. This became known colloquially as the Chicken and the Egg debate: Which came first—the facilities that were sited or the communities that were/would be disproportionately impacted?[27, 28, 29, 30, 31, 32, 33] Wolverton (2009) noted: "When plant location is matched to current socioeconomic characteristics, results are consistent with what the environmental justice literature predicts: Race is significantly and positively related to plant location, while income is significantly and negatively related to plant location. When plant location is matched to socioeconomic characteristics at the time of siting, empirical results suggest that race is no longer significant, though income is still significantly and negatively related to plant location."[34] This change might be due to people relocating or other socioeconomic factors over time.[35, 36] There is, however, a strong correlation

23  United Church of Christ—Commission for Racial Justice. "Toxic Wastes and Race in the United States: A National Report on the Racial and Socio-Economic Characteristics of Communities with Hazardous Waste Sites." 1987. Reproduced from the UCC archives. https://new.uccfiles.com/pdf/ToxicWastes&Race.pdf.

24  Kojola, Erik, and David N. Pellow. 2020. "New Directions in Environmental Justice Studies: Examining the State and Violence." *Environmental Politics* 30 (1-2): 100-118. https://doi.org/10.1080/09644016.2020.1836898.

25  Hendricks, Marccus D., and Shannon Van Zandt. 2021. "Unequal Protection Revisited: Planning for Environmental Justice, Hazard Vulnerability, and Critical Infrastructure in Communities of Color." *Environmental Justice* 14 (2): 87–97. https://doi.org/10.1089/env.2020.0054.

26  Wolverton, Ann. 2009. "Effects of Socio-Economic and Input-Related Factors on Polluting Plants' Location Decisions." *The B.E. Journal of Economic Analysis & Policy* 9 (1). https://doi.org/10.2202/1935-1682.2083.

27  Mohai, Paul, and Robin Saha. 2015. "Which Came First, People or Pollution? Assessing the Disparate Siting and Post-Siting Demographic Change Hypotheses of Environmental Injustice." *Environmental Research Letters* 10 (11): 115008. https://doi.org/10.1088/1748-9326/10/11/115008.

28  Williams, Kirsten. 2022. "The Impact of Foresight: Reframing Discriminatory Intent to Properly Remedy Environmental Racism." *Houston Law Review* 59 (5): 1231–61. https://houstonlawreview.org/article/36549-the-impact-of-foresight-reframing-discriminatory-intent-to-properly-remedy-environmental-racism.

29  Zhang, Ruohao. 2023. "Behind Environmental Injustice: Disparate Siting Industries and Post-siting Demographic Transformation." Presented Friday, January 6, 2023, at the Environmental Justice and Inequality session at the American Economic Association Conference in New Orleans, Louisiana. https://www.aeaweb.org/conference/2023/program/powerpoint/EYDFa2hz.

30  Pastor, M., Sadd, J., and Hipp, J. 2001. "Which Came First? Toxic Facilities, Minority Move-In, and Environmental Justice." *Journal of Urban Affairs* 23 (1): 1–21. https://doi.org/10.1111/0735-2166.00072.

31  Billias, Christopher. 1998. "Environmental Racism and Hazardous Facility Siting Decisions: Noble Cause or Political Tool?" *Washington and Lee Journal of Civil Rights and Social Justice* 4 (1): 36. https://scholarlycommons.law.wlu.edu/crsj/vol4/iss1/5.

32  Taylor, Dorceta E. 2014. *Toxic Communities: Environmental Racism, Industrial Pollution, and Residential Mobility.* NYU Press. http://www.jstor.org/stable/j.ctt9qglv9.

33  Zhang, Ruohao. "Behind Environmental Injustice: Disparate Siting Industries and Post-siting Demographic Transformation." December 10, 2022. https://www.ruohaozhang.com/uploads/1/3/1/0/131057686/siting_and_migration.pdf.

34  Wolverton, Ann. 2009. "Effects of Socio-Economic and Input-Related Factors on Polluting Plants' Location Decisions." *The B.E. Journal of Economic Analysis & Policy* 9 (1). https://doi.org/10.2202/1935-1682.2083.

35  Banzhaf, S., Ma, L., and Timmins, C. 2019. "Environmental Justice: Establishing Causal Relationships." *Annual Review of Resource Economics* 11 (1): 377–98. https://econpapers.repec.org/article/anrreseco/v_3a11_3ay_3a2019_3ap_3a377-398.htm.

36  Banzhaf, S., Ma, L., and Timmins, C. 2019. "Environmental Justice: The Economics of Race, Place, and Pollution." *Journal of Economic Perspectives* 33 (1): 185–208. https://doi.org/10.1257/jep.33.1.185.

between racial discrimination and siting[37, 38, 39, 40] found in the literature.[41]

Scholars have argued that environmental injustices happen because of the way racial groups are distributed across areas.[42, 43] Hundreds of studies conclude that, in general, ethnic minorities, Indigenous persons, people of color, and low-income communities experience a relatively higher burden of environmental exposure from air, water, and soil pollution from industrialization, militarization, and consumer practices.[44] Being able to distinguish between intent, which requires demonstrated motivation, and impact, which requires a causal relationship, would become a subject of future debates.[45]

## B. Federal Action

### 1. The First Executive Order

On February 11, 1994, President Clinton issued Executive Order 12898: Federal Actions to Address Environmental Justice in Minority Populations and Low-Income Populations. The purpose was to bring federal attention to the environmental and human health effects of federal actions on minority populations and low-income populations, and the order established an Interagency Working Group on environmental justice.[46]

*Sec. 1–101. To the greatest extent practicable and permitted by law, and consistent with the principles set forth in the report on the National Performance Review, each Federal agency shall make achieving environmental justice part of its mission by identifying and addressing, as appropriate, disproportionately high and adverse human health or environmental effects of its programs, policies, and activities on minority populations and low-income populations in the United States and its territories and possessions, the District of Columbia, the Commonwealth of Puerto Rico, and the Commonwealth of the Mariana Islands.*

*Sec. 2–2. Each Federal agency shall conduct its programs, policies, and activities that substantially affect human health or the environment, in a manner that ensures that such programs, policies, and activities do not have the effect of excluding persons (including populations) from participation in, denying persons (including populations) the benefits of, or subjecting persons (including populations) to discrimination under, such programs, policies, and activities, because of their race, color, or national origin.*

It was not until President Clinton's next term that U.S. federal government policy began publishing a singular definition for EJ. The term "environmental justice" was not used in the *Federal Register* in 1990, 1991, or 1992, suggesting that the 1993 publication was the first time this term was used publicly by federal agencies. The term

37  Iceland, John. 2019. "Racial and Ethnic Inequality in Poverty and Affluence, 1959–2015." *Population Research and Policy Review* 38 (5). https://doi.org/10.1007/s11113-019-09512-7.

38  Brown, M.A., Soni, A., Doshi, A.D., and King, C. 2020. "The Persistence of High Energy Burdens: A Bibliometric Analysis of Vulnerability, Poverty, and Exclusion in the United States." *Energy Research & Social Science* 70 (December): 101756. https://doi.org/10.1016/j.erss.2020.101756.

39  Baldwin, Davarian L., and Emma S. Crane. 2020. "Cities, Racialized Poverty, and Infrastructures of Possibility." *Antipode* 52 (2): 365–79. https://doi.org/10.1111/anti.12600.

40  Faber, Jacob W. 2020. "We Built This: Consequences of New Deal Era Intervention in America's Racial Geography." *American Sociological Review* 85 (5): 739–75. https://doi.org/10.1177/0003122420948464.

41  Mohai, Paul, and Robin Saha. 2015. "Which Came First, People or Pollution? Assessing the Disparate Siting and Post-Siting Demographic Change Hypotheses of Environmental Injustice." *Environmental Research Letters* 10 (11): 115008. https://doi.org/10.1088/1748-9326/10/11/115008.

42  Pulido, Laura. 2000. "Rethinking Environmental Racism: White Privilege and Urban Development in Southern California." *Annals of the Association of American Geographers* 90 (1): 12–40. https://doi.org/10.1111/0004-5608.00182.

43  Vaz, E., Anthony, A., and McHenry, M. 2017. "The Geography of Environmental Injustice." *Habitat International* 59 (January): 118–25. https://doi.org/10.1016/j.habitatint.2016.12.001.

44  Mohai, P., Pellow, D., and Roberts, J.T. 2009. "Environmental Justice." *Annual Review of Environment and Resources* 34 (1): 405–30. https://doi.org/10.1146/annurev-environ-082508-094348.

45  Mohai, P., Pellow, D., and Roberts, J.T. 2009. "Environmental Justice." *Annual Review of Environment and Resources* 34 (1): 405–30. https://doi.org/10.1146/annurev-environ-082508-094348.

46  Exec. Order No. 12898, 59 FR 7629 (1994). http://www.archives.gov/federal-register/executive-orders/pdf/12898.pdf.

became more popular throughout the late 1990s and into the 2000s.

Nonetheless, to date, there is no landmark federal EJ legislation, and efforts in the movement to seek judicial remedy may have been limited by this. Previous attempts to pass federal law, such as the previously proposed *Environmental Justice Act of 1992*,[47] lacked the votes necessary to pass in Congress. The next attempt at federal EJ was the law introduced in 2018 and again in 2021, entitled the *Environmental Justice for All Act*.[48] While sweeping legislation supporting EJ has faced political challenges, the movement has leveraged other areas of existing law to build jurisprudence to address environmental injustice claims. These include the 14th Amendment to the U.S. Constitution (Equal Protection Clause), the Fair Housing Act of 1968, and the Civil Rights Act of 1964.

## 2. Making Inroads Through the Civil Rights Act of 1964

Title VI, Sections 601 and 602 of the CRA of 1964,[49] have been the primary mechanism for pursuing remedies for claims related to policies and decisions that have been associated with discriminatory practices and/or led to disproportionate impacts being borne by marginalized, disadvantaged, or otherwise minoritized communities.

*Sec. 601. No person in the United States shall, on the ground of race, color, or national origin, be excluded from participation in, be denied the benefits of, or be subjected to discrimination under any program or activity receiving Federal financial assistance.*

*Sec. 602. Each Federal department and agency which is empowered to extend Federal financial assistance to any program or activity, by way of grant, loan, or contract other than a contract of insurance*

*or guaranty, is authorized and directed to effectuate the provisions of section 601 with respect to such program or activity by issuing rules, regulations, or orders of general applicability which shall be consistent with achievement of the objectives of the statute authorizing the financial assistance in connection with which the action is taken.*

Throughout the 1970s and 80s, Title VI had been EJ advocates' primary tool for litigating perceived injustices. In 2001, the U.S. Supreme Court severely limited this mechanism with a pivotal ruling in *Alexander v. Sandoval*.[50] Previously, EJ advocates would have been theoretically capable of leveraging Title VI (Sections 601 and 602) to claim discrimination via disparate impacts, where the programs that had impacted them had received federal funding as a way to seek EJ remedy. However, Section 601 had less utility for EJ litigants in that discriminatory intent had to be proven, whereas interpretation of 602 allowed for disparate impacts as the determining factor.

In *Alexander v. Sandoval*, the Supreme Court did not decide whether promulgation of Section 602 regulations would prohibit decisions or actions with disparate outcomes and instead focused on what was necessary to bring a private right to action under Section 601. In deciding that Section 601 did not "create a freestanding private right of action to enforce regulations," private litigants were only able to move forward under Section 601 by demonstrating intentional discrimination, which is a high burden of proof. Alternatively, some litigants chose to utilize the 14th Amendment or had to rely on governmental bodies bringing forward claims against other agencies on the private parties' behalf. The enforcement of EJ claims for disparate impact, therefore, was limited by agency capacity to investigate, respond to, and sanction federal funding recipients.[51]

47  Hasler, Claire. 1994. "The Proposed Environmental Justice Act: 'I Have a (Green) Dream.'" *Seattle University Law Review* 17 (2): 417. https://digitalcommons.law.seattleu.edu/sulr/vol17/iss2/8/.

48  U.S. Congress, U.S. House. "S.2360: Environmental Justice Act of 2021," 117th Congress, 1st Session, introduced in House August 5, 2021. https://www.congress.gov/bill/117th-congress/senate-bill/2630.

49  "Civil Rights Act (1964)." National Archives. https://www.archives.gov/milestone-documents/civil-rights-act#transcript.

50  "Alexander v. Sandoval." (99-1908) 532 U.S. 275 (2001) 197 F.3d 484, reversed. Supreme Court of the United States. https://www.law.cornell.edu/supct/html/99-1908.ZS.html.

51  Monsma, D. 2006. "Equal Rights, Governance, and the Environment: Integrating Environmental Justice Principles in Corporate Social Responsibility." *Ecology Law Quarterly*, Vol. 33(2); 443-498 https://www.ecolex.org/details/literature/equal-rights-governance-and-the-environment-integrating-environmental-justice-principles-in-corporate-social-responsibility-ana-079574/.

## 3. Federal Orders

Where legislative votes have been lacking, federal action has been encouraged by EJ advocates through Executive action. Several Executive Orders issued, beginning with the Clinton administration (EO 12898), and continuing into the Biden administration (EO 14008), have tasked individual agencies with developing stewardship and responsibility metrics that hope to address the root cause of environmental injustices and to correct the "disproportionate health, environmental, and economic impacts that have been borne primarily by communities of color," President Biden noted in 2022.[52]

Under the executive orders, each agency has been tasked with developing a jurisdictionally specific mission statement that achieves the outcomes mandated in the orders. For the Environmental Protection Agency (EPA), EJ is focused on addressing the environmental vulnerabilities for disadvantaged communities, including quality, access, sustainability, and equitable development. The Department of Energy (DOE) focuses their EJ pursuits on the aspects related to energy justice. Specifically, DOE is developing plans addressing the impact to job security facing energy communities, developing procedures for equitable access to future energy in underserved communities, and safeguarding against the disproportionate impact of new energy infrastructure development falling on already impacted communities.[53, 54, 55, 56] For the Department of Agriculture, the focus of EJ will be purposefully aimed at improving food supply chains and access to food stocks, building climate

## THE MEANING OF ENVIRONMENTAL JUSTICE

With growing awareness of environmental injustices and the mainstream consciousness to the EJ movement, the term "environmental justice" has come to mean many different things to different people. EJ is primarily and historically a movement for equitable treatment led by Black grassroots leaders. The term EJ is also used to describe specific communities that may have faced disproportionate and cumulative negative environmental impacts and burdens. EJ has also been adopted as an academic term and a policy framework. "Apart from how competing notions of environmental justice shape ongoing interpretations of social justice or civil rights, 'the quest for environmental justice' presumably does not end with 'an equitable distribution of negative externalities.'"[a]

Note:

a. Heiman, Michael K. 1996. "Race, Waste, and Class: New Perspectives on Environmental Justice." Antipode 28 (2): 111–21. https://doi.org/10.1111/j.1467-8330.1996.tb00517.x.

resiliency into climate-safe agricultural practices, and improving equity and equality among farmers and ranchers.[57, 58, 59, 60] The Department of Justice is focused on improving enforcement and prosecutorial mechanisms for environmental law violations, with a special task force targeting investigations in, or on behalf of, EJ.[61]

52  Biden, Joe. Earth Day Speech. April 22, 2022. https://www.whitehouse.gov/environmentaljustice/

53  DOE. "Creating Clean Energy Union Jobs." https://www.energy.gov/creating-clean-energy-union-jobs.

54  DOE. "Promoting Energy Justice." https://www.energy.gov/promoting-energy-justice.

55  DOE. "About Community Benefits Plans." https://www.energy.gov/infrastructure/about-community-benefits-plans.

56  DOE. "Fossil Energy and Carbon Management Domestic Engagement Framework: Engaging Communities, Stakeholders, and Tribes in Clean Energy Technologies." https://www.energy.gov/fecm/fossil-energy-and-carbon-management-domestic-engagement-framework-engaging-communities.

57  USDA. "Equity at USDA." https://www.usda.gov/equity.

58  USDA. "Climate Solutions." https://www.usda.gov/climate-solutions.

59  USDA. "Equitable Systems." https://www.usda.gov/nutrition-security/equitable-systems.

60  USDA. "Environmental Justice." 1997. https://www.usda.gov/directives/dr-5600-002.

61  "Memorandum for Heads of Department Components United States Attorneys From: The Associate Attorney General Subject: Comprehensive Environmental Justice Enforcement Strategy." 2022. https://www.justice.gov/d9/pages/attachments/2022/05/05/02._asg_strategy_memorandum.pdf.

## C. Evolution from EJ to Energy Justice to Climate Justice to JUSTICE40

The White House Environmental Justice Advisory Council was created by the Biden administration and tasked with providing "recommendations to the White House Environmental Justice Interagency Council established in Section 220 of [Executive Order 14008] on how to increase the federal government's efforts to address current and historic environmental injustice, including recommendations for updating Executive Order 12898."[62] Concurrently, the White House Environmental Justice Interagency Advisory Council was amended, under EO14008, to develop "a strategy to address current and historic environmental injustice by consulting with the White House Environmental Justice Advisory Council and with local environmental justice leaders."[63] EO14008 also mandated that 40% of the overall benefits from certain federal investments flow to disadvantaged communities, under a newly created initiative called Justice40.[64] In addition to moving EJ into mainstream consciousness, the latest governmental actions have expanded justice to include energy justice, climate justice, and intersectional movements that have joined with EJ over the past several decades.

There is currently no national database for tracking state- and municipal-level EJ legislation—something sorely lacking from the public sector considering the focus on local decision-making. As of 2022, 14 states have developed or were currently developing EJ legislation.[65, 66] However, there is significant diversity in the aims of these laws.[67] Some call for EJ impact assessments, while others focus on enhancing stakeholder engagement in decision-making.[68] Several states have mandated—and developed—state-specific screening tools to help capture unique dynamics at a local level that national tools (i.e., EJScreen or Climate and Economic Justice Screening Tool) do not capture. The latest trend has been focused on permitting reforms and utilizing cumulative impact assessments to address potential risks related to disproportionate siting or expansions of future projects in self-described overburdened communities.[69] There is a risk that unharmonized legislation could create contradictions between state and federal efforts.[70] For example, how a state defines EJ populations could be different from national definitions of disadvantaged communities.[71, 72] If designed in a complementary manner, state-based EJ efforts can provide missing localized information, legislation, regulation, and enforcement that strengthens EJ considerations in the absence of federal authority

62  The White House. "Executive Order on Tackling the Climate Crisis at Home and Abroad." Sec 221.d. January 27, 2021. https://www.whitehouse.gov/briefing-room/presidential-actions/2021/01/27/executive-order-on-tackling-the-climate-crisis-at-home-and-abroad/.

63  The White House. "Executive Order on Tackling the Climate Crisis at Home and Abroad." 219.d. January 27, 2021. https://www.whitehouse.gov/briefing-room/presidential-actions/2021/01/27/executive-order-on-tackling-the-climate-crisis-at-home-and-abroad/.

64  The White House. "Executive Order on Tackling the Climate Crisis at Home and Abroad." Sec 233. January 27, 2021. https://www.whitehouse.gov/briefing-room/presidential-actions/2021/01/27/executive-order-on-tackling-the-climate-crisis-at-home-and-abroad/.

65  Griffin, Nicholas. 2022. "Scorecard of Environmental Justice Policies in Northeast-Midwest States." Northeast-Midwest Institute. July 2022. https://www.nemw.org/wp-content/uploads/2022/08/Environmental-Justice-Report-and-Scorecard-August-5-2022.pdf.

66  Bruce, Dylan. 2021. "Analysis: State Laws Are Codifying Environmental Justice." *Bloomberg Law.* https://news.bloomberglaw.com/bloomberg-law-analysis/analysis-state-laws-are-codifying-environmental-justice.

67  "Emerging State-Level Environmental Justice Laws." *New York Law Journal.* May 12, 2021. https://www.law.com/newyorklawjournal/2021/05/12/emerging-state-level-environmental-justice-laws/.

68  Torres-Sota, Elissa. "2022 in Review: State Environmental Justice Laws and Policies." Environmental Law Institute. January 9, 2023. https://www.eli.org/vibrant-environment-blog/2022-review-state-environmental-justice-laws-and-policies#:~:text=To%20date%2C%20there%20are%2014.

69  "New York State Senate Bill S8830." 2022. New York State Senate. https://www.nysenate.gov/legislation/bills/2021/S8830.

70  Perls, Hannah. 2020. "EPA Undermines Its Own Environmental Justice Programs-Environmental & Energy Law Program." Harvard Law School. November 12, 2020. https://eelp.law.harvard.edu/2020/11/epa-undermines-its-own-environmental-justice-programs/.

71  Majumder, Myisha. "Environmental Justice Is a Growing Operational Factor. How Are Federal and State Agencies Defining It?" February 22, 2023. *Waste Dive.* https://www.wastedive.com/news/environmental-justice-definition-epa-disadvantage-community/642809/.

72  Fernandez-Bou, A.S., Ortiz-Partida, J.P., Dobbin, K.B., Flores-Landeros, H., Bernacchi, L.A., and Medellín-Azuara, J. 2021. "Underrepresented, Understudied, Underserved: Gaps and Opportunities for Advancing Justice in Disadvantaged Communities." *Environmental Science & Policy* 122 (August): 92–100. https://doi.org/10.1016/j.envsci.2021.04.014.

or action. As former EPA administrator Bill Reilly stated: "Any effort to address environmental equity [justice] issues effectively must include all segments of society: the affected communities, the public at large, industry, people in policy-making positions, and all levels and branches of government."[73]

Beyond pursuing governmental intervention, EJ organizers remain focused on grassroots mobilization in the movement-policy cycle.[74] The movements, while focused on addressing localized issues, have sought international tactical collaboration to build support. With broader movements such as energy justice, climate justice, and second-generation EJ advocacy, new groups and movements have found intersections with each other. Those connections have led to the development of coalitions,[75] alliances, and global awareness of EJ issues. [76, 77, 78]

While EJ has been a uniquely focused, activist-led effort in the United States, it is important to note that these concerns are not only a domestic issue, with a broader, international dialogue having developed simultaneously. However, unlike the United States, many countries have less well-developed environmental and civil rights protection frameworks to leverage. Internationally, this lack of institutionalized environmental and civil rights protection frameworks and policies

has engendered a more grassroots-based, cross-movement strategy. In 2001, EJ leaders piloted a grassroots approach by consciously working with environmentalists and conservation organizers focused on Amazonian concerns, with social justice advocates representing urban concerns.[79] These Amazonian mobilization efforts resulted in intersections with issues, policies, or sensitivities from different ideological and historical contexts. This approach is referred to as "intersectionality" and is increasingly an important organizing methodology for EJ. Just as early organizers, such as Cesar Chavez[80] and Martin Luther King, Jr.,[81] worked to create intersectional coalitions between environmental and civil concerns and labor movements, organizers today are seeking to build coalitions and multifront campaigns that address EJ, labor, civil rights, climate justice, sovereignty concerns, and many others at the same time.[82]

Some EJ advocates have been involved since the inception of the movement with mobilized protestations, such as the aforementioned Warren County PCB landfill siting decision. These organizers view EJ as an intersection of civil rights, labor rights, and the need for stronger environmental protections for overburdened communities.[83] Consequently, their organizations are deeply rooted in addressing systemic issues, building equity, and centering community

73  Letter from EPA Environmental Equity Workgroup to EPA Administrator, which covers the EPA Environmental Equity report: "Reducing Risks for All Communities." June 1992.

74  Kane, Melinda. 2003. "Social Movement Policy Success: Decriminalizing State Sodomy Laws, 1969–1998." *Mobilization: An International Quarterly* 8 (3): 313–34. https://doi.org/10.17813/maiq.8.3.q66046w34wu58866.

75  Pellow, David N. "Transnational Alliances and Global Politics: New Geographies of Urban" in *In the Nature of Cities*, 1st ed. 2005. https://www.taylorfrancis.com/chapters/edit/10.4324/9780203027523-21/transnational-alliances-global-politics-new-geographies-urban-environmental-justice-struggles-david-pellow.

76  Pellow, David N. 2005. *In the Nature of Cities Urban Political Ecology and the Politics of Urban Metabolism.* Routledge.

77  Martínez-Alier, Joan. 2012. "Environmental Justice and Economic Degrowth: An Alliance between Two Movements." *Capitalism Nature Socialism* 23 (1): 51–73. https://doi.org/10.1080/10455752.2011.648839.

78  Walker, Gordon. 2009. "Globalizing Environmental Justice." *Global Social Policy* 9 (3): 355–82. https://doi.org/10.1177/1468018109343640.

79  Porto, Marcelo Firpo. 2012. "Movements and the Network of Environmental Justice in Brazil." *Environmental Justice* 5 (2): 100–104. https://doi.org/10.1089/env.2011.0012.

80  Chavez, Cesar. 1986. "Four Freedoms Curriculum Resource." https://learn.nrm.org/media/1242/cesar-chavez-wrath-of-grapes-speech.pdf.

81  "'I've Been to the Mountaintop' by Dr. Martin Luther King, Jr. American Federation of State, County and Municipal Employees (AFSCME)." April 3, 1968. https://www.afscme.org/about/history/mlk/mountaintop.

82  Thomas, Leah. *The Intersectional Environmentalist.* The Hachette Book Group. 2021. https://www.hachettebookgroup.com/titles/leah-thomas/the-intersectional-environmentalist/9780316281935/?lens=voracious.

83  Obach, Brian K. 2004. *Labor and the Environmental Movement.* The MIT Press. https://doi.org/10.7551/mitpress/4080.001.0001.

decision-making.[84] Other organizers are being shaped by a broader environmentalism perspective that arose after the 1970s. These organizers push racial, social, and climate justice as a globally unifying platform.[85] The new-wave EJ movement still leverages protest tactics,[86] but has moved to a more global focus; these organizations describe their missions as trying to address climate vulnerabilities, democratic participation, community sovereignty, and equitable adaptation,[87] and are broadly against future pollution and industrialization.[88]

For local organizers, mobilizing is focused on directing activity to address procedural issues related to public participation, holding governmental agencies accountable to rules and environmental laws related to pollution or exposure to hazardous products, and, wherever possible, opposing new industrial facilities being sited in their communities. For international players, organizations may focus on nation-state intervention.[89] In doing so they may seek to highlight lack of state action in addressing displacement of harm on hemispheric divides,[90] exportation of hazardous products,[91] exploitation of sovereign resources,[92] and lack of adherence to EJ programs.[93] Organizations may also focus on publicity via "name and shame"[94, 95] campaigns or other documentarian methods.

In the future, the EJ lexicon may become more prescriptive and the definitions around EJ, energy justice, and climate justice may be normalized to ensure clarity in both the usage and application of these principles and frameworks across local, regional, national, and transnational environments. Environment, social, and governance (ESG) information reporting provides one such framework that could be leveraged to encourage voluntary adoption of, and adherence to, normative EJ principles through public commitments that are linked to community engagements and stakeholder responsibilities. As stated by Showalter and Antoniolli (2023), "EJ falls at the intersection of the "E" and "S" of ESG and good Governance is required to manage exposure to EJ risks."[96]

Many corporate risks are managed through good risk management practices that are made available to the public and investors. Investors

84  Wilgosh, B., Sorman, A.H., and Barcena, I. 2022. "When Two Movements Collide: Learning from Labour and Environmental Struggles for Future Just Transitions." *Futures* 137 (March): 102903. https://doi.org/10.1016/j.futures.2022.102903.

85  As an example, see: "A Movement for Racial Justice." Rainforest Action Network. https://www.ran.org/issue/a-movement-for-racial-justice/.

86  Baptista, A.I., Jesudason, S., Greenberg, M., and Perovich, A. 2022. "Landscape Assessment of the U.S. Environmental Justice Movement: Transformative Strategies for Climate Justice." *Environmental Justice* 16 (2). https://doi.org/10.1089/env.2021.0075.

87  Schlosberg, David, and Lisette B. Collins. 2014. "From Environmental to Climate Justice: Climate Change and the Discourse of Environmental Justice." *Wiley Interdisciplinary Reviews: Climate Change* 5 (3): 359–74. https://doi.org/10.1002/wcc.275.

88  Dawson, Ashley. 2010. "Climate Justice: The Emerging Movement against Green Capitalism." *South Atlantic Quarterly* 109 (2): 313–38. https://doi.org/10.1215/00382876-2009-036.

89  Koliev, F., Park, B., and Duit, A. 2022. "Climate Shaming: Explaining Environmental NGOs Targeting Practices." *Climate Policy* 23 (7): 1–14. https://doi.org/10.1080/14693062.2022.2143315.

90  United Nations. "Plastic Pollution Disproportionately Hitting Marginalized Groups, UN Environment Report Finds." *UN News.* March 30, 2021. https://news.un.org/en/story/2021/03/1088712.

91  Wang, K., Qian, J., and He, S. 2021. "Contested Worldings of E-Waste Environmental Justice: Nonhuman Agency and E-Waste Scalvaging in Guiyu, China." *Annals of the American Association of Geographers,* 11 (7): 1–20. https://doi.org/10.1080/24694452.2021.1889353.

92  Valencia, Robert. "She Grew up in the Amazon, and Now She's Fighting for Its Life." *Earthjustice.* January 6, 2023. https://earthjustice.org/article/she-grew-up-in-the-amazon-and-now-shes-fighting-for-its-life.

93  Perls, Hannah. "EPA Undermines Its Own Environmental Justice Programs-Environmental & Energy Law Program." Harvard Law School. November 12, 2020. https://eelp.law.harvard.edu/2020/11/epa-undermines-its-own-environmental-justice-programs/.

94  Barnes, Ash, and Rob White. 2020. "Mapping Emotions: Exploring the Impact of the Aussie Farms Map." *Journal of Contemporary Criminal Justice,* 36 (3). https://doi.org/10.1177/1043986220910306.

95  "'We Don't Have Any Choice': The Young Climate Activists Naming and Shaming U.S. Politicians." *The Guardian.* October 16, 2020. https://www.theguardian.com/environment/2020/oct/16/sunrise-movement-wide-awakes-us-climate-activists.

96  Showalter, Michael J., and Amy Antoniolli. "What Do ESG and Environmental Justice Actually Mean?" *National Law Review.* February 23, 2013. https://www.natlawreview.com/article/esg-and-environmental-justice.

often leverage nonfinancial, nonregulated ESG ratings as a differentiating factor for their investment decisions; several companies have taken the step to "incorporate equity and EJ [principles] holistically into their operations and across their supply chains, in furtherance of corporate social responsibility goals and as strategies for market differentiation."[97] The lack of industry disclosure of EJ does not mean there is a lack of awareness or consideration of these tenets. In fact, EJ principles and tenets are incorporated into some companies' broader commitments or approaches to managing environmental and socioeconomic impacts, as well as through formal economic development programs. In some cases, these programs are specifically designed to be supportive of local communities particularly vulnerable to industry activity. Just as community best practices encourage highly participatory local engagement processes, incorporating EJ principles into ESG as an explicit disclosure depends upon dialogue and collaboration, and on the position investors and corporate operators take toward addressing and upholding EJ tenets and principles.

97  Halliday, S., Redd, J., and Glickstein, J. "Addressing Environmental Justice as Part of ESG Initiatives," *Law*360. May 24, 2021. https://www.law360.com/articles/1384123/addressing-environmental-justice-as-part-of-esg-initiatives.

## CASE STUDY OF THE TRADE-OFFS COMMUNITIES EXPERIENCE SPECIFIC TO NATURAL GAS DEVELOPMENT ACTIVITIES

A study of the social consequences in the Marcellus Appalachia region documented community responses of positive and negative impacts of natural gas development activities. Economic benefits were the number one positive benefit according to communities. These benefits were not limited to monetary value, but included elements like training opportunities for youth to remain in the local region, thereby creating generational family stability and enhanced financial stability for the elderly, etc. The indirect benefits included themes like long-term business development for alternative sectors, like agriculture—which allowed the community to retain its identity. These factors contributed to improved indicators of enhanced quality of life.[a]

The negative consequences reported in the study were concentrated around the "ramp-up" stages of development when drilling activities commenced. This included traffic congestion, dirt, noise, damage to existing infrastructure, population increases with "newcomers," increase in crime rates, lack of housing and utility infrastructure, and a lack of trained workers to support the development activities. Some of the negative impacts extended to the operational or post-production stages of activities, including unfair/unequal treatment of homeowners by energy companies (i.e., signing bad leases), minimal royalties, and negative environmental impacts.

Note:

a.  Gorman, Mary. "Social Consequence, Stakeholder Influence, and Resource Needs for Marcellus Shale Communities." ScholarWorks. December 2014. https://scholarworks.waldenu.edu/cgi/viewcontent.cgi?article=1102&context=dissertations.

# Appendix T

# IMPLEMENTING COMMUNITY ENGAGEMENT BEST PRACTICES

*The joint* Charting the Course *and* Harnessing Hydrogen *study task group analyzed several community and stakeholder engagement best practices and guidance reference documents, referenced throughout Chapter 7 and in this appendix. The analysis resulted in the identification and elevation of the following characteristics and formed the basis of the community engagement model that both studies developed.*

## I. IMPLEMENTATION OF BEST PRACTICES

The following guidance is for the implementation of best practices for all stakeholders—federal and state agencies, local governments, Tribal governments, private citizens, public interest groups, and industry—to strive for better community engagement, as well as to meet and accomplish the regulatory objectives more effectively.

### A. The Four-Step Framework

#### Step 1: Prepare

Project developers should begin by identifying potential impacts, both beneficial and adverse, and all potentially impacted communities. Developers should also identify stakeholders to understand their history, culture, land use, socioeconomic activities, political organization, relationships with prior developers, past economic development efforts, and the community members and neighborhoods that will be most affected by the project. Doing so is part of an authentic intent to deepen understanding and build trust.

It is also important to develop a deep understanding of the community's values—what matters to them and how the project might advance local interests. This should be studied well before community engagement and refined as the project developers engage with community. In addition, to cultivate a collaborative process of engaging with communities, project developers should aim to obtain early endorsement of the processes rather than the project itself.[1] Project developers should be ready to discuss potential impacts, both positive and negative.

Integration of Indigenous and/or local knowledge, through literature review and subsequent field research, should be undertaken. This may include broad categories such as local livelihoods and culture, sociodemographic and socioeconomic data, traditional resources, ecosystem services, culturally sensitive environments, and potential social project needs. The list is nonexhaustive and should be informed by local circumstances and needs. Recommended Reading: *UN Declaration on the Rights of Indigenous Peoples* (2007).[2]

In undertaking preparation and community impact assessments, the initial screening (desktop research) can make use of tools available at the federal and some state government levels. It is important to note there is not a single tool, but various agencies have tools available, including EPA, DOE, and the White House Council on Environmental Quality Climate and Economic Justice

---

1    Chavez, Marques. "Vermillion Wind Energy Project." Keystone Policy Center. February 2023. https://www.keystone.org/vermillion-wind-energy-project/.

2    United Nations. 2007. "United Nations Declaration on the Rights of Indigenous Peoples." https://www.un.org/development/desa/indigenouspeoples/wp-content/uploads/sites/19/2018/11/UNDRIP_E_web.pdf.

Screening Tool.[3] None of these tools replace the full preparation work described above, but they can help identify existing or potential environmental justice (EJ) considerations for communities and associated risks/needs. Refer to Chapter 7: Societal Considerations, Impacts, and Safety for additional information.

## Step 2: Listen

To establish and improve the value of a proposed project, communities affected by a project must have opportunities to communicate with developers. While many meetings begin with sharing early plans or intentions, active listening is a continuous practice that starts with observing as much as possible.

Positive community engagement also involves acknowledging the role of communities and their voices, being open to active listening, and developing a good understanding of community members during the preparation step.

## Step 3: Understand and Respond

For developers to understand and respond authentically, it may be necessary to identify methodologies for selecting the right messenger(s). Bringing colleagues with diverse perspectives and experiences can encourage community members to engage more openly and help equip developers to better understand what is being said or interpreted.

Ensure that leaders are chosen by their respective communities to make certain the process maintains representation and accountability.

Gathering notes, reflecting upon the full range of feedback, and asking clarifying questions are important steps. Having follow-up conversations and sharing back to the community what you've heard are equally important parts of this process.

Wherever communities have expressed needs that are within a developer's purview and capability to address, developers could strive for finding mutually beneficial solutions. Where community interests are difficult to accommodate, the developer may take care to convey the reasons for the lack of accommodation, including cases where the industry may not be able to adequately address community concerns or needs.

Be ready to have a community build upon (or reject) the understanding that is shared back to them and continue pursuing mutually recognized understanding. As conversations progress, redouble efforts in active listening.

## Step 4: Learn

Commit to continued learning and reflection on the stakeholder engagement practices. As conversations progress, expect that engagement plans will need to evolve and improve as those proposing the action and the community learn how best to work together and the needs of the community come into better focus.

Identifying and responding to community input (as is discussed below as a principle) is recognized to be an important part of learning, requiring project team flexibility.

Note that beyond best practice community engagement, flexibility is also important for addressing justice concerns. Agility, or the ability to shift gears and adjust plans as needed to meet the needs of the community, is invaluable. In fact, it is impossible to predict at the outset of a project, or at the project application stage, what a complete stakeholder engagement strategy will be. Stakeholder engagement plans need to allow for flexibility and should be allowed to change over time to accommodate the dynamic nature of stakeholder engagement. For example, concerns in the activation phase of hydrogen development will be very different than concerns and needs in the at-scale phase; a static engagement would be insufficient to address the myriad concerns across that period.

## B. The Iterative Aspect

Although the four steps (prepare, listen, understand/respond, learn) imply iterative or even continual improvement processes, this aspect is itself a required element of best practice community engagement. An ongoing venue for addressing

---

3   "Climate and Economic Justice Screening Tool." *U.S. Climate Resilience Toolkit.* 2023. https://toolkit.climate.gov/tool/climate-and-economic-justice-screening-tool.

grievances, as well as opportunities, should be present during project design, permitting, construction, and operation. This will look different for every project, depending on the scale, size, and type of project being proposed. Some options include community advisory boards, town halls, reporting web portals, or hotlines. The same due diligence will be required for these programs to ensure accessibility and support effective community use. Listening and/or understanding without response and learning would not align to the principles that accompany this framework. On the other hand, responding well helps bring alignment to these principles.

## C. The Five Principles of the 4-Step Framework

### Principle 1: Bringing Authenticity; Building Trust and Goodwill

Communities that have suffered discrimination or are disadvantaged seek recognition of historical injustices and will look for this as part of building deep trust. Industry proposals that seek to reduce inequities may garner more support and foster more trust. Stakeholders should be supported as needed and have access to the same opportunities that industrial activities may bring to a community. Beyond technical knowledge, behaviors that are authentic, respectful, and nonextractive reduce mistrust, particularly from communities that have been exposed to industrial impacts. Demonstrating plans to create and utilize better processes is an early trust-building step in engagement. For example, meaningful dialogue may lead to identifying areas of mutual interest, such as minimally invasive development practices that preserve and protect sacred sites and sensitive ecosystems or improving supplier diversity and local worker participation through training and other workforce development practices.

Note that the "Prepare" element of the 4-Step Framework is important not only for effective listening, but specifically for building trust and bringing authenticity. In addition, an effective community engagement process will vary because no two projects or communities are alike, and solutions that address EJ will not look the same for each project given these differences. Work-

ing to address EJ requires meaningful community engagement, especially with collaboration among project partners, impacted community members and organizations, businesses, multiple levels of government, and sometimes other third-party resource partners (e.g., facilitators).

Meeting the community where they are, in places where they commune regularly, will help identify leaders and representatives. These different stakeholders will each have roles to play in advancing meaningful community engagement. Industry engagement that seeks to address EJ goals can build authenticity, goodwill, and trust within the community. Where possible, working in partnership with local organizations that have relationships with the community, including a diverse range of leaders, will help to define a stakeholder engagement strategy well suited to the local context.

Local organizations can help with identifying representative voices of the community, navigating local politics, advising on message development, and serving as a bridge to the people. Project developers should make sure that representatives of the community are respected and that those who will be directly affected by a project are treated fairly and have meaningful involvement in decision-making, planning, and plan execution. Industry should work with community groups and members to codefine the vision and scope of a community-driven engagement process. Establishing a long-standing, trusted relationship takes time, commitment, and perseverance, and developing strong relationships with local organizations can be an important first step. During this process, to signal true cooperation with community, project developers may benefit from early engagement after optioning the site, but before land easement acquisition and project site map finalization. Engaging communities via political leadership and public relations pathways that lack a listening element may not build trust or good will.

### Principle 2: Transparency

All parties involved in community engagement should be transparent about the interests they are representing. Different individuals will define transparency in different ways. For this reason, transparency guidelines should be defined with the community.

When approaching a meaningful process, industry should be transparent about the intentions, commitments, objectives, and anticipated outcome of the engagement, with the recognition that there are specific forms of information that are confidential for specific reasons. For example, certain details about infrastructure are not disclosed because they would increase infrastructure vulnerability from a safety or security perspective. Transparent disclosure by industry should include a discussion about the potential risks and limitations associated with the proposed project.

Industry should use community-informed planning and implementation processes to solicit engagement that involves openly communicating desired outcomes and soliciting community input early and at defined points throughout the project implementation. Industry should communicate its intentions clearly and ensure the community understands the purpose of the proposed action and has opportunities for their voices to be heard. The community should be made aware of the proposed schedule for implementation, what they can expect during each phase of the action, and plans for accountability to the community members once the action is complete. To do so, industry should consider creating documented engagement plans that are regularly updated with outcomes and checkpoints in a phased approach. Documentation allows for clear communication and the opportunity to refer to commitments and agreements, and/or changes. Keeping communities engaged throughout all levels of planning and implementation is key to demonstrating that they too, have an instrumental role in the process and outcome and are treated as respected partners and their local expertise is valued.

## Principle 3: Early, Open, Responsive, and Accessible Engagement

Engaging early and often with the impacted and surrounding communities is key to building relationships. Providing consistent, transparent, and easy-to-understand project information while soliciting feedback are equally critical, as is both the communication of benefits and the determination of whether a community recognizes those benefits.

To do this, the mechanism and accessibility, as well as the inclusivity of stakeholder voices, will be fundamental to successful engagement. Ensure there are effective and sufficient means to reach the community by considering potential communication or participation barriers, including language, technology, transportation, and temporal barriers (childcare or competing priorities).

In the United States, regulatory public comment processes have a formal structure and tend to occur after project design is well underway. As mentioned above, these processes cannot be taken as sufficient engagement. Their formal nature—which often includes written comments submitted via government websites or public hearings where participants must request to speak and stand at a microphone—can be an obstacle to maximizing community participation. Developers should be mindful of the formality barrier when they consider the input gathered in these processes.

Best practice community engagement should place particular emphasis on facilitating participation by underrepresented communities. For example, developers should plan on providing educational and informational resources, including their direct community engagement processes, according to local needs. This may mean providing multilingual resources and materials to facilitate engagement with non-English speakers, or adaptive accommodations for disabled individuals such as live American Sign Language translation for in-person events or TeleTypewriter (TTY) and/or TTY Relay Services for telephone engagements. Fortunately, there are many national and local community-based organizations serving these diverse groups that can provide guidance on specific accommodation-based best practices.

Incorporate plans that address skepticism, especially communities that have been harmed by similar actions previously or see little value in the action for them. This additional effort might take the form of meeting communities where they are, rather than expecting them to go to an event, or reaching out over time with information to help build a relationship of trust.

In engaging communities throughout the life of the project, it is also important for project leads to examine, understand, and honestly articulate answers to the following questions:

- Who is participating? Who is missing from the discussion and why?

- What are the primary modes and methods of communication and decision-making being utilized here? How well do these methods fit the purpose?

- How much influence do participants have in the decision-making or actions taken? How well do participants understand their influence or responsibility?

Successful engagement and communication also ensure that all voices are heard and included in project input, including a variety of community leaders as well as disenfranchised communities and community members. Strive toward a diversity of viewpoints and experiences that provide a full sweep of those impacted by the project, as not all opinions are represented in community leadership or government.

Likewise, industry needs to be timely and responsive to requests, input, grievances, and feedback. It may take time for community members to be comfortable providing input and it may take various formal and informal methods (individual side conversations, emails, letters, etc.) to achieve true engagement.

### Principle 4: Identifying and Responding to Community Input and Concerns

Creating a mechanism to track community feedback and needs is important to ensure actions are aligned with community requests, issues, and grievances. This is critical for establishing credibility and is a core area of the United Nations Guiding Principles. The International Petroleum Industry Environmental Conservation Association (IPIECA) has a detailed document covering this important work.[4] Having a community feedback tracking mechanism is cru-

cial for identifying trends, ensuring resources are addressing the appropriate issue area, and adjusting engagement and response strategies as needed. A Plan-Do-Check-Act (PDCA) management system can be used to measure this. The PDCA includes creating strategies and plans, executing them, checking actions for conformity, and using results to adjust the next generation of plans. Learning from experiences and continuous improvement using PDCA are essential to measure and convey how feedback and actions are being considered and addressed properly.

### Principle 5: Articulation of Community Value (by Developer) and Recognition of Value (by the Community and Government)

Community engagement is crucial for ensuring trust, credibility, and effectiveness in the engagement process. All involved are accountable for the outcomes of the engagement process. This includes following through on commitments made, providing updates on progress, and ensuring that the process leads to tangible results and improvements.

Each community has unique social and economic needs based on a variety of factors, including demographics, geographical landscapes and ecosystems, civic and political views, and media use. Understanding community members, identifying what they value, and prioritizing historical, current, and future needs of a community and/or region is critical.

At the community and stakeholder level, there may be various concerns across the hydrogen supply chain. The magnitude and nature of local concerns and potential impacts or benefits vary by project type, size, technology, and regional context, requiring that community impact and perceptions be assessed on a project-by-project basis. As community needs are identified through the input and feedback from community members, resources—including community investments and volunteerism—and responses can be aligned. The inset "Example Scenario of Balancing Multiple Community Perspectives and Differing Concerns for a Single Project Element" provides a scenario and potential response to a given community's concern.

---

4    IPIECA. "Community Grievance Mechanisms in the Oil and Gas Industry." May 1, 2014. https://www.ipieca.org/resources/community-grievance-mechanisms-in-the-oil-and-gas-industry.

## EXAMPLE SCENARIO OF BALANCING MULTIPLE COMMUNITY PERSPECTIVES AND DIFFERING CONCERNS FOR A SINGLE PROJECT ELEMENT

**Scenario:** Throughout the engagement process, community members express broad support for a new project in their community due to the jobs and indirect economic benefits, but some have concerns related to the potential risks and uncertainties of blending hydrogen into natural gas for transport using the existing natural gas pipeline in their community. However, the underlying reasons for the concerns vary by individual stakeholder group.

| Interviewed Groups | Concerns Expressed During Community Engagement Process |
|---|---|
| (A) Local chapter of an environmental nongovernmental organization | Expresses a desire to phase out fossil fuel production and to proceed to end-of-life; they believe that blending $H_2$ into the existing infrastructure will only prolong the utilization of fossil fuels and will delay an energy transition. |
| (B) Landowners group immediately adjacent to the pipeline route | Expresses concerns about what could happen during an unplanned release and the compounding risks associated with adding hydrogen into the natural gas stream; they are concerned about the potential damage and if it will prevent them from using their land at any point in the future. |
| **Identified Group Needs** | **Potential Response Plan to Consider** |
| (A) Addressing pollution and proceeding with the energy transition | Engage in direct dialogue about the pros and cons of hydrogen blending into existing infrastructure versus developing new infrastructure, including potential environmental footprints, project timeliness to address local emissions sources and decarbonization, and what measures are being used to evaluate lifecycle emissions of the $H_2$-blending process. Consider discussing alternative developments and how these may or may not be feasible for the specific project needs; look for mutual opportunities to take feedback into the project design. Be prepared to discuss end-of-life plans for the existing infrastructure, so far as is feasible without constituting a breach of privilege and with the appropriate cautionary statements for any forecasting that may be discussed in the process. Be prepared to identify other ways to work together that could be accommodated in a Community Benefits Plan. |
| (B) Safety and environmental health concerns | Work with community leaders, local emergency response service providers, and landowners to conduct public education and to codesign a community response plan in the event of an unplanned release. If community members express a willingness and would welcome additional education, bring company safety officers and/or environmental scientists into a townhall setting to answer questions directly. Be prepared to explain the rules, regulations, applicable laws, and the assessment processes the firm may undertake to address these concerns. |

# Appendix U

# COMMUNITY BENEFITS HUBS: THE HOUSTON ADVANCED RESEARCH CENTER MODEL

**C**ommunity Benefits Hubs (CBH) will serve as structural, physical, and virtual centers to engage with community values and needs, build capacity in local community assets, provide connections with technical assistance and available funding, and build trust to activate community participation in clean energy hub development and planning. Structural support will be provided by low carbon intensity energy hub development while additional funding will be identified to support other community needs. With respect to permitting, infrastructure, and governance, impacts to communities during hydrogen deployment may best be addressed through interactive participatory governance and enhanced corporate prioritization of community engagement.

Lower-resourced communities are competing with their wealthier peers to meet ever more complex philanthropic and federal funding proposal hurdles that may require intensive negotiations with the private sector, including community benefit agreements, as well as stakeholder engagement plans, metrics, and other technical documents above and beyond the already rigorous engineering, financial, and environmental information required to apply. While these additional steps are laudable in their intent and potential to improve projects, they require significant time and effort for communities that are already facing resource constraints.

As billions of dollars are invested in new clean energy hubs to decarbonize the Industrial sector, we must also build up the connective social infrastructure and support systems to ensure the benefits of those investments flow to disadvantaged communities that are most affected by climate change. The CBH framework illustrated in Figure U-1 aims to uplift disadvantaged communities through capacity building and technical assistance to empower community representatives through participation and agency in decision-making processes, and to ensure accountability of benefits flowing to those communities.

The CBH framework encompasses three participatory bodies:

- **The Community Advisory Board** (CAB) should consist of leaders and stakeholders from local communities who will guide CBH development and represent community interests throughout project planning, development, implementation, and operations.

- **The Industry Council** should be an organized association of industry participants across projects to develop common frameworks for community engagement, share lessons learned and best practices, and engage with the CABs and other community and labor benefits stakeholders through the Community Benefits Roundtable Forum.

- **The Community Benefits Roundtable** is intended to serve as a forum for members of the industry council, labor and workforce development representatives, and the CAB. The community benefits roundtable can be used to co-develop hub-wide frameworks for benefits flows, review and make recommendations to project plans, target opportunities for good paying jobs and workforce development opportunities, evaluate options for investment in existing community assets, review benefits metrics and scorecards, and coordinate with other hubs.

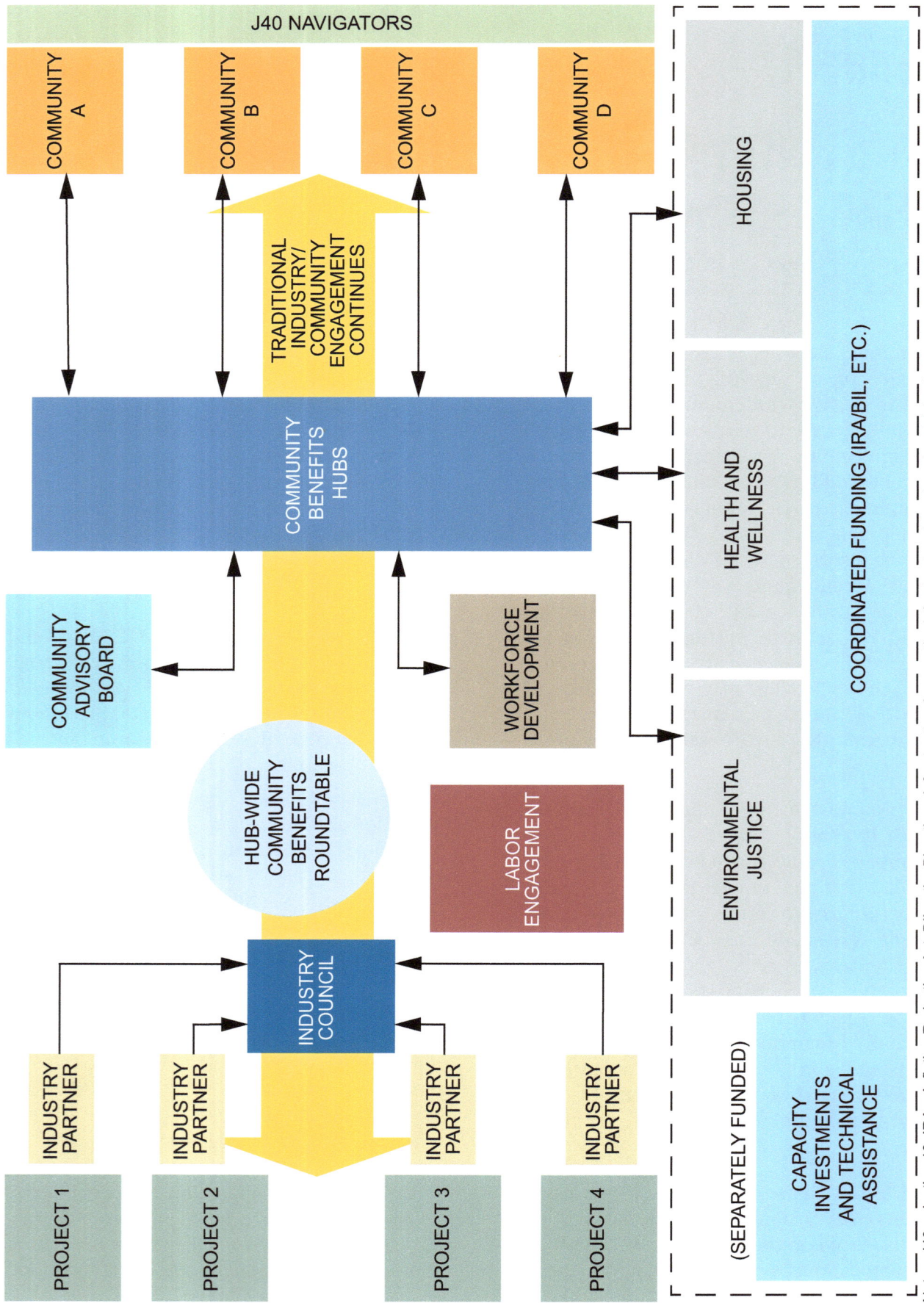

Figure U-1. The Community Benefits Hub Framework

Notes: J40 = Justice 40; IRA = Inflation Reduction Act; BIL = the Bipartisan Infrastructure Law, or the Infrastructure Investment and Jobs Act.

Source: This illustration was created by the Houston Advanced Research Center (HARC) and was adapted from *Well-Being Hub Summary*, IC2 Institute, the University of Texas at Austin.

# Appendix V

# CONSIDERATIONS FOR BUILDING AND OPERATING HYDROGEN FACILITIES

There is a reasonable probability that early hydrogen generation and usage projects will be in or adjacent to existing (i.e., brownfields) facilities because capital and operating costs are likely to be less than if a brand-new (i.e., greenfields) site were used. However, this means there is a greater likelihood that the chosen site will be in or near disadvantaged communities.[1] Nationwide, 13,581 census tracts were identified as disadvantaged communities using this approach (18.6% of 73,056 total census tracts). Additionally, federally recognized Tribal lands and U.S. territories, in their entirety, are categorized as disadvantaged communities.

Project developers planning to generate, transport, store, or use hydrogen must consider the following possible actions to address societal interests and concerns of disadvantaged communities in or near the proposed project:

- Early in a company's consideration of a new project, determine which communities (disadvantaged and otherwise) are near the proposed project area. Prior to starting construction, the project promoter should evaluate legacy pollution and planned actions of the project and share results with neighboring disadvantaged communities.

- Prior to starting project construction, the project promoter should conduct a baseline analysis of existing environmental burdens, hazards, and harms within the proposed project area and determine whether they would create negative social or environmental impacts such that the project location, size, or scale should be reconsidered.

- At that time, the company should identify the project's direct impacts, indirect impacts (those later in time or more distant), and cumulative effects of the project and the existing nearby facilities. The project operator can then determine whether and how affected or disadvantaged communities would achieve net benefits because of the project.

- A company planning to build and operate a hydrogen generating or consuming facility that would be in, or adjacent to, disadvantaged communities should initiate discussions with community groups, including those representing disadvantaged people, after the land for the facility has been acquired and/or before a final commitment to build is made. The purpose of the discussions would be to learn concerns of such groups and try to determine which ones could be satisfied at a reasonable cost of time and money.[2]

- In its discussions with community groups, the company should seek to provide estimates of local tax revenues and local expenditures from the construction and operation of the project.

---

1    "Disadvantaged communities" as used here are defined by DOE as the top 20% most burdened census tracts in each state, where 36 burden indicators are considered, and at least 30% of households are at or below 200% of the Federal Poverty Level and/or are considered low-income households as defined by the Department of Housing and Urban Development.

2    DOE has a useful August 2022 publication, "Creating a Community and Stakeholder Engagement Plan," which includes information about stakeholder and community identification, engagement methods, and related information.

- In its discussions with community groups, the company should provide the following information:

  - The expected amount and type of air emissions, their relation to any regulations, expected amount of freshwater usage and waste liquid disposal, the disposal location and amounts of any regulated substances, and the amount of any solid waste and where it will be disposed

  - The number of expected truck and/or rail deliveries per day or week to and from the facility both during construction and during subsequent operation, which give rise to concerns about accidents, noise, increased dust, increased tailpipe emissions, and potential decrease in values of homes near truck routes, and determine whether changes to reduce these impacts could be made

  - The expected noise, light, flares, and odors from the normal operation of the facility and whether there will be any infrequent but expected incidents with noticeably increased amounts of light, noise, flaring, or odors

- EPA has indicated that it "will prioritize enhanced public involvement opportunities for [an] EPA-issued permit that may involve …. significant public health or environmental impacts on overburdened communities."[3] Thus, it is suggested that the project promotor for hydrogen generation or use work with their nearby disadvantaged communities prior to initiating the permit process to share their respective perspectives and information about the project and permit requirements.

- To provide a basis for nearby communities to be supportive of the new hydrogen generation, usage, or investment, the project owner should provide continuous compliance monitoring related to its air permits and share the results with the communities.

- Companies operating a hydrogen generating or consuming facility should maintain relations and information sharing with neighboring disadvantaged communities.

- In evaluating the cost of developing the hydrogen facility, the company must analyze to what extent it could commit to hiring some percentage of its needed employees from people living within disadvantaged communities adjacent, or proximate, to the facility; to what extent the company could provide financial or technical assistance to a nearby program to train operators and other skilled employees for work, such as in the subject facility; and to what extent the company could hire apprentice workers who live within adjacent or proximate disadvantaged communities to the subject facility. The company should also evaluate whether its maintenance staff could provide fixed-duration training experience for individuals who recently completed appropriate training programs.

- In evaluating the cost of developing the hydrogen facility, the company must analyze to what extent it could commit to contributing an amount or a percent of the overall economic benefit from the subject hydrogen unit on a yearly basis to training and other nearby educational institutions or public organizations (e.g., hospitals) serving the subject area.

- In evaluating the cost of developing the hydrogen facility, the company must evaluate to what extent it could commit to installing at least one and up to four criteria air pollutant and/or toxic air pollutant measuring devices on the perimeter of the subject facility that would operate continuously, with the resulting information being shared with groups representing neighbors of the subject facility.

- In evaluating the cost of developing the hydrogen facility, the company should evaluate to what extent it can commit to allocating a percentage of the facility capital or operating cost on a yearly basis for items benefitting the affected disadvantaged communities as selected by groups representing such communities.

---

3   "EPA Region 6 Regional Implementation Plan to Promote Meaningful Engagement of Overburdened Communities in Permitting Activities." 2013. DOE has developed three very useful guides for companies applying for Funding Opportunities and considering investments near disadvantaged communities. The guides are "Creating a Community and Stakeholder Engagement Plan"; "Guidance for Project Teams on Diversity, Equity, Inclusion, and Accessibility Plans"; and "Creating a Justice40 Initiative Plan." Although companies would not be required to follow such guides if they were not seeking DOE funding, there are increasing social and public pressures on companies to take action to address issues affecting disadvantaged communities. Thus, these could be useful guides.

- In evaluating the cost of developing the hydrogen facility, the company should determine whether its location is in or adjacent to a census tract with criteria pollutants or toxic air pollutants exceeding the federal and/or state limits for such areas. If that is the case, the company should evaluate the cost of reducing its emissions of criteria pollutants or toxic air pollutants to levels below such limits to cause the total emissions of these pollutants to be reduced to closer to the overall limits. Alternatively, the company can evaluate the cost to assist a facility affecting nearby communities to reduce its emissions of criteria pollutants or toxic air pollutants to the limits for these areas. This could help reduce overall pollutants for such areas. Assuming the company agrees to make an investment to reduce pollutants, it could share the commitment with the relevant groups near its facility.

- In evaluating the cost of developing the hydrogen facility, the company must determine how far from the subject location the EPA/state monitoring device for criteria and toxic air pollutants should be. If the facility is in a disadvantaged community or adjacent thereto and distant from such a device, the company could determine with EPA how to contribute the capital and/or operating cost of a monitoring system to install adjacent to these site(s).

- Prior to starting project construction, the promoter should develop a Community Benefits Plan in partnership with neighboring disadvantaged communities and stakeholders that describes how the project will deliver tangible benefits to their communities throughout the project lifecycle.

- Recognizing that obtaining low-cost capital is a challenge for disadvantaged communities, a hydrogen project promoter should evaluate whether there are low-cost capital options for the disadvantaged community potentially impacted by the project, share such information with the community stakeholders, and consider some support for such options focused on that community.

- The project promoter should evaluate the energy resilience of its neighboring disadvantaged communities and identify ways to enhance it. They could then share this information with the communities. Together, they can assess the feasibility of advocating with the utilities serving these areas, focusing on improving resilience.

- If the project is to be in a disadvantaged community, the project operator must seek to identify issues of concern to the community in which the company could join the community in seeking local government attention to the issues.

- The project promoter should create opportunities to improve environmental and social conditions within the neighboring disadvantaged communities, including job and enterprise creation. By purchasing goods or services from a small and disadvantaged business, the project would create such opportunities.

Among the potential disbenefits or harms that a project can impose on neighboring communities that should be considered by the project owner are: a) use of limited resources such as biomass, freshwater, or land; b) environmental pollution or waste streams; c) impact on land-use patterns; d) impact on home values; and e) project land being on, or adjacent to, Tribal lands.

# Appendix W

# SELECTION OF BEST PRACTICE DOCUMENTS

- "API Recommended Practice (RP) 1185 Pipeline Public Engagement." 2024. https://publications.api.org/documents/1185_el-PubAcc/html5.html.

- "API RP 100-3 Community Engagement Guidelines API Publishes Community and Stakeholder Engagement Standard for Upstream Operations." April 4, 2024. https://www.api.org/news-policy-and-issues/news/2024/04/04/api-publishes-community-stakeholder-engagement-standard-upstream-operations.

- Federal Energy Regulatory Commission. "Suggested Best Practices for Industry Outreach Programs to Stakeholders." July 2015. https://www.ferc.gov/industries/gas/enviro/guidelines/stakeholder-brochure.pdf.

- The Aspen Institute Dialogue on Energy Governance. "Stakeholder Engagement Best Practices and Recommendations." 2019. https://www.energy.gov/sites/default/files/2022-10/Infra_Topic_Paper_3-6_FINAL.pdf.

- IPIECA. "Community Grievance Mechanisms in the Oil and Gas Industry." January 2015. https://www.ipieca.org/resources/community-grievance-mechanisms-in-the-oil-and-gas-industry.

- Department of Energy, Office of Fossil Energy and Carbon Management. "Framework Engaging Communities, Stakeholders, and Tribes in Clean Energy Technologies." https://www.energy.gov/fecm/fossil-energy-and-carbon-management-domestic-engagement-framework-engaging-communities.

- Department of Energy, National Energy Technology Laboratory. 2017. "Best Practices for: Public Outreach and Education for Carbon Storage Projects (DOE/NETL/1845)."

- Bradbury, J., Greenberg, S., and Wade, S. 2011. "Communicating the Risks of CCS." Canberra, Australia. Global CCS Institute.

- Ashworth, P., Bradbury, J., Feenstra, C.F.J., Greenberg, S., Hund, G., Mikunda, T., Wade, S., and Shaw, H. 2011. "Communication/Engagement toolkit for CCS Projects." Canberra, Australia. Global CCS Institute.

- IFC. 2007. "Stakeholder Engagement: A Good Practice Handbook for Companies Doing Business in Emerging Markets." https://www.ifc.org/en/insights-reports/2000/publications-handbook-stakeholder-engagement--wci--1319577185063.

- Forbes S, Almendra F, Ziegler M. 2010. *Guidelines for Community Engagement in Carbon Dioxide Capture, Transport, and Storage Projects.* 2010. World Resources Institute, Washington, D.C.

- Health Effects Institute Energy. 2022. "Guiding Principles for Research and Stakeholder Engagement." https://www.heienergy.org/sites/default/files/2022-04/heienergy-guiding-principles-2022.pdf.

- IPIECA. "Indigenous Peoples and the Oil and Gas Industry: Context, Issues and Emerging Good Practice." April 2012. https://www.ipieca.org.

- IPIECA. 2014. "Community Grievance Mechanisms Toolbox."

- United Nations. "Guiding Principles for Business and Human Rights." https://www.ohchr.org/sites/default/files/documents/publications/guidingprinciplesbusinesshr_en.pdf.

www.ingramcontent.com/pod-product-compliance
Lightning Source LLC
Chambersburg PA
CBHW040932050426
42334CB00050B/86